Military Agility

Foreign Military Studies

History is replete with examples of notable military campaigns and exceptional military leaders and theorists. Military professionals and students of the art and science of war cannot afford to ignore these sources of knowledge or limit their studies to the history of the US armed forces. This series features original works, translations, and reprints of classics outside the American canon that promote a deeper understanding of international military theory and practice.

Series editor: Joseph Craig

An AUSA Book

Military Agility

Ensuring Rapid and Effective Transition from Peace to War

Meir Finkel

Translated by Moshe Tlamim

UNIVERSITY PRESS OF KENTUCKY

Scholarly publisher for the Commonwealth,
serving Bellarmine University, Berea College, Centre
College of Kentucky, Eastern Kentucky University,
The Filson Historical Society, Georgetown College,
Kentucky Historical Society, Kentucky State University,
Morehead State University, Murray State University,
Northern Kentucky University, Transylvania University,
University of Kentucky, University of Louisville,
and Western Kentucky University.

Editorial and Sales Offices: The University Press of Kentucky
663 South Limestone Street, Lexington, Kentucky 40508-4008
www.kentuckypress.com

Cataloging-in-Publication data is available from the Library of Congress.

ISBN 978-0-8131-7884-4 (hardcover : alk. paper)
ISBN 978-0-8131-7997-1 (epub)
ISBN 978-0-8131-7996-4 (pdf)

This book is printed on acid-free paper meeting the requirements of the American National Standard for Permanence in Paper for Printed Library Materials.

Manufactured in the United States of America.

Member of the Association
of University Presses

For my loving and patient wife Amira

Contents

Abbreviations

AFV	armored fighting vehicle
APC	armored personnel carrier
BEF	British Expeditionary Force
C2	command and control
COIN	counterinsurgency
EBO	effect-based operation
EFP	enhanced forward presence
eNRF	Enhanced NATO Response Force
EW	electronic weapon
GHQ	General Headquarters
HEAT	high-explosive antitank
HESH	high-explosive squash head
HIC	high-intensity conflict
IAF	Israeli Air Force
IDF	Israel Defense Forces
IED	improvised explosive device
IMI	Israel Military Industries
ISR	intelligence, surveillance, and reconnaissance
J2	intelligence branch (or intelligence officer)
J3	operations branch (or operations officer)
J7	doctrine and instruction branch (or doctrine and instruction officer)
LAW	light antitank weapon
LIC	low-intensity conflict
MDB	multidomain battle
MTW	major theater war
NATO	North Atlantic Treaty Organization
NBC	nuclear, biological, chemical
OTRI	Operational Theory Research Institute
PIAT	projector infantry antitank
RPG	rocket-propelled grenade
RSO	routine security operation
SAM	surface-to-air missile

TOW	tube-launched, optically tracked, wire-guided
TRADOC	US Army Training and Doctrine Command
TTPs	tactics, techniques, and procedures
VJTF	Very High Readiness Joint Task Force

Introduction

In *America's First Battles, 1776–1965*, Charles E. Heller and William A. Stofft argue that, "With little prior warning, the Army must be capable of fighting in a variety of geographic locales against any one aggressor or a coalition of potential aggressors in joint and combined formations."[1] Since 1986, when these lines were written, the US armed forces have had to shift from peace to war a number of times. The need to enter a conflict rapidly is an enduring global demand and, given today's dynamic geopolitical environment, has become more relevant than ever.

The ability to transition swiftly from peace, or from a prolonged low-intensity conflict (LIC), to the high-intensity conflict (HIC) of war and to succeed in the initial engagements is usually discussed in terms of readiness, capability, and capacity, which are related to materiel, personnel, doctrine, and training. Every security establishment—whether state or nonstate—is familiar with these aspects. This book, however, deals with the other complementary, important, but generally neglected "soft" aspects of moving from peace to war: the mental ability to shift from peacetime to wartime, the challenge of consolidating a coherent doctrine when war erupts in the midst of an ongoing peacetime conceptual-doctrinal debate, and the difficulty of achieving proficiency on short notice when new weapons systems become available at the last minute (or even after units have deployed).

The initial phase of hostilities may seem unimportant from a broad perspective when considering prolonged conflicts such as World War I, World War II,[2] Vietnam, Afghanistan, and others, but in fact, these initial battles are *more* crucial than ever for a number of reasons. First, as John Shy contends, "The results of the first battle play a crucial role in strategy."[3] It can be argued that this is also the case in prolonged conflicts, but more importantly, "All wars involve a high level of ignorance and uncertainty . . . but it is the very beginning of war when lack of knowledge or confidence may dominate the situation, before commanders can assess the results of their first realistic test of estimates, assumptions, guesses, predictions, hopes and fears."[4] This means that, practically speaking, first battles are experiments and thus play an essential role for military organizations that are trying to be receptive and adaptive to change.

Second, in comparatively short and intense wars (like the kind Israel fights), early engagements shape the physical and mental conditions for the engagements that follow. This was the case at the beginning of the 1973 Yom Kippur War and the 2006 Second Lebanon War. Egyptian president Anwar Sadat based his 1973 campaign on the assumption that the initial battles would be of supreme importance: "We should have the upper hand in the first twenty-four hours of fighting, because, I said, he who wins the twenty-four-hour encounter will surely win the entire war. Our plan and method of execution should be based on the kind of action designated to tip the balance in our favor within the initial twenty-four hours."[5]

In late 2001–early 2002, at the peak of the Palestinian suicide bomber offensive against Israel, senior Israel Defense Forces (IDF) officers believed that fighting the terrorists inside the refugee camps would result in hundreds of IDF casualties. The first successful attacks in February 2002 in the Balata refugee camp outside Nablus by an IDF paratrooper brigade and in the Jenin refugee camp by the Golani Brigade, restored the confidence of Israel's political and strategic policymakers in combating terror in densely populated urban areas. The success of these initial engagements enabled the order to be given a week later to occupy the major cities in the West Bank as part of Operation Defensive Shield.

The 1976 version of the US Army's operations doctrine, *FM 100–5*, focuses on a central European scenario similar to the Yom Kippur War and states: "The first battle of our next war could well be our last battle. . . . The United States could find itself in a short intensive war—the outcome of which may be dictated by the results of the initial combat."[6] Winning the first battles is also important for the expeditionary units that are the first to fight. During and after the Cold War, US Army doctrine emphasized the importance of force projection and, later, the expeditionary forces' mental and cognitive challenge. The 1993 edition of *FM 100–5* states:

> Force projection usually begins as a contingency operation—a rapid response to a crisis. Alert may come without notice, bringing with it tremendous stress on soldiers and systems, accompanied by pressure from the media for information. . . .
>
> Force-projection operations will challenge Army leaders. Early critical decisions set against a backdrop of uncertainty and friction, will be required at every level—strategic, operational, and tactical—in war and in operations other than war. The commander and the force will routinely be required to plan and execute multiple concurrent activities. Decisions made early will begin to set conditions for successful mission accomplishment.[7]

Regarding expeditionary forces, the US Army's 2008 *FM 3–0* states:

> Future conflicts will include incomplete planning information, rapid deployments with little or no notice, and sustained operations in austere theaters. . . .
>
> Expeditionary capabilities are more than physical attributes; they begin with a mindset that pervades the force. Soldiers with an expeditionary mindset are ready to deploy on short notice. They are confident that they can accomplish any mission. They are mentally and physically prepared to deploy anywhere in the world at any time in any environment against any adversary. Leaders with an expeditionary mindset are adaptive. They possess the individual initiative needed to accomplish missions through improvisation and collaboration. They are mentally prepared to operate within different cultures in any environment. An expeditionary mindset requires developing and empowering adaptive thinkers at all levels, from tactical to strategic.[8]

The US Army's future concept of "multidomain battle" (see chapter 5) assumes that "adversaries can conduct armed conflict via regional campaigns with limited warning to seize limited strategic objectives and consolidate gains within days or weeks." Therefore, "Multi-Domain Battle requires a dynamic mix of forward presence forces, expeditionary forces, and partner forces to deter an adversary and, if required, to defeat his plan within days and not months."[9]

It is important to note that American military thinkers also stress the need for a rapid reaction capability by newly organized expeditionary forces, and they suggest a combination of organizational, technological, training, educational, and career management changes to achieve the necessary transformation. For example, Douglas Macgregor, in his book *Transformation under Fire*, suggests three modes of operation for these new forces: rapid intervention with minimal or no alert in places where the United States or its allies do not have a presence but, for strategic reasons, need to intervene; a constant presence in key areas in peripheral parts of the globe to enable a rapid reaction against emerging threats to US interests; and a constant presence to support the stability of important countries and prevent regional crises.[10] In a later book, Macgregor restricted his suggestions for future American intervention but still emphasized the need "to maintain powerful force-in-being—forces designated to win the first fight, because we may not get the second chance to win a second."[11] Others, such as Eliot Cohen in *The Big Stick*, suggest that decision makers in Washington should prepare the US Army for much wider intervention scenarios than those implied by the current post-Iraq and Afghanistan conventions.[12]

Third, in the oversaturated media environment that armies fight in, first impressions—on all sides—are more important than ever. Two decades ago, news reports on war would encompass a combination of initial failures and follow-up successes in a way that softened the former and highlighted the latter. Today, online news of initial failures might bring the war to an immediate halt.

Fourth, the growing ambiguity surrounding the political definition of conflict and the determination of success makes the transition from peace to war more difficult. In the Yom Kippur War, for instance, it was quite clear that the situation at hand was war. It was much harder to define the situation at the beginning of the Vietnam War or Israel's military engagement in July 2006 that, a year later, would officially be called the Second Lebanon War. The growing military literature on "understanding" attests to this challenge.[13] One could claim that in the Vietnam War or the Second Lebanon War the problem was not that the war was unrecognizable as such or that its character was unexpected but that the political and military leadership failed to sustain the readiness of the force. Be that as it may, in the end the challenge fell—and, due to the inherent political difficulties of declaring war, will probably continue to fall—on the shoulders of the military commanders who had to make the quick shift to war. These commanders are the target audience for this book.

Framing the Issue

Just as the professional conduct of war requires many kinds of transitions, success in first battles depends on many conditions. A short discussion of both issues will clarify this book's focus.

The ability to identify and adapt to a new situation is the basic and essential test of competency of every commander and every unit. The classic mode of transition is a switch between offensive and defensive operations and vice versa. This kind of transition involves changes in almost every aspect of warfare—different methods of combat, organization, mindset, and so forth.[14] Another set of transitions is implied by the American concept of "phasing"—that is, the shift from "shape" (phase 0) through "stabilization" (phase IV).[15] For example, the challenge of identifying the need to adapt to changing circumstances at the end of the successful ground invasion of Iraq in 2003 can be described as a "failed transition" between phases III and IV.[16] This book addresses a specific kind of transition—the rapid shift from peace or LIC to HIC (war).

A successful transition depends on many variables that are usually covered by the term "readiness." During the Cold War, discussions about readiness were based mostly on the American experience in the two world wars and, later, the

Korean War. Planners drew on the lessons learned in those wars to prepare a force buildup strategy for American and allied mobilization in the event of war between NATO and Warsaw Pact forces in Europe. The literature dealing with readiness for the transition from peace to war focused on the size, organization, and mobilization of forces and their training. The outcome of this effort was research-based decisions on factors such as the industrial infrastructure needed to accelerate the production of weapons and ammunition, the ratio between regular and reserve units, the reserve component's level of competency, the time required for mobilization in Europe and the United States and deployment from the United States to Europe, and so forth. The creation of the Mobilization Concept Development Center and the publication of books such as *NATO–Warsaw Pact Force Mobilization* exemplify the response to such needs at the time.[17] Probably the best analysis of readiness is Richard Betts's 1995 book *Military Readiness*.[18] Betts surveys the readiness traditions up to and during the Cold War, praises the readiness that enabled the relatively short (in American terms) force buildup that led to victory in Iraq in 1991, and provides guidelines for the future. After the Cold War, attention shifted to quick-reaction forces or rapid-deployment forces that could deploy worldwide as an initial force for a larger, heavier presence. In these scenarios, the main issues were (and still are) transportation assets for rapid deployment and the integration of multinational coalition forces, or the numbers and types of forces stationed around the world.

Although these are essential issues, this book does not deal with the size of armed forces, their level of training, transportation assets for deployment, or the stationing of units around the globe for immediate intervention. Assuming that all this has been accomplished, I argue that to conduct a successful transition from peace to war, other "softer" aspects of readiness, such as cognitive and mental flexibility, must be addressed.

The concept of "adaptation" is usually related to change during war, as discussed in the growing literature on the subject, which includes Williamson Murray's *Military Adaptation in War, with Fear of Change* and my own *On Flexibility: Recovery from Technological and Doctrinal Surprise on the Battlefield*.[19] The rapid transition from peace to war generally requires a much faster recognition of the new situation and a much more extensive change in force employment compared with adaptation during war. This aspect of adaptation is not part of the current literature. As Murray points out, adaptation "is a phenomenon of indeterminate length, which presents the opportunity for the contestants to adapt to their enemy's strategy, operations and tactical approach."[20] In the case of the transition from peace to war, the interval is much shorter compared with the case studies presented in the literature. For example, in his book on the US military in Iraq, Chad Serena describes an adaptation that took years.[21]

In addition to the short time available to adjust, another difference between battlefield adaptation and the rapid transition from peace to war involves the unique combination of changing one's mindset (peace versus war), which is a cognitive-mental process, and dealing with the professional challenges of improvisation, such as assimilating new weapons or tactics or consolidating an unvalidated concept. Probably the worst case is encountering the combination of both challenges in the event of a surprise attack, as occurred in the Yom Kippur War.

A few other cognitive-mental challenges exist when making the rapid switch from peace to war, as opposed to battlefield adaptation. For example, there is the need to define the new situation as war (which sounds easy but is not), the need to persuade one's superiors in the rear that there is a war on the front, and the need to revise the basic mode of action from the one used and assimilated in peacetime and routine security missions.

This book's aim is to fill the existing gaps in the literature. To that end, I identify four main challenges when making a successful transition from peacetime to wartime. First, there must be a successful mental transition from peacetime or routine security activities to a higher-intensity mode of action for combat. This is an enduring human and organizational challenge that stems from the need for preconceptions and organizational stability.

Second, if prewar debates over concepts and doctrine are still unresolved when war breaks out, these issues must be quickly resolved. Peacetime conceptual and doctrinal debates are essential for the healthy development of a military force's fighting ability. As General Donn Starry, commander of the US Army Training and Doctrine Command (TRADOC), noted in the 1970s: "Operational concepts are the stuff on which armies feed and nurture themselves. And so a dialogue about them is essential to the Army's well-being."[22] But continuing the debate into actual combat operations can be disastrous. This is mainly a leadership challenge. The ambiguity concerning where, when, and against whom the next conflict will take place, as well as that conflict's shape and form, is becoming a prominent challenge.

Third, new weapons systems—those delivered at the last minute before hostilities begin or even while the conflict is ongoing—must be integrated and employed. This challenge increases as the pace of technological change creates more opportunities.

Fourth, there must be a balance between the need to win every tactical engagement in LICs (which often call for mindsets, organization, and doctrines different from those needed in HICs) and the preparation of forces for a war scenario.

Why Does Israel's Experience Matter?

In World War I, World War II, and the Gulf Wars, the United States had remarkable strategic depth in time and space. In Israel, neither exists. For most of its modern history, the major threat to Israel has been land invasion, similar to the situation of other countries whose land borders have been threatened, such as Finland, West Germany, Poland, and South Korea. Each country solved its own challenge with a unique solution by combining organization (Finland's reserve system), physical obstacles (South Korea's Demilitarized Zone), doctrine (American active defense and, later, the air-land battle of the 1980s and 1990s), allied support (the American air defense systems in eastern Europe), and the like.

Today, the strategic threat from Hamas and Hezbollah rockets nullifies even the pre–Yom Kippur War presumption of a forty-eight-hour early warning. Except for a short period (in Sinai), Israel has always lacked tactical depth. Israel's wars occur on its borders and in the vicinity of Israeli civilians. Because they usually erupt in a matter of hours to days, Israel's wars demand a very rapid transition from peacetime deployment to full-scale mobilization and wartime deployment. Israeli military history therefore exemplifies the worst-case scenario: the need for a rapid transition from peace to war. Furthermore, Israel's experience in making the transition is more complex than that of most armies because of the inherent contradictions between the methods and mindsets required in long-term routine security activities and those required for a rapid escalation to high-intensity warfare. This is complicated by the possibility that the escalation in hostilities might be only a temporary spike within the lower-intensity warfare framework. During the first ten to twelve hours of the Yom Kippur War, for instance, many Israeli commanders thought they were facing raids and artillery bombardments of the kind often encountered in the War of Attrition rather than an invasion. Many Israeli tactical decisions were compromised due to this misunderstanding.

The Israeli worst-case transition scenario provides valuable lessons for countries such as South Korea, the Baltic States, and Finland, as well as for US Army forces in Europe and other first-reaction forces. Although there are strategic cultural and structural differences between the United States and Israel (such as the fact that 70 percent of IDF ground forces are reserve units), I believe that many Israeli lessons are applicable to the United States.

Organization of the Book

The book is arranged according to the four abovementioned challenges. Chapter 1 looks at the challenge of incorporating new equipment into existing units when war is in sight or already in progress. Unlike the material challenges of accelerated research and development, production, and delivery of new machinery or software, the issues here are fast learning and implementing the new asset so that it becomes part of the existing fighting machine. The cases analyzed are the 1956 Sinai War and American aid to Israel during the Yom Kippur War.

Chapter 2 discusses a major obstacle in a successful transition: prolonged low-intensity or counterinsurgency (COIN) operations.[23] The effect of such operations on the ability to shift rapidly to high-intensity war was a concern during the US Army's decade in Iraq and Afghanistan. Israel's experience prior to the Yom Kippur War and the Second Lebanon Wars is presented here.

Chapter 3 analyzes the situation of an ongoing peacetime conceptual or doctrinal debate that continues during war. Here, the challenge lies in identifying gaps between commanders or forces and bridging them in ways that enable coordinated action yet give commanders enough space to function independently. The chapter opens with a detailed discussion of Israel's experience in the Yom Kippur War and continues to the Second Lebanon War. The focus is not on whether the concept or doctrine was suited to the military's needs but on its acceptance throughout the force so that coherent and synchronized action in a multiechelon and joint-force military organization could take place.

Chapter 4 assesses the cognitive and mental challenge of recognizing a given situation as war and then pushing this understanding up and down the echelons of command to implement a change in the mode of action. The case studies of the Yom Kippur War and the Second Lebanon War show how difficult this seemingly simple task can be.

Chapter 5 describes the global, persistent nature of the phenomena discussed throughout this book by providing brief US Army historical anecdotes. It examines the current challenges for the US Army's rapid transition to war in Europe and concludes with specific recommendations for overcoming these challenges. Most of the historical examples are at the tactical level, but in a few cases they reach the strategic and operational echelons.

The conclusion offers a few broad suggestions for improving military organizations' ability to successfully transition from peace or LIC or COIN operations to war.

1

Hastening Force Buildup before and during War

Military force design—which includes the elements of doctrine, organization, training, materiel, leadership and education, personnel, and facilities—entails many levels of risk management. This chapter focuses on two major risks: miscalculating the outbreak date of the next war, and planning for a particular scenario when a different scenario might occur (based on a mistaken assumption).

Throughout Israel's history, the likelihood of the eruption of a full-scale confrontation has arisen every few years, causing the Israel Defense Forces to hasten preparations for war; these preparations are termed "force buildup." This chapter examines three events—the Sinai War, the Six-Day War, and the Yom Kippur War—where the decision to augment the army's readiness (professional competency, basic organizational suitability, weapons upgrade, and improved stockpile levels) was put to the test, followed by a discussion of what can and cannot be done when war appears on the horizon.

These three events were chosen because they can be analyzed within the limits of declassified information. They illustrate a range of time factors and types of action taken—for instance, the time interval between a decision to prepare for war (based on the perception that a fundamental change has occurred and war is imminent) and the actual outbreak of hostilities. Preparation for the Sinai War lasted a whole year—from the public announcement of the Egyptian-Czech arms deal in late September 1955 to the outbreak of war on October 29, 1956. Preparation time for the Six-Day War was shorter—roughly three weeks—from the alert on May 15, 1967, to the outbreak of war on June 5. Preparations for the Yom Kippur War continued for half a year—from the announcement of the "Blue-White" alert on April 16, 1973, to the Egyptian-Syrian attack on October 6.[1] In addition, the chapter discusses the airlift that took place in the midst of the Yom Kippur War and the effort to assimilate new weapons in the course of fighting.

A determination that war is likely to erupt within a few months or a year enhances tensions in certain areas. (Note that this chapter deals with wartime scenarios, when the main force has to be deployed at the onset of hostilities, and not in a limited or pinpoint operation, where such tensions may be more circumscribed.) The main tension is between the heightened readiness for the approaching clash and the future relevancy of the weapons procured (as well as supplies and structural organization) if war does not occur at the expected time. Given that the army receives funding to improve its readiness in the face of impending war and that cutbacks routinely occur after hostilities abate, investment in the immediate time frame—that is, to procure weapons and supplies and undertake relevant training exercises for the expected confrontation—comes at the cost of developing military capabilities for a more distant clash whose nature cannot be known in advance.

In the case of weapons, the dilemma is whether to increase stocks of existing weapons or wait for newer and better ones to become available. For example, should an army upgrade its tank cannons and procure ammunition to improve its immediate military capability or take a risk and wait to acquire more advanced weapons that are better suited to oppose the new tanks the enemy will presumably receive after the war has ended. It should be remembered that every new weapons system requires a learning period. An additional element in risk management is the balance between the quantity of primary weapons (tanks and planes, for example) and the amount of ammunition and spare parts purchased for training and operational use.

Another tension is the reliance on a foreign source for weapons, ammunition, and replacement parts versus reliance on domestic production. The dilemma revolves around the relatively high costs of developing, maintaining, and expanding independent production versus reliance on a foreign state in an emergency, with the inherent risks of embargo, delayed delivery, partial or gross incompatibility with the army's needs, and so forth. This is one of the most complex tensions, and it involves an assessment of the political situation and long-term economic considerations. Although this aspect is irrelevant to the United States, it is a major consideration for America's smaller allies, and US decision makers must understand this.

Training and exercises for assimilating new weapons are necessary steps whether those weapons are acquired from foreign sources or domestically. The dilemma is whether to gain proficiency in the use of a current weapon or wait for a more advanced weapon to become available, at the price of less time for assimilation and training. It must be remembered that the transition from a known weapons system that the forces are skilled in operating to a new weapons system often entails not only learning new procedures but also unlearning or overriding old habits.[2] Another issue is the diversity and scope of the retraining required. For example, training pilots to fly new aircraft demands many flight hours. In addition, ground-crew technicians need time to learn how to identify and fix problems in the new aircraft. There are other tensions related to the supply of ammunition and weapon operability (due to the numerous replacement parts and the time needed to repair breakdowns that occurred in the training period) and between the desire to train as much as possible and the need to maintain a sufficient degree of readiness in case of sudden war. Another source of tension is the ability to modify trainers (instruction teams), training areas, and training aids.

In the area of force organization, the dilemma is whether to restructure the forces based on the specific needs of the coming conflict (even though this lengthens the time needed to assimilate changes and bring them to fruition on the battlefield) or to act within known frameworks that may be less suited to the specific threat. (This refers to the establishment of new units, headquarters, and so forth—not to manning the combat forces.)

A final risk involves a low level of compatibility between the force elements: weapons replenishment (which includes several factors, such as the number and quality of weapons, the amount of ammunition, and the availability of replacement parts), the level of proficiency in their use (training and exercises), and the level of maintenance. When compatibility is low, the weak link in the chain dictates a unit's operability. For example, there is no sense in maintaining a highly trained division equipped with the latest weapons if ammunition is in short supply.

I claim that once a decision has been made, readiness can be significantly improved within a matter of months. The main improvement results from the force's increased competency and not from the assimilation of new weapons. This chapter analyzes the IDF's accelerated force buildup after the decision had been made to prepare for war. Strong points and shortcomings are identified, and rules are presented for future scenarios. Although the focus is on the IDF's experience, other events in other armies could have been used, for example, the Red Army's preparation for war after the German invasion of Poland and France, the preparation of American armed forces for war between September 1939 and the attack on Pearl Harbor in December 1941, or the Allied landings in North Africa in late 1942.

The Sinai War

The year before the Sinai War (which started in October 1956) was a special period for the IDF in terms of force design and buildup. Armor's operational order of battle increased more than twofold, and the Israeli Air Force (IAF) was in the midst of converting from piston-engine (propeller-driven) aircraft to jet planes. The accelerated force buildup taking place under the constant threat of war involved numerous risks and therefore serves as a model, allowing us to analyze risk management and learn the necessary lessons. All the while, the fledgling state of Israel was struggling to absorb massive waves of immigrants and recuperate economically from the lengthy War of Independence. Economic measures at the time included gasoline and food rationing.

During most of the first half of the 1950s, the IDF operated based on the assumption that war was unlikely in the near future (within two or three years); therefore, the 1953 three-year plan was built on this premise.[3] A dramatic change in the regional balance of power occurred in September 1955 when Egyptian president Gamal Abdel Nasser announced a huge arms deal with Czechoslovakia. Prior to that deal, Egypt enhanced its armored force by acquiring British Centurions and upgraded cannons for its Sherman tanks. Israel estimated that Egyptian armor would increase from 130 tanks in late 1955 to between 310 and 430 tanks with the addition of Russian T-34s and Stalins to the British Centurions and French AMX-13s.[4] Furthermore, the Egyptians were scheduled to receive a large number of modern Mig-15s and Mig-17s.[5] The Syrian army, too, would be replenished with tanks and armored fighting vehicles (AFVs). On October 18, 1955, Israeli prime minister Moshe Sharett announced that "something has happened in the Middle East that portends the bleak prospect of our strongest enemy state gaining a decisive military advantage that will confront us with dangers unlike any we have known since the War of Independence."[6] At a government meeting in December 1955, Prime Minister David Ben-Gurion (who had returned to office after Sharett's resignation) stated that the Egyptians would be ready for war in a few months and would attack Israel in the spring or summer of 1956. While Israel studied the possibility of an Israeli-initiated war before Egypt could assimilate its new weapons, it attempted to purchase offensive arms to counterbalance the Egyptian acquisition.

Armor Buildup

In September 1955 the IDF had 86 operational tanks (76 Shermans with M-3 cannons and 10 AMX-13 reconnaissance tanks); in addition, there were 131 nonfunctioning tanks without armament. The IDF planned to organize the Shermans in four tank battalions and to attach three of the battalions to armored brigades (the 7th, 27th, and 37th), with the fourth as a general support to the infantry units.[7]

In May 1955 the French government expressed a willingness to sell a large number of aircraft, tanks, and antitank missiles to Israel. The deal was stymied, however, due to opposition from the French Foreign Office and gaps in Israeli financing. In early November these obstacles were overcome (the reasons for the removal of French opposition have been studied in detail elsewhere) because of the shock of the Egyptian acquisition. The director of Israel's Ministry of Defense, Shimon Peres, went on a procurement mission to Europe and succeeded in signing sales agreements for French Ouragan and Mystère aircraft, 60 AMX-13 tanks, 40 Super-Shermans, 175 75mm M-50 cannons for mounting on the Shermans, SS-10 missiles, and 500 73mm bazooka rockets.[8] "Some of the items, such as the Super-Shermans and bazookas would be taken out of French army stores and units and quickly supplied, while the rest, the planes, light tanks and missiles, were still in production which meant that their delivery would take a few months."[9] The French put a freeze on the deal after signing it, but in April, after learning that Egypt was aiding the rebels in Algeria and determining that strengthening Israel would be in France's interest, French and Israeli negotiators agreed on the sale of 72 Mystère-4s, 120 AMX-13 tanks, 40 Super-Shermans (with 76.2mm cannons), and 18 self-propelled cannons. Delivery was scheduled for late July to late September 1956.

Within a year, the IDF's number of operational tanks had more than doubled, from 86 in 1955 to approximately 181 tanks that took part in the Sinai War (120 Shermans of various models and 61 AMX-13s). The IDF's total tank force rose that year to nearly 450, more than twice the number in September 1955. Between late July and the opening of hostilities in late October 1956, 233 tanks arrived: 120 AMX-13s, 40 Super-Shermans, 25 Sherman M-50s, and 48 Sherman M-1s.[10] Israel's beefed-up strength made a major impact on the order of battle (the establishment and dismantlement of units), crew training, and unit exercises with the new weapons. All this was carried out mainly between July and October while assimilating the weapons.

Tank Procurement and Upgrade

The case of the AMX-13 illustrates the problems inherent in the rapid procurement of an existing weapon with limited capabilities, when taking into account the enemy's threat and serious technical serviceability weaknesses. Israel complied with French demands to purchase 180 light tanks, a larger number than its operational needs called for (112, according to the original plan) at a very high price (nearly $150,000 per tank), compared with a smaller number of Shermans at $25,000 per tank.[11] The relatively new AMX-13 tank (production began in France in 1951) had a three-man crew, weighed fourteen tons, offered a high speed and high muzzle velocity, and had the only shell that could penetrate the Egyptians' Centurion armor. Nevertheless, the tanks' protective armor was very thin (a 0.5-inch machine gun bullet could penetrate it), and it was unsuited for Israel's combat conditions of heat and dust. Because of these limitations, the AMX-13 was originally defined as an antitank (or tank destroyer) weapon and not as a battle tank.[12] After testing and trials, the ordnance branch concluded that basic changes were needed to improve the tank's durability in Israel's soil and climate conditions: modifying the cooling system, switching the air filters to oil filters, and replacing the gear system. The decision was made to buy the tank before the necessary changes and repairs had been finalized. It should be noted that some of the modifications that were considered essential required further examination. Another complication was that many of the tank's parts were being produced in factories spread across France and Germany.

In mid-1955, after the contract had been signed, it was revealed that production and delivery would take longer than expected. "Israel faced a dilemma: whether to wait and insist that the tanks not be sent until the modifications were introduced or receive them as soon as possible regardless of their limitations."[13] Israel decided to obtain the tanks before the modifications had been made so that assimilation and training could begin and the tanks could be rendered operable as early as possible. After the improved systems were developed, Israel would install them. The decision to develop crew proficiency before the adaptations had been completed had a profound effect on the tanks' capability while the army was preparing for war.[14] The incomplete modifications for desert fighting were a factor during the war. A tank company of regulars in the 9th Battalion, 7th Brigade, that was attached to a paratrooper brigade suffered many types of breakdowns. For example, on October 27 "the tank crews had to deal with an unexpected problem: instead of Browning .30 caliber machineguns that fire parallel to the cannon, they received, without warning, a new French Lebel-model machinegun they had never seen before."[15] Only seven out of thirteen tanks survived the trip when the brigade moved from Ein Husub (Hatzeva) in the Arava (Israel's southern border with Jordan) to Kunteila in Sinai: "All the rest had their gears burnt out or their filters clogged with dust."[16] Only three tanks reached the Tamed area in Sinai's depth because "the three others had gotten stuck due to clogged filters."[17]

The IDF's acquisition and assimilation of the AMX-13 highlight the downside of trying to attain a higher degree of readiness for an approaching battle with an available weapon—in this case, the relatively unsuitable AMX-13 tank (excluding the cannon). This consideration overrode the potential benefit of obtaining a better weapon, such as the Sherman tank, in the future. The large number of AMXs that were purchased (40 percent of the IDF's total order of battle at the start of hostilities) exceeded the amount needed by one and a half times. The AMX-13's service in the IDF was fairly short-lived. Before the Six-Day War, the army had already begun to transfer them from the armored brigades to regional command armored battalions. The AMX-13's flaws were blatant in the Six-Day War: its inadequacy in dealing with the enemy's advanced tanks (T-55s and Stalins), its light armor plating, difficulties in command and control (C2) at the company commander level and higher, and maintenance problems. They were taken out of the order of battle at the first opportunity, and many were sold to foreign countries in 1968–1969.[18]

The Sherman tank's life expectancy was extended after being converted to the Sherman M-51. The gun barrel was replaced with a 105mm cannon, the gasoline engine was replaced by a Cummins diesel engine, rotation and elevation were upgraded to a hydraulic system, and the tracks were widened for improved maneuverability. When the Six-Day War broke out, 178 M-3s had been already been converted to M-51s, and the engines of 186 M-50s had been replaced.[19] The M-51s with the 105mm cannons also fought admirably in the Yom Kippur War. The Shermans were employed in the mechanized brigades' tank battalions (three M-51 companies and a platoon of M-50s). The 4th, 9th, and 670th Mechanized Brigades fought on the Golan Heights; the 11th Mechanized Brigade in the northern sector of Suez Canal; and the 875th Mechanized Brigade battled in the canal's southern sector.[20]

The conversion of the Sherman cannons was another example of very complex risk taking. The decision to substitute the short-barreled 75mm M-3 cannon (originally designed for infantry assistance because of its relatively low armor-penetrating capability) with the long-barreled 75mm M-50 cannon (the AMX-13's cannon, with improved armor-penetrating ability) contributed significantly to the IDF's readiness. "The idea to mount the M-50 cannon on Sherman tanks, which began in September 1953, was still incomplete after two years." By June 1956, "the IDF had approximately 70 operable Shermans (without cannons) that were waiting for the tests and checks of the mounted M-50 cannon to be completed."[21] Although the M-50 cannon had arrived from France with mounting instructions in late 1955, it was still far from being operational. In mid-March 1956, even after additions and modifications such as smoke canisters and a new telescopic sight, field tests revealed that twenty alterations were still needed. "The tank's testing in Israel and the changes that had to be made, pushed back the start of the ordnance work by a few months. On August 7 the chief quartermaster estimated that the first twenty tanks with M-50 cannons would be ready only on September 1, 1956 (about six months after the cannons' arrival in the country)."[22] Be that as it may, in the months preceding the Sinai War, the ordnance branch accelerated its pace and succeeded in converting twenty-four Shermans to the M-50 model. A few weeks before hostilities began, fourteen were delivered to Major Moshe Brill, the commander of A Company, 82nd Battalion, 7th Brigade (the brigade that would capture the Ruefa Dam).[23] During the retraining exercise, a serious flaw was discovered: the cannon's weight caused cracks in the screws connecting the elevation arch to the turret. The problem was fixed before the war.[24]

The length of time that passed until the armored battalions were equipped with M-50 cannons proved to be crucial. Even as the IDF was planning offensive operations and was in a state of alert against an Egyptian or Egyptian-Syrian armored attack, the battalions were in short supply of Shermans. A June agreement with France regarding the arrival of forty Super-Shermans (with 76.2mm cannons) starting in late July was key in bridging the quantitative and qualitative gap during the long wait for the M-50s.[25] This illustrates the tension that arises when weighing the risks of waiting for advanced weapons with long-term operational durability versus attaining a high level of readiness with technologically inferior weapons.

The M-10 tank destroyers were an example of a threefold problem: the acquisition of low-cost, secondhand equipment; the need to budget for replacement parts; and a manpower shortage in the ordnance layout. This weapon was purchased from Britain in late 1951, entered service in late 1955 (four years after its purchase),[26] and was withdrawn from service in the mid-1960s following the procurement of 100 additional Shermans from Iran.

Organization of the Armored Units

The reestablishment of the 7th Brigade as a basic armored formation of regulars contained all the elements of combined-arms warfare (after the brigade had been disbanded in 1954, its units came under the command of the armored corps). This process began before the Czech arms deal was announced and continued until the war broke out. The 7th Brigade's commander, Colonel Uri Ben Ari, writes that the AMX-13 tanks reached the 9th Battalion on October 24, 1956, six days before the war began.[27] The 52nd Battalion, an infantry battalion that had been transferred from the dismantled Givati Brigade in early September, had to be converted into a mechanized infantry battalion. The 61st Motorized Infantry Battalion, made up of reservists, had never trained as a motorized infantry battalion attached to an armored brigade. The reconnaissance unit that was designated to fight from AMX-13 tanks went into battle in jeeps. "According to IDF plans the 7th Brigade would be fit for war only in early 1957!"[28]

The establishment of the 27th Armored Brigade (reservists) took five years. The brigade already had armored battalions, but now the brigade headquarters had to be formed, the mechanized infantry and maintenance units had to be trained, and the reconnaissance company had to be converted to the AMX-13. The process culminated with a brigade exercise in May 1956. The assimilation of new weapons continued until just before the war. Colonel Haim Bar-Lev, who assumed command of the brigade only in mid-October,[29] recalled that "the Super-Shermans arrived a few days before the general mobilization [and] the M-50s two days before the operation."[30]

The formation of the 37th Brigade (reservists) began in April 1955. The battalions were being built while the brigade's headquarters and combat support units were still only partially manned. The brigade assimilated the new tanks and half-tracks only two weeks before the war,[31] which had an unfavorable effect on the brigade's proficiency. When it went into action on November 1, "the brigade had just completed its basic replenishment that morning and still lacked equipment, mainly communications gear."[32]

Seven AMX-13 companies were organized on the basis of existing tanks and those that were supposed to arrive. The companies were scheduled to operate within the framework of regional command reconnaissance battalions and a General Headquarters (GHQ) "reserve" battalion. Forming tank crews with troops who lived in the area where the unit was expected to be deployed, and transferring troops from existing units for retraining, encumbered both the companies being established and the units that had lost soldiers for retraining.[33]

The armored corps was not alone in undergoing organizational change. It was decided to reduce the number of "elder" infantry brigades (six at the time) and raise the proficiency level of those that remained. It was also decided to convert the 202nd Paratroop Battalion into a brigade on the basis of four battalions: the jump-school battalion, the 890th Battalion, the Nachal Airborne Battalion, and a reservist battalion.[34] During the reorganization of the regulars' order of battle, the 5th Brigade (Givati) was disbanded, and two battalions of regulars reinforced the 7th Brigade and Golani (Infantry) Brigade (which consisted of only two regular battalions). Most of the Givati Brigade's combat support units became the foundation of the new 202nd Brigade.[35]

Two events related to unit organization stand out as important with regard to risk management in force buildup. The first was the formation of the armored corps in early 1954. This involved the dismantling of the command echelon of the armored brigade as a basic formation and the subordination of armored battalions to the new armored corps, which would allocate them as battle teams to headquarters according to their missions. Amiad Brezner, the corps historian, writes: "The changes that the armored forces underwent cannot be separated from the rosy evaluation that prevailed in late 1953 that chances were slim that war would break out in the coming years. Only an army that is not under the threat of an approaching war can opt for long range preparations instead of maintaining immediate readiness, and embark on deep structural changes that entail dismantling the existing organizational system and building units to be organized and employed in an untested formation."[36] The return to an organization in which the brigade was the basic formation began unofficially in July 1954, a few months after the start of the reorganization, and was officially approved in late April 1955, almost half a year before the IDF began preparations for war.[37]

The second event was the dismantling of the reconnaissance companies of five-man crews on Staghound armored cars and their conversion to three-man crews on AMX-13s before the tanks arrived. The change required splitting up the crews and the platoons or companies and transforming the machine gunners into the more demanding roles of tank commanders, loaders, and drivers. A worrisome situation was created by the delay in the tanks' delivery from France. This was not the first time delivery had been held up, but "unlike the other occasions, no preliminary actions that were so comprehensive had been taken that disrupted the existing combat formation." In this case, "the regional command's armored battalions, which were supposed to supply armored forces to the commands, were non-operational because the previous organization had been thrown into disarray (the Staghounds could not be used and the crews that had been converted to tanks were still without the AMX-13s). The dismantlement of the Staghound companies that had seemed a calculated risk, turned out to be genuinely unsound."[38] The general staff and the armored corps scrambled to remedy the situation by taking the following steps: the remnants of the Staghound crews in the reconnaissance battalions were mustered into company frameworks, the untrained manpower was channeled to the formation of new companies, and some of the crews that had already undergone retraining on tanks were sent back to the armored cars.

The Rotem event is another example of the problems that can arise when there is no overlap between the removal of outdated equipment from service and the addition of new equipment. In early March 1960 the IDF learned that the Egyptian 4th Division was deployed in forward positions in Sinai. In light of this surprising development, the IDF heightened the level of alert in certain areas. At the same time, it was replacing World War II–era antitank cannons with newer jeep-mounted 106mm recoilless cannons. The transition was taking place without overlap—that is, the old cannons had been withdrawn from the regulars' units, and the recoilless cannons were only beginning to enter service. The Golani and Nachal infantrymen, however, were unfamiliar with the old weapons and inexperienced in the use of the new ones. Southern Command allocated one week for rapid training exercises.[39]

Training and Exercises

The new AMX-13 posed a great training challenge to the armor school. New courses had to be developed for tank commanders, drivers, and loaders, and the crews had to undergo intensive training. Many mishaps occurred during training, especially because of the disproportionate number of trainees to available tanks and the lack of sufficient training facilities, such as open-range firing areas. Thus, training was only partially completed. An AMX-13 commander who was sent to France completed a mere two-week crew training course on the new tank, plus an additional two-week instructors' course. Upon his return to Israel, he was given the responsibility of converting infantrymen into tank crews in a three-week course.[40] The first company commanders' course opened in March 1956. When the Sinai War erupted, the second course was canceled, so the first course was the only training company commanders received before the war.[41] The low proficiency of the AMX-13 companies led to the creation of an instruction staff made up of commanders and instructors who had trained on the tank in France. The staff's goal was to oversee training for autonomous armored units—brigade reconnaissance and AMX tank companies. In reality, due to the delayed delivery of the bulk of the tanks and snags with the existing ones, only one reconnaissance company and two armored car companies had undergone training by the time the war broke out, and an emergency call-up order was sent to reserve officers to act as instructors.[42] "As a rule it was decided to train the maximum number of units this year and make sure they familiarized themselves with enemy territory. The task was assigned to the IDF's head of the instruction branch, Major General Yitzhak Rabin. The emergency mobilization of reservists was meant to continue for half a year."[43]

In May 1956 a full armored brigade exercise was carried out for the first time since 1952. During that interval, only battalion formations had been deemed necessary for training exercises.[44] But the exercises encountered numerous difficulties (see below). The Merkava exercise for airborne units in March 1956 was also of major importance. This exercise for the remodeled 202nd Airborne Brigade tested its airborne and seaborne capabilities, which would be employed in the war.[45]

Complicating matters was the need to bolster the units' readiness through training despite the growing wear and tear on their weapons. The combination of intensive training, relatively new (and more sophisticated) weapons, and limited maintenance experience created a major operational problem in 1956. The number of engine hours in 1956–1957 was more than twice that of the previous year, with the extra hours attributed to the new tanks.[46] The May 1956 Pelet exercise that concluded the training of the newly established 27th Brigade (reservists) ended with a crisis in mechanical serviceability. In an attempt to limit damage to the AFVs' operability, the armored corps' training AFVs were used in the exercise instead of the brigade's combat vehicles. The combination of AFVs in need of repair after training, reservists who were generally lax about vehicle maintenance, and a brigade maintenance system that had not been trained to perform under pressure led to the "final undoing of the armored forces' level of readiness as far as tanks were concerned. . . . Of the 60 AMXs, about 40 were rendered inoperable; 13 of them from this exercise," wrote chief of staff Moshe Dayan in his diary.[47] A report on June 14 noted that approximately half of the armored corps' Shermans, AMX-13s, and half-tracks were no longer fit for action.[48] The armored corps, which used the AFVs, and the ordnance branch, which was responsible for their maintenance, blamed each other for the situation.[49] Dayan accused the armored corps commander of putting Israel's survival at risk.[50] He ordered that 100 tanks remain continuously operable and on full alert; this, in effect, canceled all training until new tanks arrived.[51]

Tactics, techniques, and procedures (TTPs) and training for the AMX-13 encountered problems due to mistranslations of the tank's operating instructions from French to Hebrew. The tactical training material also had to be translated. "In mid-1956, the amount of official instruction material that was published reached its low point," for two reasons:[52] the volume of armored corps headquarters' training and organizational assignments in recent years, and the shortage of professional officers at headquarters.

Regarding efficient force buildup, a quantitative imbalance existed between the number of tanks acquired and the number of trained crews. At the beginning of the Sinai War, the IDF had 104 fully manned AMX-13s out of 180 tanks (58 percent); it had 120 fully manned Shermans of various models out of 166 operational tanks and 205 in total (72 and 58 percent, respectively).[53] "Although the replenishment of the main fighting equipment was impressive, armor lacked certain items (ammunition for the M-1 cannon, refueling pumps, fillers for loading the cartridge belts, lubrication equipment, and camouflage netting) that prevented it from exploiting the large number of AFVs and hampered the fighting units from realizing their potential."[54]

Organization of the Antitank Units

When Israel grasped the full extent of the threat from Arab armor, it accelerated its force buildup and went further than just upgrading its medium tank force and purchasing AMX-13 light tanks.[55] It now increased its tank destroyer layout and acquired antitank cannons, missiles, and rocket launchers. The cutbacks of the previous years had resulted in the concentration of antitank platoons into brigade antitank companies, the truncation of regular army antitank units (which subsequently created a manpower shortage in the reservist units), and a gap between the number of cannons (57mm or 6-pounder) in service and the table of equipment. Instead of purchasing additional cannons, Dayan acquired light AMX-13s from France, upgraded the Sherman cannons, and waited for Israel Military Industries (IMI) to produce rocket launchers. The light tanks' disadvantage was their price tag—$150,000, compared with $5,000 for antitank cannons—and the relatively long assimilation period. The development of the 82mm rocket launcher also proved more troublesome than envisaged, and replenishment was scheduled for the beginning of 1957 at the earliest. As an interim solution, 500 73mm rocket launchers were acquired in 1954 and concentrated in company-level antitank squads. Although they were effective, they were too few for Israel's needs.[56]

Antitank Cannons

In late 1955 the antitank battalions' situation was flawed. Although the battalions' manpower status in the infantry brigades was acceptable, most of the antitank units had undergone training only at the crew and battery level, not as battalions. Furthermore, the transfer of batteries between battalions in the first months of 1956 detracted from their combat proficiency. In 1955–1956 six antitank battalions of the elder infantry brigades were established without undergoing combat training. Another drawback was the need for vehicles to tow the antitank cannons. The vehicle fleet allocated to this task and to transporting the crews and ammunition was unsuited for the job. Nearly one-third of the ammunition carriers were civilian vehicles that had been conscripted, and their use was limited because of their diversity, the shortage of spare parts, and the absence of towing hooks on many of them. Mobility was especially problematic for the heavy 17-pound cannons, which had a greater penetrating ability than the 6-pounders and were more effective against the enemy's heavy tanks (Stalins and Centurions). Half-tracks were supposed to be used for towing, but instead, five-ton 6-by-6 trucks—unsuited for towing heavy antitank cannons—were allocated. To make matters worse, the 6-pounders failed to receive proper technical maintenance: their sights were not calibrated, and their range tables were found to be off. Thus, in May–June 1956 a frantic effort was made to calibrate the cannons and correct the range tables. According to Ze'ev Elron, the weakness in the antitank and armor layout, as revealed by the Pelet exercise in May, was probably one reason that Ben-Gurion decided not to initiate hostilities and opted instead for a defensive posture.[57]

SS-10 Missiles

Israel purchased SS-10 antitank guided missiles from France in late 1955. In early 1956 it was decided that the artillery branch would establish four antitank battalions, each with three batteries: three regional command battalions and one as a general staff reserve. In March thirty-five missiles and two launchers arrived from France, and the first unit was set up under a veil of secrecy. In early April the trainees returned from France and began to organize the unit. The first battery was expected to be operational in July 1956, the second in August, and three more by July 1957. However, the organization took longer than planned, and in the end, the missiles were not used in the Sinai War.[58]

Rocket Launchers

In early 1955 the IDF had 560 73mm rocket launchers and 3,000 PIAT launchers, far short of the 5,000 launchers and 100,000 rockets it required. To close the gap, Israel decided to purchase American 3.5-inch rocket launchers and additional 73mm rocket launchers and to order 1,000 82mm rocket launchers and 20,000 rockets from IMI. France agreed to supply an additional 500 73mm rocket launchers. With these acquisitions and the possibility of purchasing thousands of rocket launchers of various models, discussions were held regarding the units' table of equipment. Four types of rocket launchers were acquired and produced in this period:

1. American 3.5-inch (89mm) rocket launchers. In November 1955 the director of the Ministry of Defense, Shimon Peres, recommended buying these launchers because of their low price. At the same time, he warned that the manufacturer might be unable to supply them within the one month promised. The 350 launchers that arrived in July 1956 turned out to be inferior to the French 73mm ones, and they were assigned to regional defense and noninfantry units.
2. Belgian 83mm rocket launchers. The IDF purchased 1,000 rocket launchers from Belgium before testing them. The ammunition that came with them had apparently passed the expiration date, and two years after the transaction, one-third of the rockets were deemed unfit for use.
3. Israeli 82mm rocket launchers. Despite the plan to produce 60 to 90 rocket launchers and 1,000 rockets each month, the IDF had only six launchers in its inventory in early October 1956. Distribution to the units began only in early 1958—a major miscalculation in planning.
4. French 73mm rocket launchers. The IDF doubled the number of these weapons (compared with early 1955) to 1,090 launchers and 19,000 rockets. The 200 launchers that were taken out of the French army and urgently sent to Israel proved to be inoperable. One thousand additional launchers and 30,000 rockets arrived on the eve of the Sinai War but came too late to be used in combat.[59]

Given the sense of urgency, some of these weapons were acquired before their suitability to Israel's professional needs or technical conditions had been thoroughly examined, only because their price was attractive or an early delivery date was promised.

Given the pace of events, there was little opportunity to discuss the new equipment's assimilation and employment before it arrived in the country. Thus, the army had to develop doctrine for using equipment it had not requested or that it suddenly found itself in possession of—often in quantities far exceeding its needs. Instead of an orderly procedure in which equipment is acquired because of its applicability to a fighting concept, in this period, the IDF had to devise a combat doctrine for the weapons it already had.

The basic change in the work plans was necessitated by the acquisition of tanks in June 1956 that far exceeded the army's needs. The procurement was incompatible with professional requirements, devoured huge sums of money, and weighed heavily on the maintenance budget in the following years. The funds required for this tank acquisition were thus not available for vital investment in the readiness of many defensive weapons purchased in early 1956 or for ammunition, operational accessories, and the training of their operators.[60]

Dismantlement and Reestablishment of Southern Command Headquarters

The proposal to eliminate Southern Command and save 400 manpower positions was broached in September 1954. Two months later, Central Command assumed responsibility for the southern half of the country and all the units attached to Southern Command. In place of Southern Command, a newly formed Negev Headquarters was established in Beer Sheva to deal with routine security matters. A few months after this major shift, however, second thoughts were expressed, and there was talk of reestablishing Southern Command due to Central Command's need to deal with the rising Egyptian threat owing to the escalation of incidents on the Gaza border.[61]

"In November 1954 Moshe Dayan dismantled Southern Command and subordinated it to Central Command in order to cut expenses. . . . [The following summer] he realized that his decision had been a gross mistake."[62] On the eve of the Khan Yunis operation (August 31, 1955), a heightened state of alert was declared, and Southern Command was reinstated.[63] "Southern Command's headquarters was hastily restored to the former framework of 1954, although at this stage it was still called the 'Negev Headquarters' within Central Command. The headquarters' commander was Colonel Meir Amit, who had headed General Staff Directorate until then. His first task was to evaluate the likelihood of war."[64]

According to Amit, he reestablished Southern Command in stages, first as the head of a setup team composed of people he knew and trusted. On

October 28, 1955, Amit was formally appointed commander of Southern Command. "The first thing we did was build the command from scratch," he wrote.[65] Simultaneously, they had to cope with attacks by fedayeen (Arab infiltrators) and reinforce the regional defense layout. Amit recalled that Southern Command focused its war preparations on the offensive: "We carried out frequent maneuvers and prepared intelligence files on vast areas in Sinai for the units."[66] "Because Southern Command had been mothballed, the team that was supposed to keep close tabs on the Egyptian forces consisted of only one officer and two soldiers who were reinforced with three reservists at the start of tension."[67] On August 5, 1956, Amit was replaced by Colonel Asaf Simchoni, whose first assignment was to transfer the command from Kastina to Beer Sheva.[68]

The Air Force

In aerial combat, the more complex the weapons, the more difficult their assimilation. In the months preceding the war, the IAF was transitioning from World War II piston-driven aircraft to jet aircraft. The head of the IAF's history branch, Motti Habakuk, notes that the IAF was in the midst of assimilating advanced jet aircraft—the Ouragan and Mystère IV—while it was also scrupulously preparing for war. Thus, the number of pilots qualified to fly the new aircraft was insufficient, and the use of these planes was minimal. On October 29, 1956, the day the war broke out, of the sixty Mystères in the country, only fourteen were operable, and even they were limited by their imprecise gun-firing capability.[69]

Weapons

As noted earlier, the main difficulty in risk management is deciding whether to replenish troops with readily available weapons (as war approaches) or wait for more advanced weapons that are expected to become available. General Ezer Weizman describes how the French army urged the IDF to procure the Mystère II, a fighter plane that could not be converted into an attack aircraft. Although the Mystère II was available for immediate delivery, it was plagued by sundry problems.[70] The Mystère IV, a more advanced model with multipurpose capability as both a fighter and an attack plane, would be available in a few months. According to Weizman, despite pressure from Dayan, Peres, and many others who insisted that the Mystère II should be purchased, IAF commander Dan Tolkowsky "displayed obstinacy in the face of all the counter-arguments that stood between the IAF and the Mystère II procurement."[71] Eleven years later in the Six-Day War, the Mystère IV proved invaluable in Operation Moked. Though planned to be utilized until 1973, it was taken out of service in 1970.[72]

The decision to back down on the Mystère II and wait for the Mystère IV apparently came at the price of readiness for the Sinai War. In his book *There Will Be War in the Summer,* Motti Golani describes a conversation in early July 1956 between Prime Minister–Defense Minister Ben-Gurion and Tolkowsky about a Mystère squadron with twelve pilots: "six who can fly and six who are still learning." Later, in answer to Ben-Gurion's question about how much time it would take for sixty pilots to be ready for war, Tolkowsky replied, "A year, at the very least."[73]

Some of the Ouragan pilots, too, were inexperienced; six of the eighteen pilots had spent only eight hours flying the aircraft.[74] Weizman describes how he piloted the Ouragan in the war after only ten hours of training and learned some of the aircraft's capabilities while in flight.[75] "Even though Israel had enough Mystères for three squadrons, only one was operational—Squadron 101 [under the command of Major Benny Peled]—and this too was achieved at the cost of the Meteor and Ouragan squadrons that had been reduced to only a dozen pilots each."[76] The IDF was fortunate that the rest of the new Mystères were flown by French pilots in the Sinai War.[77] French assistance proved priceless in carrying out air reconnaissance; this freed the Israeli squadrons for offensive missions, such as attacking the retreating Egyptian convoys.[78]

The Mystères' 30mm cannon ammunition arrived from France in limited supply just one or two days before the war. The "Mystères' bombs were unavailable and only a handful of 68 mm rockets had arrived. The newest plane in our arsenal had not been installed [with the necessary equipment] to drop bombs."[79]

Lieutenant Ran Ronen (Pekker) describes his first combat mission in a Mystère squadron in the Sinai War, which he carried out with insufficient knowledge of the aircraft he was flying: "Only after we crossed the Israeli-Egyptian border east to Gaza did I realize that we were actually headed for war! I found myself seated in a new plane that I'd accumulated only 15 hours in the air with and was just beginning to learn its maneuverability in aerial combat or in attacking ground targets. I'd never operated its weapons systems. . . . This was a lethal combination of flying too low for strafing, uncontrolled deviation of the new and unfamiliar aircraft, and precarious terrain."[80]

The ground crew also had problems with the new aircraft: "'Jettisoning drop tanks!' I looked at the wings and was horrified to see the detachable fuel tanks were still locked in place and what was plunging to the ground were the rocket pods. . . . The munitions crew definitely got it wrong when they connected the jettison system which they were obviously uninstructed in. . . . The series of foul-ups in the aircraft was quite large. The technicians had lots to learn yet about the new plane. . . . The Mystère had just been assimilated and was already engaged in actual combat."[81]

Lieutenant Yosef Tzuk, a young Mystère pilot, recalled: "We received our first air-to-surface training at a firing range only on the Saturday before the war. We didn't have a clue what to do. The rockets were put into regular (and unfitted) launching pipes and some of them fell out in the flight to the range."[82]

The IAF's control and monitoring system was being remodeled while the air force was undergoing a force buildup and switching to jet planes. The air force's communications services, which were based on line links, were also in the midst of being upgraded. Work on the infrastructure of underground communications cables had begun in 1955, but the section between Tel Aviv and Haifa was halted in the final stage when hostilities broke out. Therefore, the IAF's main control station suffered from excessive communications breakdowns and even cutoffs during the fighting.[83]

Organization and Training

According to the Absalom training plan, which went into effect on September 25, 1956, and raised the level of alert, the propeller squadrons that had been mothballed in the Bedek storage facility in Lod in June–July 1956—the 69th (B-17s), 105th (Mustangs), and 110th (Mosquitoes)—were prepared for active flight. The ten days planned for training were shortened to just three.[84] To man the jet planes and prepare the best pilots to fly the newest aircraft, pilot training on the propeller-driven planes was minimized, operational training on the Mustangs was canceled, and flight-school graduates went directly from piston-driven Harvards to Meteors. One Ouragan squadron was fully designated for instruction.[85] "Preparation for war was hastily carried out before the force buildup with the new equipment was completed. All of Israel's weapons had to be put to maximum use; the piston-powered aircraft had to be restored to combat capability and the air crews had to be quickly refreshed. Ironically, the air force went to war in the midst of a lull in its operational fitness and tactical preparedness."[86]

Israel was lucky that it could rely on the air capabilities of its coalition allies France and Great Britain; thus, its operational shortcomings were not conspicuously apparent. Weapons upgrade is a fact of life for every military organization. The fact of the matter is that every war catches an army in the middle of change. The IAF's story is a classic example of war erupting when the military is undergoing a dramatic overhaul that temporarily diminishes its capabilities. The lesson to be learned is that before implementing an upgrade, the implications of the transition from tried and tested capabilities to new ones must be taken into consideration. Translating this principle into reality is complex and expensive because it often demands twice the amount of training. In other words, it entails employing old and new weapons simultaneously, maintaining two weapons inventories, and so forth. Naturally, the newer the weapons (or C2 systems), the more resources needed to assimilate them and the more convoluted the process becomes. Changing an infantryman's personal weapon is much different from replacing an aircraft. The more complex a weapon's technology, the more difficult its assimilation is, the longer the time required, and the greater the risks involved.

Besides the basic changes in the armored corps, the IAF, the antitank systems, and so forth, a number of senior commanders assumed new roles before the war broke out. Bringing in new players at the start of a war is a risky undertaking. In Israel's case, the head of the J3 branch and deputy chief of staff, General Haim Laskov, was transferred to the armored corps to oversee the rapid force buildup (he later commanded the 77th Division based at the armored corps headquarters). Laskov's former position as head of GHQ was assigned to Major General Meir Amit, the commander of Southern Command. Amit's role was taken over by Colonel Asaf Simchoni in early August 1956.[87]

The Six-Day War: The "Waiting Period"

In February–March 1967, on the basis of the Maccabee Multiyear Plan, the GHQ reviewed the assessment that an all-out Arab-initiated war was unlikely until 1970, although limited operations were possible.[88] This evaluation radically changed on May 19 when Egyptian advances in Sinai heightened the possibility of hostilities.[89]

Ammunition Shortages and Tank Upgrades

The Bnei Or (Sons of Light) Multiyear Plan was designed to expand the Centurion and Patton order of battle to more than 600 tanks. Optimal operation of the 105mm Shreer (Muscle) tank cannons required 250,000 shells of various types. This amount was difficult to obtain because of the high cost of ammunition in Britain. At the conclusion of the arms deal with the United Kingdom in April 1965, and with domestic production by IMI, the total would be around 50,000. Therefore, the IDF signed another deal with Britain for 86,000 shells. This would bring the 105mm Shreer ammunition up to the standard (full tank belly and battalion-level truck reinforcement) for three days of fighting. The problem was that the supply of the ammunition was spread out through 1970 and 1971. Another complication was Britain's development of a new kinetic energy armor-penetrating L-52 shell that was superior to and more expensive than the L-28. After weighing its options, Israel decided to acquire the new L-52.[90]

In early 1965 the armored corps commander, General Tal, dramatized the situation estimate to Prime Minister–Defense Minister Levi Eshkol: "The armored corps is good for inspections and parades but it's not ready for war if it lacks ammunition."[91] Upon hearing this, Eshkol agreed to add another 22,500 shells to the budget. Tal flew to Britain to facilitate the acquisition. Use of the shells in training exercises was banned because of the shortage of ammunition (20-pounders were used instead). In reality, and for myriad reasons, on May 15, 1967, the start of the alert preceding the Six-Day War, the full inventory of Shreers stood at 24,200 kinetic energy armor-penetrating shells, 16,500 high-explosive antitank (HEAT) shells, and 5,230 high-explosive squash head (HESH) shells. This was the approximate standard (excluding armor-penetrating shells) for three days of combat.

During the waiting period from May 15 to June 5, 1967, while the country held its breath to see whether President Nasser of Egypt would recall his troops from Sinai or the Israeli government would declare war, an impressive number of tanks were upgraded with Shreer cannons (sixty-five Centurions and fifteen Pattons). This effort "emphasized the urgent need for ammunition, especially HESH shells, in order to close the widening gaps. Britain, the source of these rounds, conditioned their delivery on the rate of production. Now the supply would have to come from the British army's current stock."[92] Britain largely fulfilled Israel's requests. By June 4, 3,670 HESH shells had arrived in Israel by air, and 4,700 arrived by sea the following day. The delivery of these munitions during the waiting period and after the war began had a substantial effect on the armored units. For example, a company of Centurion tanks that was hastily cobbled together by the chief armor officer's headquarters and attached to the 10th Brigade on the eve of the war was armed with only armor-penetrating shells. On the morning of June 8, when the company reached Jericho, the first HESH shells finally arrived.[93]

A similar problem was the shortage of HEAT shells for the 105mm cannons of the Sherman M-51s. On May 15 the ammunition inventory stood at 6,120 HEAT and 9,650 HESH shells. Thus, each of the 175 tanks was armed with only 34 HEAT shells and had enough HESH shells about three days of fighting.[94] As a result, "each Sherman in the 45th Brigade received only half a belly of HEAT shells (19–20 to a tank) and at the battalion and company level the stock was non-existent. Another delivery of the shells arrived on June 4."[95]

Brezner states that, as these data show, no meticulous planning had been performed to match ammunition stocks to existing tanks or the expected number of Centurions. At times, this led to an acute ammunition shortage and a critical threat to the effective operation of first-line tanks if war erupted in the near future. Although vast resources had been invested in improving the Centurions, given the lack of ammunition, their optimal combat capability could not be realized. In an extreme case, all efforts to upgrade the tanks would be in vain. Not only the new tanks but also the Sherman M-51s suffered from an ammunition deficit due to the long wait between placing the order and receiving the product. Some of the ammunition (HEAT shells) was still being developed, and the IDF had to stand by until research and development were completed. The Ministry of Defense hoped IMI would begin producing some of the ammunition and thus broaden the range of its products, which would save foreign currency and avoid lengthy delivery delays. Finally, budget cutbacks played a role in the dire shortfall in ammunition.[96]

In ten hectic days (May 16–25) the ordnance workshops managed to upgrade 115 tanks, including 16 Centurions. When Central Command received them, they were still armed with 20-pound cannons, just as they had been when shipped from Britain. The tanks' 20-pounders were not replaced with 105mm cannons after it was realized that Central Command had enough 20-pounder shells.[97]

The three-week waiting period leading up to the war were of major significance because they enabled critical shortages to be filled. "The armored corps' ammunition deficit taught Rabin that force buildup demands a planned parity between weapons' replenishment and the acquisition of ammunition and spare parts. . . . 'Better thirty tanks less and having what we possess with the necessary amount of ammunition and spare parts.'"[98]

Force Organization

During the waiting period, the chief armor officer's headquarters established two battalions and three companies made up of Armor School staff instructors and the armored corps' testing unit. The headquarters made optimal use of the 900 officers and men who had trained in Israel or had returned from abroad by reinforcing the armored divisions with 197 additional crews.[99]

The formation of the Eshkolot Landing Force (named after its commander, Ze'ev Eshkolot) on May 23 was also an important step. This force was designated to make a seaborne landing during the 55th Paratrooper Brigade's airdrop in the El-Arish area in the event the 84th Division was delayed on the roads. The force consisted of two AMX-13 companies from the 60th Brigade, a platoon of 120mm towed mortars, an SS-11 missile platoon, and a motorized infantry platoon on half-tracks from the 55th Brigade. Much work went into ensuring the improvised force's supply of fuel, ammunition, communications equipment, and machine gun mounts, as well as sealing (waterproofing) the AFVs and other vehicles. The tank crews underwent training at the Armor School's firing range. The landing force carried out maneuvers in the Ashdod Port, completed its preparations and exercises by June 4, and assembled in the port on the night of June 4–5.[100] The next day the El-Arish landing was canceled, and the Eshkolot Landing Force came under the command of the 11th Brigade and participated in the capture of the Gaza Strip.

Training

Training exercises in the waiting period were limited in order to conceal force preparation. The limitations applied mainly to heavy weapons. Absolute radio silence was maintained, and movement to concentration and training areas was reduced and done without radio communication. Training focused on proficiency enhancement and operations in special areas and under NBC (nuclear, biological, chemical) conditions.[101] The infantry (especially in Southern Command) underwent intensive training related to attacking fortified objectives. The IDF planned for an NBC threat because of its deep concern about Egypt's use of chemical weapons in Yemen. A commander of a tank company, Lieutenant Avigdor Kahalani, recalled that, during the waiting period, "they surprised the hell out of us with anti-gas systems. . . . We carried out hasty training sessions in holding our breath while hooking up to the system."[102] Captain Yossi Peled, the commander of a mechanized infantry company, remembered that "they suddenly gave us these weird masks. What's this? Protection from gas. . . . So how does it work? What's it like under fire? What about training? How am I supposed to remember the drill? What if the radio suddenly conks out and I have to improvise, was I thoroughly trained for this?"[103]

The 94th Battalion, 200th Brigade, which was still not completely formed, continued its program of instruction and refresher training into early June.[104]

Intelligence Measures

Southern Command's intelligence aids are of special interest. After ten years of quiet following the Sinai War, Southern Command was suddenly ordered to commence hasty planning for an IDF attack in May 1967. Zalman Gandler writes that since the start of the waiting period, IDF military intelligence had been working around the clock to prepare up-to-date material, and the quantity collected after two weeks equaled that normally compiled in an ordinary year.

The area was photographed only at the end of the waiting period, and only some of the forces received the updated photostats. Even then, it was too late.[105]

To sum up the Six-Day War case, the high level of readiness the IDF attained in three weeks enabled it to win the war. Good relations with European countries (France, Britain, Germany, and Holland) allowed Israel to narrow some of the gaps in aircraft equipment, tank ammunition, and NBC equipment.

The Yom Kippur War: The "Blue-White" Alert

At the April 16, 1973, general staff meeting, the chief of intelligence reported that the latest findings predicted war for May 15. His assessment, however, was that the likelihood of war was low. The chief of staff, Lieutenant General David (Dado) Elazar, decided to undertake a wide range of preparations, executed discreetly. These included increasing the available order of battle in Sinai and the Golan Heights; updating operational plans; advancing training schedules planned for later in the year; forming new reserve units and canceling orders for the dismantling of regular units; accelerating weapons replenishment; and speeding up the completion of operational infrastructure such as roads, fortifications, and antitank obstacles.[106] This section discusses some of the tensions involved in these preparations, and it highlights what can be accomplished in a relatively short time.

Organization

The formation of the 210th Division was originally planned for March 1974. On May 14, 1973, the date was brought forward to June 15.[107] The buildup of the division included the establishment of division headquarters, the 312th Communications Battalion, two tank battalions (the 106th and 183rd) in the 164th Shot (105mm L7 Centurion) Brigade, the headquarters of an artillery regiment (the artillery battalions had already been formed), the 923rd Engineering Battalion, and an improvised supply regiment headquarters.

The formation of the 418th Ivri Missile Unit, originally planned for 1974, was moved up to 1973, and the formation of the 440th Division headquarters, which was part of the Ofek A Multiyear Plan, was brought forward to August 1973. Similarly, the formation of three armored reconnaissance battalions for the 143rd, 146th, and 162nd Divisions, which had been planned for August–November 1973, was advanced to June–July.

In the corps of engineers, two assault roller bridging units were established in June 1973 (not originally planned for 1973). In addition, the formation of two reserve engineering battalions for the 252nd and 210th Divisions was advanced from October–December 1973 to June–August 1973.

The 1973 work plan called for the demobilization of the regular 75th Battalion, 7th Tank Brigade, but during the 1973 alert it remained a regular battalion.[108]

Operational Infrastructure

The following infrastructure was present:[109]

- Twelve kilometers of antitank trenches in Northern Command.[110]
- One hundred twenty-one kilometers of roads on the Golan Heights for artillery and tanks.
- Communications lines stretching between Nafakh-Safed (Northern Command) and Yalek-Refidim and Yalek-Dveila (Sinai).
- Reserve stores units at Abu-Rudeis (Sinai) for an infantry battalion, tank company, and battery of 122mm cannons, and at Bir Tmada (Sinai) for sixty-four tanks.

The 679th Brigade's reserve stores unit advanced to Corazim (northern Galilee),[111] and the 179th Brigade's reserve stores unit moved to the Filon Base (northern Galilee). After the war, the Agranat Commission report stated that advancing the reserve stores units of Northern Command's armored brigades contributed decisively to their speedy arrival in the Golan and blocking of Syrian forces.[112]

Weapons and Equipment

The following weapons and equipment were available or added:[113]

- Hundreds of vehicular and portable radio communications sets were added.
- Water-crossing equipment—twenty-one carriages for transporting Unifloat pontoons—was brought forward, and a fifth Yiftach roller bridge was ordered.
- The Ivri Missile Unit received an additional four launchers and twenty rockets.

It should be noted that until the war broke out, the attempt to develop towing hitches that would enable the roller bridges to traverse the steep, sandy slopes in the Suez Canal area took place at a frenetic pace, regardless of cost, yet ultimately proved unsuccessful.[114]

Another area of tension during the force buildup was the development and replenishment of night-vision devices for tanks (Arab armies had been equipped with them since the Six-Day War). There were no plans to acquire infrared sights that could be procured in the West (such as those in Russian-made tanks) because, according to intelligence estimates, war was not expected. Instead, Israel planned to wait until its own technology for starlight enhancers was developed. However domestic production of electro-optic systems was beset by delays and cancellations,[115] which put IDF tank crews at a grave disadvantage in the Yom Kippur War.

Training

The amount of prior training naturally had a major impact on the units' competency. Among the various exercises were task-oriented maneuvers for the canal-crossing units. Avshalom Levi describes the 257th Armored Battalion, 421st Brigade, a reserve unit formed in April 1973 and commanded by Lieutenant Colonel Shimon Ben Shoshan. The battalion's initial training lasted ten days. Officers at the platoon commander level and higher participated in a divisional skeleton exercise in August that gave an invaluable boost to the battalion's proficiency. The 275th Battalion was scheduled to receive its tanks and equipment in 1974.[116]

Alert Level

Raising the alert level is not a factor in force buildup, but to complete the picture, the following should be noted: On May 25, 1973, the GHQ operations branch ordered that steps be taken to prepare for mobilizing the reservists.[117] These steps included checking the emergency mobilization procedures and evaluating the regular army headquarters' level of readiness to call up the reserve units. A plan was issued to hold mobilization drills, verify reserve soldiers' addresses, and monitor the alert level of all reserve units during June–August 1973. Unit deployment exercises were carried out, reserve storerooms were readied, self-propelled artillery was sent to Sinai, crossing equipment was hastily deployed, and so forth.[118]

The Blue-White alert lasted four months (from mid-April to August) and concluded as planned. The cost of the alert was 69 million Israeli lira (in 2019, approximately $66 million),[119] and it had a major impact on the IDF's readiness for the Yom Kippur War.[120] According to deputy chief of staff Tal, "The IDF entered the Yom Kippur War a stronger army than what was planned for October 1973, even more powerful than the design for 1974–1975."[121]

The American Airlift

The American airlift is a different type of issue from that discussed up to this point. Much can be learned from the attempt to introduce brand-new weapons into combat, illustrating what can and cannot be achieved during fighting. After many delays, the American airlift began on October 14, 1973. Most of the equipment was brought over on US Air Force Galaxies and Starlifters, as well as civilian aircraft. Between October 14 and 24, 8,775 tons of ammunition, weapons, spare parts, and other supplies reached the country.[122] On October 8 the IDF ordered 120 TOW antitank launchers at a cost of $10 million. A few months earlier, Tal had vetoed a request for a small number of TOWs for testing.[123] Seventy launchers arrived on October 16, and a team was trained in their operation. The test firings proved successful.[124] According to an American report, Israel received eighty-one launchers and 2,000 missiles.[125] The IDF christened the missile Orev (Raven) and mounted it on Israeli-made reconnaissance jeeps. Within twenty-four hours of the jeeps' and missiles' arrival at the IDF Repair and Maintenance Center, the first antitank jeep model was produced. Officers and noncommissioned officers recently returned from training in the United States took the jeep and, accompanied by ordnance personnel, test-fired the missiles. Lessons were learned on the spot, and the ordnance branch began manufacturing dozens of replacement parts.[126] The jeeps were rushed to the southern Golan Heights to reinforce the thin defensive line being held by the aging Sherman tanks.[127] Nevertheless, not a single missile was fired during the war.

Another weapon provided by the airlift and rushed to the battlefield was the LAW antitank launcher. Given the difficulties of assimilating even so-called user-friendly weapons in the midst of fighting, the complexities involved in this task were readily apparent. According to an American report, the IDF obtained 16,000 launchers during the war.[128] "The [890th] battalion received two pallets of LAW rockets replete with English-language instructions attached. We were lucky that Egyptian tanks didn't show up because no one had a clue what to do with the rockets."[129] Two occasions on which the LAWs were fired illustrate the problem. On the night of October 21–22 Israeli naval commandos carried out a fourth attack on the Egyptian port of Hurghada and fired a LAW that had arrived the previous day. Their mission was to sink an Egyptian missile boat. The commandos reached the objective in swift attack boats. According to Ze'ev Almog, commander of the Red Sea sector:

> Since we were given only 20 rockets, we had to use them for both training and combat operations. The weapon's allocation was decided in this way: ten missiles for training . . . and ten for the mission. Only

> one fighter in each attack boat would undergo "sniper" training. . . . We didn't know what the rocket's range would be from inside a fast boat. . . . Therefore, on the morning of October 21 we practiced firing on a seaborne target. The effective range was calculated at 100 meters max. Then we decided to carry out a nighttime test on a firing range to determine the launching range. . . . During the operation the first eight rockets missed the target and the last two hit a Komar-class missile boat and destroyed it.[130]

Captain Shaul Mofaz, commander of the paratrooper reconnaissance company in Operation Kutonet (Nightgown), recounted another occasion when the LAWs were used immediately after their arrival. The night operation took place deep behind Syrian lines on October 12 and was designed to hit Iraqi convoys reinforcing the Syrians on the Golan Heights. He recalled:

> A few hours before setting out, weapons (including LAW rockets) arrived at the Tel Nof Airbase on the American airlift. The Americans are very organized. When they send weapons to foreign countries they include all the instruction paraphernalia. The LAW also came with blue plaster rocket training aids. We were the first IDF unit to receive this weapon. We didn't exercise with them but some of the soldiers managed to read the operating manual before setting out on the mission. When a tank and the tank carrier overturned, one of the officers gave the order to fire the LAWs. Two rockets were fired and a large white stain spread across the tank. The soldiers were amazed and thought it was a secret weapon that fragmentized tanks or something like that, but in the debriefing it turned out that these were plaster training rockets.[131]

Even though Israel received thousands of LAW launchers, dozens of TOW launchers, and 2,000 missiles, almost none of them were used in the war.

Another new weapon that arrived was the Chaparral surface-to-air missile. This was an air-to-air Sidewinder missile repurposed as a mobile surface-to-air missile. Two Chaparral systems came in on the airlift, and the American operating instructions were quickly translated. The weapon was test-fired forty hours after its arrival, and eight hours later the force employed it operationally, defending a Hawk battery by ambushing Egyptian helicopters. This took place on October 23, one day before the end of the war. A week earlier, a contingent of fifty-four commanders, soldiers, and technicians had been dispatched to the United States. They completed a nineteen-day crash course on the Chaparral rather than the usual seven-week course. Upon their return they were deployed in the Israeli bulge in Syria.[132]

These case studies illustrate what can and cannot be done, as well as the dilemmas and tensions inherent in a hasty force buildup.

Investment in the Present versus a Solution for the Future

In some cases, priority was given to acquiring available weapons, even if their effectiveness remained uncertain; in other cases, replenishment was postponed until a more suitable weapon arrived. The large purchase of AMX-13 tanks and rocket launchers was an example of the first choice, while waiting to acquire the Mystère IV and the long-barreled Sherman M-50 tanks represented the second choice. The rule is that hasty procurement in wartime is of limited value, and the equipment usually ends up remaining in service after the war because of insufficient funds to replace it. Upgrading existing weapons is generally less complicated and often provides an unmistakably greater contribution, as was the case with the dieselization of the Shot tank engines (105mm L7 Centurions), which was competed just before the Yom Kippur War.[133]

Two cases illustrate the problem of mustering out old weapons before assimilating new ones. First, in the period preceding the Sinai War, replacing the Staghound armored car with the AMX-13 tank forced the IDF to make a volte-face. Second, the difficulty in assimilating and operating new jet fighters pushed the propeller squadrons, which were gradually being replaced, out of service. The rule should be: new takes priority over old, but only after the new has been assimilated. And assimilating new weapons just before or during a war is problematic. Their effectiveness is generally minimal. This was the case with the Mystère aircraft, the AMX-13 tanks, the LAW rockets, the TOW missiles, and so forth. The rule should be: do not introduce new weapons into service immediately before or during a short war. Another lesson is that a balance has to be maintained among all the elements: main weapons systems, ammunition, spare parts, users' proficiency.

In the future, increasing the number of main weapons systems (such as tanks and aircraft) will become increasingly difficult due to the greater complexity of producing them. On the one hand, for Israel (and for small states in general), relying on the domestic production of AFVs, for example, significantly limits the ability to expand production. On the other hand, banking on foreign production creates dependency on an outside supplier that may decide to freeze sales (examples include France's boycott of Israel after the Six-Day War and American political pressure in exchange for the supply of weapons and ammunition in the Yom

Kippur War). The conclusion is that when war is expected, the working assumption should be that increasing the force size is impossible.

The prewar upgrade of weapons has also grown more complex. For example, the pace of technological advances in the computer software that supports a wide range of combat systems exacerbates the difficulty of upgrading sophisticated weaponry. The integration of a new component into a complex system, such as a tank or advanced aircraft that was produced a decade before the upgrade, is more challenging than ever. In addition to the engineering and mechanical hurdles that have always had to be overcome, adapting software and dealing with electromagnetic spectrum management issues present new challenges.

2

The Effect of Prolonged Routine Security Operations on Wartime Capabilities

Routine security operations (RSOs) in the Israeli context comprise a wide variety of activities, including border defense against terrorists, detentions and targeted killings in the West Bank (under IDF doctrine, referred to as limited conflict), and brigade-sized raids similar to those carried out during reprisal operations.[1] Specific examples of RSOs include the 1968 Karameh raid in Jordan, brigade-sized operations in the Israeli security zone in Lebanon (under IDF doctrine, limited-scale offensive operations), and Israeli operations against surface-to-air missiles (SAMs) on the Egyptian front during the 1967–1970 War of Attrition. The American equivalent to an RSO is a counterinsurgency operation, similar to those conducted in Iraq and Afghanistan, despite the absence of border issues in those cases.

In Israel, RSOs are relatively long lasting and are characteristic of every interwar period. RSOs must be successful for a number of reasons: to protect against the perpetual threat to Israeli citizens, to ensure relatively few casualties, to deter adversaries, and so forth. The need for success in RSOs usually compels commanders to do the following:

- Operate according to a detailed command and control (C2) approach that minimizes performance error.
- Prefer elite units.
- Request and employ state-of-the-art weapons.
- Adjust to fighting norms unsuited to wartime situations (for example, low casualty rates rather than mission accomplishment).[2]

Tension is created between operational success in limited conflict and reduced fighting capabilities in a future war, as the following points illustrate:

- The detailed command philosophy and measures used in small, intense actions in RSOs are the antithesis of the mission-oriented command that should be employed by an army in wartime. Therefore, the army's ability to carry out large, complex, tightly scheduled operations is inhibited.

- The adoption of RSO norms, such as giving priority to the treatment of wounded rather than mission completion, is liable to spill over into wartime.
- The insistence on specific (sometimes special) units for offensive RSOs can harm the sense of competence in the rest of the army, which is burdened with numbing, repetitious activity that limits the opportunity to gain diversified military experience.
- The use of sophisticated weapons in RSOs risks their exposure, thus enabling the enemy to develop the means to neutralize them before the next war. This stands in stark contrast to the surprise revelation of such weapons in the next war.[3]

These actions are the responsibility of the regional brigade and division commanders. The bodies responsible for force design (the air force, army, and so forth) must also be aware of these problems and provide solutions that entail training for war and maintaining secrecy, among other things. However, the problem is aggravated when the bodies responsible for force design are focused on RSOs and the army loses its fighting capability in many areas. Diverting attention from war preparation often leads to the following:

- Investing more time on training and acquiring proficiency for RSOs than for wartime missions.
- Forming special RSO-designated units.
- Developing weapons geared primarily to RSOs.

Almost every war the IDF has fought took place after several years of RSOs. For example, the 1956 Sinai War began after retaliatory raids and defensive operations against fedayeen, and the Six-Day War broke out after the "battle" over the Jordan River's water (1964–1967). Two wars in which the IDF's performance was considerably influenced by the preceding routine security periods were the Yom Kippur War, which occurred after six years of defensive operations on the borders, especially in the Jordan Valley and Suez Canal region (including the War of Attrition on the canal front), and the Second Lebanon War, which erupted more than two decades after the First Lebanon War.[4] In the latter case, the IDF had been engaged mainly in RSOs on the northern border (the Israeli security zone in southern Lebanon) and in Judea and Samaria (the West Bank) and the Gaza Strip. This chapter analyzes the effect that years of RSOs had on the army's combat capability in these two major wars. It does not deal with the psychological strain involved in shifting from daily security to wartime, as occurred in these two events (see chapter 4).

Impact of 1967–1973 RSOs on the Yom Kippur War

At the end of the Six-Day War, the IDF found itself engaged in operations on the new borders. Activity was concentrated in two regions: the Jordan Valley (against Palestinian terrorist squads) and the Suez Canal (against Egyptian artillery attacks, commando raids, ambushes, and sniper fire). A major air battle also ensued above the canal.

Edward Luttwak and Dan Horowitz write, "The conflicting demands of long term force design on the one hand and daily operations on the other were all the more acute because of the new defensive tactics that were coming to the fore." They note, "In 1968–70 the army had to devise new tactical methods, retrain officers and men, absorb much new equipment—and do all this while fighting a conventional war on one front [the Suez Canal] and counter-guerilla on three [Lebanon, the West Bank, and Gaza]."[5]

Yoav Gelber's analysis of these competing demands is similar. He describes a sharp decline in the amount of time devoted to training periods. Originally, training consumed approximately 90 percent of the army's time; this percentage dropped to 50 percent, with the time being equally divided between training and RSOs.[6] It should be noted, though, that this was still far more training than was performed before the Second Lebanon War, when almost 90 percent of the army's time was allocated to RSOs. Another major difference between the 2000–2006 and 1967–1973 periods is that before the Yom Kippur War, armored units conducted their RSO missions on tanks and split into platoons on the Suez Canal and the Golan Heights. Between 2000 and 2006 they operated as infantry squads. Nevertheless, despite the dramatic change in the allocation of time and resources, training and weapons assimilation strengthened the IDF before the Yom Kippur War.

C2 Aspects

The IAF's attacks against SAM sites on the canal in the War of Attrition were comparable to ground raids that require careful planning and elite units. In Israel's case, new Phantom squadrons were formed. The air force's missions, both along the Suez Canal and deep in Egypt, were meticulously prepared by the IAF headquarters, whereas most wartime operations (excluding specific cases such as Operation Moked—the IAF's liquidation of Arab air forces at the start of the Six-Day War) were planned at the squadron level. Shmuel Gordon describes the difference between IAF operations in the War of Attrition (limited war) and in the Yom Kippur War (full-scale war). In limited wars and RSOs, operations are executed by a very small number of forces relative to higher headquarters' C2 capability. Headquarters deals with each threat the moment it arises, changing targets, routes, and other microtactical details for flight leaders. It makes numerous decisions that flight leaders are capable of making themselves. Its ability to exert hands-on control in limited fighting addresses numerous restrictions and sensitive issues that are absent in a large-scale war, such as determining a certain line that must not be crossed or prohibiting aerial combat. But the need for constant supervision in limited fighting inhibits flight leaders' freedom. They grow accustomed to obeying orders, leading to a diminution of their operational judgment and decision making. Because the orders for RSOs are precisely planned for each mission, they leave squadron leaders no room to introduce changes. Gordon explains:

> In all-out war the situation is very different. Operational activity is much more intense. With hundreds of planes, helicopters and airborne assistance systems aloft simultaneously, the central command post has to instruct planning teams, approve operational plans, and perform other duties. Since its ability to control operations in real time is greatly reduced, it focuses only on vital decisions.
>
> Given the combination of the central command's inability to control all the forces and the expendability of such control, the flight leaders suddenly have freedom of action and decision-making that they are unaccustomed to. They are unprepared for responsibility and authority so unlike the patterns of conduct they had grown used to in the long period of limited warfare. Lieutenant Colonel Ben-Nun, the commander of the IAF planning branch for most of the offensive operations in the year before the Yom Kippur War, describes the situation: "In RSO we reviewed every order that the squadrons had to carry out down to the last detail. The squadrons became accustomed to receiving everything spoon-fed and neatly packaged. Everything was elaborated even for the smallest operation. During the [Yom Kippur] war I saw how we had failed to prepare the squadrons to act independently. The shift from RSO to wartime conditions became a cognitive issue."[7]

The challenge lies not only in making the transition from RSOs to a war situation; the biggest challenge is the loss of the ability to act independently, a skill that cannot be acquired on the fly. The need for success in every operation during

RSOs exacted its price in wartime. The crisis in trust between squadrons and IAF headquarters stemmed, in part, from the unpreparedness for headquarters-squadron contact in an all-out war.[8]

IDF ground forces found themselves in a similar situation. "In peacetime or in periods of relative peace, armies are sidetracked by demands that becloud their true purpose and divert them from developing the ability to fight effectively in wartime." Veteran military personnel discovered that their accumulated experience was of little value when they were forced to make decisions far weightier than those in peacetime.[9] According to Hanan Shai: "In the interwar period, armies conduct RSO whose main task is border defense that often involves the suppression of guerilla forces or paramilitary armies. Tactical, small-size fighting bodies generally conduct these operations in narrow time frames. During the interwar period neither senior nor junior officers acquire operational skills and practical experience in commanding large fighting formations. The political level is chiefly responsible for this phenomenon by placing limitations on the military echelon in order to preclude tactical mistakes developing into strategic problems that might escalate into a major war."[10]

Although the ground forces' methods in the War of Attrition enabled junior officers to act independently, it reduced the freedom of action of midlevel officers (battalion and brigade commanders). On the one hand, the split-up of formations into platoon-sized forces in the Suez Canal strongholds instilled self-reliance in junior officers. On the other hand, offensive operations (raids) at all levels (Operations Raviv and Victoria in the canal sector, Operations Asuta and Tofet in Jordan, Operation Kiton 10 in Syria, Operations Kalachat 2 and 4 in Lebanon) were characterized by centralized C2 and drawn-out battle procedures (although senior commanders gained invaluable experience).

Chief of staff Haim Bar-Lev's summary of Operation Tofet (Karameh) on March 21, 1968, expresses the inherent tension between C2 in RSOs and in wartime: "In a war you order a force to carry out a mission, and move on even if contact with the force is interrupted for half an hour. But in retaliatory actions, the high command has to be involved in every detail. . . . It isn't enough to report 'mission accomplished.' It may be enough in wartime or in an across-the-border intelligence foray, but [in a retaliatory raid] every change in plans has to be reported and approved."[11]

In RSOs, orders become tedious, detailed documents that dictate the modus operandi, the order of individual vehicles in each force, and the timetable in each stage of the fighting. The battle procedures in Operation Raviv show that the armored corps commander and his staff planned the operation down to the last element, whereas the commander of the operation was, in effect, merely a "mission contractor." Furthermore: "After 1967 the commanders and staffs that specialized in the planning and direction of raids internalized this form of battle and the centralized command procedures. . . . When war came they had to employ other forms of battle such as attack, advance, and delay—maneuvers that are based on the ability to work with hasty battle procedures. They lacked the professional experience to plan and conduct these forms of battle. The senior commanders' role in RSO caused them to use similar methods in wartime since they [had reached their present positions having] advanced in the chain of command over the years."[12]

The Agranat Commission commented on the effect of years of RSOs on C2 in the Yom Kippur War. It criticized the command approach in the first days of the war, which was influenced by RSO activities—specifically, issuing orders from war rooms in the rear and employing communications systems rather than leading from the front.[13] It also found that the influence of RSOs in the prewar years had molded battle procedures, which were characterized by a disinclination to delegate authority and responsibility to subordinate command echelons. "The IDF's standard working procedures in RSO in this period were mainly based, for various reasons, on the centralization of authority and responsibility."[14]

Elite Units versus an Operationally Experienced Army

Another phenomenon related to RSOs is the use of special units and state-of-the-art weapons in pinpoint operations because of the need for 100 percent success. The price of meeting this demand was paid twice over in wartime: first, by failing to provide a large number of units with operational experience, and second, by detracting from the forces' sense of competency by having them sit on the sidelines during the fighting.

During the War of Attrition between Israel and Egypt (September 1968–August 1970), the air campaign involved deep penetrating operations and pitted Israel's American-made Phantoms against Egypt's Russian-made SAMs. The air strikes, which began in July 1969, quickly escalated. During the first two months of the campaign, all IAF offensive aircraft took part in missions. In Operation Boxer, along the Port Said–Qantara line on July 20, 1969, Skyhawks and Mirages went after the SAM batteries, while Ouragans, Vautours, Mystères, and Super-Mystères hit other targets.[15] On July 24, in Operation Boxer 2, Skyhawks targeted SAM batteries and Egyptian strongholds on the canal, and Mirages and Mystères took out other targets.[16] With the arrival of the first Phantoms on September 5, the older aircraft were withdrawn from operations. In March 1970, when Egyptian entrenchments and SAM-3s joined the bank of targets, orders changed: French planes—Mystères and Super-Mystères—would no longer be used against SAM dugouts or adjacent targets but would be flown only by lead pilots in missions close to the canal. The Skyhawks operated only with appropriate air protection and continued to be sent into action until one was hit when it failed to detect an incoming missile, "at which point the Skyhawks were taken out of operations against manned, active missile dugouts and batteries." The Mirages continued to conduct high-altitude aerial photography.[17]

The Phantoms were used exclusively for two types of missions during this period: attacking SAM batteries and attacking Egypt's infrastructure. Both missions were vital because they could achieve two of the IAF's basic goals. With strategic bombing, Israel could force its will on the enemy—in this case, an end to the War of Attrition—while attacks against the missiles could achieve air superiority in the fighting area. However, beginning in December 1969, the other types of planes were removed from combat, and missions were handled exclusively by the Phantoms. From this point on, the Skyhawks were used in air-to-air assignments, and the attack planes were limited to operations along the canal. Viewing each mission as unique might explain why the toughest jobs were given to the best "problem solver" at the time: the Phantom. Once the division of labor became entrenched, the pilots' competency on the other combat aircraft began to slacken—at least psychologically. A month or two after the "obsolete" aircraft had been deemed unfit for the more difficult attack assignments, no decision maker or command echelon was willing to consider the possibility of integrating them into battle. Thus, 85 percent of the aircraft became irrelevant for essential missions. Without realizing it, the air force had ceased to be versatile.[18]

According to Yiftach Spector, "Naturally, we of the inferior planes sat in the bleachers distraught at what was happening on the playing field. . . . To date no one has provided an answer as to why the Mirages, which destroyed all the airfields in the Middle East three years earlier, were eliminated from the ground fighting in this critical period. Something also happened to the Super-Mystères and Skyhawks that were supposed to attack ground targets. We all stopped at the canal line and only the Phantoms penetrated the Egyptian and Syrian depth."[19] It should be noted that the Phantoms were superior to all the other aircraft for these missions, so their use seemed to be the right decision. The price, which was hard to determine, was the eroded self-confidence of the pilots of the other planes when they had to operate under the extreme conditions of the Yom Kippur War.

"Motti [General Mordechai Hod] directed the war and was keenly aware that this was the 'final game.' There was no room for error. He wanted only the aces, only the marksmen."[20] "Hod demanded that the squadrons send their best men on each mission. Even [the 117th Squadron commander] had to get the all-stars ready, I mean send out the best of the best . . . and if you didn't get the aces then you were out of the game and he'd take a quartet from another squadron. . . . What's an all-star team? The squadron commander, deputy squadron commander A, deputy squadron commander B and number four in the squadron."[21]

The ground forces' parallel to Hod's "all-stars" before the Yom Kippur War was a limited number of units that conducted long-range operations inside Arab countries. Haim Nadal, deputy commander of the 35th Paratroopers Brigade during this period, states that "in all of the special operations only 500–800 ground force troops took part, mostly commanders and crack paratroopers."[22] Even operations close to the border, such as Operations Sergeant (March 13–15, 1970) and Victoria (June 10–11, 1970) on the Suez Canal, were carried out by the elite Shaked reconnaissance unit in conjunction with naval commandos. In the north, only the 188th (Barak) Tank Brigade participated in Operation Kalachat 2 in Lebanon (May 12, 1970) and Operation Kiton in Syria (June 26, 1970).

One solution to the aversion to employing a variety of units was the use of elite commanders (from a relatively large number of units), as was done in several operations in Lebanon in the 1980s. This allowed commanders to gain experience, hone their military skills, and raise the competency level of the regular units. The price entailed certain changes in the force's organic structure.

Exposing New Weapons

In 1995 Dr. Ilan Amit of the Israeli arms company Rafael posed the following dilemma:

> After a new weapon is developed, and before it's revealed on the battlefield [or procured by another army], the question is when to use it and risk its exposure to the enemy? A too early exposure undermines the element of surprise and provides the enemy with an opportunity to study, familiarize himself with it, and perhaps even produce a counter-weapon. The result of exposure could be the loss of the weapon's full potential in a crisis. . . . On the other hand, a delay in the use of a new weapon is tantamount to turning a blind eye to the present crisis, its challenges, and the people who could be hurt because the decision was made to retain the weapon for a future crisis. However, the future crisis is not here now and may never arrive.[23]

Amit also claims that if a secret weapon that can change the outcome of a major battle is exposed too soon, one must take into account the benefit of the early success compared with the price paid for potentially aggravating the difficulties in a future full-scale war. "How can these considerations be strengthened in the army? Today's commanders are judged first and foremost by their success in the one war that they have command in, and not by their influence on other commanders in future wars. Why should they risk certainty in the present for an uncertain advantage in the future?"[24]

By way of example, Amit presents the debate in the First Lebanon War over whether to employ the air force's new unmanned aerial vehicles and precision-guided munitions to attack the Syrian SAM batteries or wait for a war that might be more perilous for Israel, such as a Yom Kippur War–type scenario. In the case of the First Lebanon War, Israel decided to use its surprise weapons. Amit notes that use of a surprise weapon does not necessarily "burn" it. The enemy has to unravel the weapon and devise a response through drills or counterweapons. Either way, this is generally a time-consuming process. Other possibilities are that the enemy learns about the new weapon from a third party or through published material even before it is employed, or that the enemy procures the same technology or a similar weapon from foreign sources.[25] Referring to Axelrod's study, Amit notes the extreme difficulty of holding on to a surprise weapon solely in anticipation of that rare instance when its use might be of high specific value at a later date. The difficulty stems from both human and bureaucratic factors. In a bureaucratic system such as the military, "people serve in their position for a limited time and are evaluated by what they achieve and accomplish in that period. There is an overriding tendency in such a system to exploit the resources at your disposal in order to improve an event that in your estimation is of the most serious consequence or greatest value in the period of your tenure."[26]

Most of Amit's examples of such dilemmas relate to wars, such as the British use of the tank and the German use of chemical weapons in World War I, the British use of chaff against German radar in World War II, or Israel's use of naval electronic weapons (EWs) in the Yom Kippur War.[27] As for the use of weapons in isolated nonwar events, Amit avows that "in some situations it is unquestionably preferable to delay or avoid revealing the use of a weapon . . . in clashes that are not actual wars even if the short-term military gain is appealing and lucrative." An example is the sinking of the Israeli destroyer *Eilat* on October 21, 1967, by Styx missiles fired from an Egyptian Komar-class missile boat. This was the first time in history that a missile boat used an antiship missile, and it hastened a conceptual transformation in the IDF.[28] The change included the conversion to missile boats, the development of Israeli EWs,[29] and the production of the Gabriel antiship missile at Israeli Aerospace Industries. The Gabriel was based on the Hazelnut (in Hebrew, *Luz*) missile, which Rafael had worked on after the Sinai Campaign and became operational in 1969.[30] The Gabriel missile (with a range of twenty kilometers) and its application doctrine closed the range imbalance between Israeli missiles and the Styx (with a range of approximately fifty kilometers).[31] This, together with Egyptian and Syrian complacency stemming from a sense of superiority, led to the Arabs' naval defeat in the Yom Kippur War. During the war, three Syrian and four Egyptian missile boats were sunk, without any damage to the Israeli vessels. According to Mahmoud Fawzi, the Egyptian defense minister during the war, the Israelis, in conjunction with American experts, succeeded in devising electronic countermeasures against the Styx missile, which had caused a surprising amount of damage in sinking the *Eilat.* The countermeasures were installed on Israeli ships armed with Gabriel missiles.[32] The Egyptians' reason for employing a state-of-the-art weapon in a nonwar event was apparently the army's need to prove its capabilities after the stinging defeat in the Six-Day War.

Another example deals with the IAF's application of EWs in the War of Attrition and the price it exacted in the Yom Kippur War. The IAF was aware of the existence of SAM-2s in the Six-Day War. In the first months of the War of Attrition, Israeli pilots coped with them successfully thanks in part to the Americans' lessons in Vietnam; in addition, the missiles' size and limited maneuverability made them readily identifiable and enabled pilots to take evasive action. This success came at the price of immediate escalation: the introduction of SAM-3s into the theater. "The [SAM-3] missiles' arrival went directly against all previous agreements according to which the Soviet Union would not compromise its latest technological development in the Middle East by having it fall into Israel's hands and, indirectly, into American hands."[33] Israeli pilots thus faced the challenge of two types of missiles and an antiaircraft cannon layout that called for the most advanced response available. The technology included an electronic system in the form of Yabelet (Blister), a French-made area blocking system designed specifically for the IAF's Vautour squadron in the War of Attrition. Yabelet also neutralized the airborne emitter locating systems in SAM-2 batteries. Another EW blocking system, the Shoulder, blinded ground radar to penetrating aircraft; it was mounted in various configurations on a number of planes and helicopters.[34]

Unlike the Americans' warning and disruption systems developed at breakneck speed to counter SAM-2s, there were no American solutions to SAM-3s, which were not deployed in North Vietnam. The Americans upgraded the Phantoms' warning systems and sent the new software to the IDF, but there was no active technology capable of disrupting the radar. The IAF had to come up with its own solution.[35] The Russians' entry into the fray led to the introduction of hundreds of SAM-7 Strela missiles and thousands of antiaircraft cannons of various calibers, some of them radar guided.[36] The Russians moved at night, camouflaged their equipment, maintained strict electronic silence, and activated the systems only against perceived attacks.[37] On June 30, 1970, the first SAM-3s were fired at Israeli planes during a photo reconnaissance mission. The Russians employed a previously unknown doctrine: launching fifteen missiles from the batteries on the Phantoms' flight path. "This new method of launching a missile barrage would have a grave impact on the IAF's ability to attack the missile batteries."[38] The Russians were fast learners. That day, two Phantoms were downed over Egypt, one after the other. Eitan Ben Eliyahu, deputy commander of the 201st Phantom Squadron, describes the upheaval this caused in early 1970: "We suddenly realized that the array was employing new tactics that included overlapping battery protection, dense anti-aircraft defense, mobile ambushes, and deceptive systems such as sham dugouts. . . .Our intelligence lost its effectiveness because the pace of battery movement was faster than the pace of the photo reconnaissance flights."[39]

The answer included the development of a new offensive doctrine. Israel sent an urgent order to the United States for electronic weapons. In the meantime, the idea was to shift from pop-up bombing, where the aircraft flies over the target, to loft bombing, where the pilot releases the bombs before reaching the target while accelerating. The latter technique reduced the plane's exposure but also diminished its accuracy and increased the uncertainty of hitting the target. The first loft-bombing attack failed. Photographs later showed that the batteries were empty and the bombs off target.[40] A second attack produced the same disappointing results. At this point, it was decided to make a low-altitude attack and return to base at the same altitude.[41] On July 4 Phantoms approached the target at low altitude, released the payload, immediately increased altitude, and succeeded in hitting the target while maneuvering away from the large missile barrage.[42] Based on these results, sixty planes were sent up the next day to attack Egypt's most strongly defended area between Abu Suwayr and Suez. Some of the batteries were empty or dummy sites, and "the air force paid a heavy price in these low altitude flights. . . . The IAF took it hard—not only the loss of pilots and planes but also the inability to find a suitable military solution to the sophisticated missiles. The new American pods—'the electronic wonder of the age'—were still on their way to Israel and many people pinned their hopes on them."[43]

The ALQ-82 (Sweet Pea) pods (external tanks designed to carry equipment) arrived on July 10. Two American experts and a technical team accompanied the thirty containers and instructed the Israeli Phantom technicians from the 69th and 201st Squadrons how to install and operate the weapon. A new procedure was devised using relatively tight flight patterns. The pods were designed to take out both the original and the improved SAM-2s but not the SAM-3s. In the meantime, the IAF's EW engineers had worked out an answer to the SAM-3, although production was still a long way off. The media publicized Israel's receipt of the EW systems a few days after the pods' arrival. It is important to note that the pods had already fallen into the hands of the North Vietnamese, who passed them on to the Russians. Therefore, the Americans could transfer their "secret weapon" to the IAF knowing that if an Israeli plane were shot down, the damage to the US Air Force would be minimal.[44]

On July 18 the new tactic was used in Operation Etgar (Challenge) in a high-altitude attack that evaded SAMs. The secrecy of the mission and the compartmentalization of its planning bear witness to the IAF's fear of discovery by the enemy. The use of active EW systems was divided into two parts:

1. Aerial EWs against the SAM-2s consisted of individual Sweet Pea pods on the Phantoms, various Shoulder systems activated from Super Frelon helicopters and Bell-205s, and Yabelet jamming systems on two Vautours. Against SAM-3s, a special Yabelet model with secret Israeli-developed jamming systems for the Vautours was used, and Shoulder systems adapted to jam the SAM-3s' communications systems were mounted on Super Frelon helicopters. The new antimissile systems were not installed in aircraft that crossed the border because they were highly classified, and the biggest fear was that a plane carrying them might fall into enemy hands.
2. Ground EW systems that were designed to throw the operation of the two types of SAMs into disarray were installed at Umm Hashiba Mountain.

In practice, the Yabelet jamming system failed to neutralize either the SAM-3s or the improved SAM-2s.

As stated, the operation of the anti–SAM-3 systems was top secret. Compartmentalization was strictly observed, and none of the pilots, including the squadron commanders, was privy to the secret information. The system would be used only if the sensors picked up signals that a missile attack was imminent.[45] According to Yosef Naor, the IAF officer in charge of EWs at the time, "We had to safeguard the secrecy . . . pilots on a mission were [sometimes] captured. We tried to divulge as little information as possible so that if the pilots were taken prisoner they'd give away nothing of importance to the Russians."[46] Shmuel Chetz, commander of the 201st Squadron, briefed the pilots on the new flight configuration—direct and horizontal flights and exact distances between planes—and told them that the pods were effective against SAM-2s. "Chetz made no mention of the SAM-3 batteries in the target area, probably because he didn't know about them."[47] In reality, the new EW systems were able to interrupt the SAM-2s but not the SAM-3s. Six of the seven batteries were hit, but Chetz was killed and the navigator captured. Israel immediately asked Washington for radar-guided Shrike missiles, although at this stage, they were ineffective against the Russian threat.[48] On August 3, in Operation Hair 265 against missile batteries in the Abu Suwayr area, IAF planes flew into a sophisticated Russian-planned ambush that included faux positions with dummy explosions that simulated live fire, camouflaged mobile batteries in agricultural areas, and the dowsing of launch areas with water to reduce the signature of the fire. One Phantom was brought down in the ambush, and another was hit.[49] "Intelligence personnel had the most frustrating job in the attack . . . having to cope with Russian innovations such as randomly leapfrogging batteries, day and nighttime camouflage, and [creative] deception."[50]

Toward the end of the War of Attrition, advanced SAM-6 batteries were deployed around the Aswan Dam, but as far as we know, they were not used against Israeli aircraft.[51] In the three years between the end of the War of Attrition and the Yom Kippur War, SAM-6s became a key element in Egyptian and Syrian air defenses. The IAF had no information about their capabilities and was naturally concerned. The introduction of SAM-6s, which caught the IAF by surprise in the Yom Kippur War and prevented it from attaining air superiority, was the Russian response to Israel's success in dealing with SAM-2s.

The memoirs of senior Egyptian army officers and Soviet air division staff officers who assisted the Egyptians in the War of Attrition explain the success of the Arab air defense layout in the Yom Kippur War. These memoirs reveal that the Egyptians and Syrians learned from Israel's successful fighting methods and use of new EWs in the War of Attrition and exacted the price from Israel in the Yom Kippur War.

The Egyptians and Soviets realized the need to acquire as much information as possible about the enemy's systems. The Egyptian chief of staff stated on August 7: "The downing of the advanced planes that were carrying sophisticated electronic devices was a golden opportunity for our experts and engineers to study the equipment and take immediate countermeasures to reduce their effectiveness and increase our success and superiority." Although this statement was made on the last day of the war, it shows that Egyptian and mainly Russian experts collected every shard of equipment and quickly conveyed it to intelligence and research and development centers.[52] Major General Alexei Smirnov, commander of the Soviet air defense division in Egypt, wrote, "The Soviet air defense units received full cooperation from the Egyptians in the form of productive studies that resulted in improved air defense equipment and [an improved] air defense mechanism in general."[53]

Dima Adamsky, an expert on Soviet intervention (known as Operation Kavkaz–Caucasus) in the War of Attrition, found that the Soviets learned quickly. Given Israel's successes, the Soviets concluded that their operating concept, which was based on their experience with similar systems used against American Phantoms in Vietnam, was ineffective against the IAF. Therefore, instead of setting up a line of overlapping battery coverage, they deployed a cluster layout of batteries and depended more on camouflage, mock positions, and alternating radio frequencies to trick the Israeli pilots.[54]

On September 17, 1971, more than a year after the official end of the War of Attrition, the Egyptians shot down an Israeli Stratocruiser that was equipped with EWs. General Saad El Shazly, the Egyptian chief of staff in the Yom Kippur War, recalled:

> The enemy response came, predictably, the next day. It reassures us. We had guessed that they would try to knock out our SAM radar, which were set back some ten miles west of the canal by using Shrike air-to-ground missiles Israel obtained from the United States. We had devised electronic means of countering Shrike and were quite keen to test them. On September 18 Israel did as we had expected. Their aircrafts launched their missiles from six miles east of the canal. Shrike only has a range of ten miles. The missiles fell hopelessly short. Clearly, we were beginning to establish a cordon sanitaire east of the canal too.[55]

Admittedly, the Shrike missile performed poorly. Even the advanced model, which was used later in the First Lebanon War, failed to hit the target. Its most effective use was in suppression, but it only caused the enemy to switch off the radar and shift to optical and manual mode.[56]

According to Egyptian defense minister Fawzi, the Egyptian air defenses acquired new fighting capabilities from their direct contact with Israeli aircraft between July 1969 and the cease-fire on August 8, 1970. More important, they grew familiar with the Israelis' offensive modus operandi (including approach to the target, aerial maneuvering, and use of electronic jamming and guiding devices). He claimed the Egyptian air defense forces never would have gained so much experience had they not been involved in daily confrontations with the IAF. In October 1973 Egypt's air defense forces came to battle equipped with vital information that enabled them to paralyze the IAF's strength and movement in the air and neutralize its maneuverability, which was based on mobility and air superiority in the battle zone. The Egyptians were also armed with technical data, especially the ability to conceal gaps in the radar's field at low altitudes and establish integration between air defense units and fighter planes. Fawzi also notes that in addition to the SAM-2, SAM-3, SAM-6, SAM-7, and double- and four-barreled 23mm cannons, a major Soviet contribution to Egypt's response to Israel was "the electronic devices that boosted the air defense capabilities and rendered them invulnerable to the enemy's improved jamming techniques and US-supplied air-to-surface missiles."[57]

Regarding secrecy, Haitham al-Ayoubi, an Arab officer, notes that the Egyptian and Syrian air forces kept their SAM-6s out of the September 13 air battles three weeks before the war. The did so not only to maintain secrecy but also to gain, at the proper time, a greater physical and moral surprise. And indeed, that surprise was attained.[58]

Israel Tal analyzed the influence of the War of Attrition on the IDF's abilities in the Yom Kippur War and concluded that, given the Russians' generous supply of antiaircraft fighting systems in the War of Attrition, direct Russian command of air defense weapons systems in Egypt, and the development of combat doctrines, the Egyptians were able to plan for the Yom Kippur War in such a way that the IAF's airpower would be unable to stop them from crossing the canal. "The Egyptians and the Russians gained experience in the War of Attrition and came to the Yom Kippur War well-trained and full of confidence in their air defenses."[59]

The IAF fought determinedly, employing all available weapons and every method in the book, including some ad hoc ones. It chalked up superb tactical gains and a partial operational-strategic success as well. It acquired considerable experience in dealing with the Egyptian surface-to-air layout, but the effort in the War of Attrition had two grave ramifications on the IAF's effectiveness in the next war. First, technological and operational escalation in the form of an accelerated arms race transformed the situation from one the IAF knew how to cope with (SAM-2s) to one in which the air force lost its ability to operate against antiaircraft cannons integrated with a new, partly unfamiliar (SAM-6), dense missile layout. Second, the War of Attrition revealed the greater part of the IAF's combat tactics and weapons, thus enabling the enemy to study the material and improve its defenses. The IAF was keenly aware of the price it might have to pay for immediate victories in the War of Attrition and therefore made a great effort to limit the exposure of new weapons. This is a classic example of the trade-off between achieving success in limited, albeit intensive confrontations and paying a potentially heavy price in some future war. It is impossible to know whether the interval between exposure of the new weapon and the outbreak of war will allow sufficient time to develop an answer to the enemy's learning.

Force Design for War in the Interwar Period

Although the IDF had to defend the new 1967 borders, it rigorously prepared for the next war through acquisition, replenishment, and training. The Sinai Division's armored brigades underwent a three-month rotational schedule of operational duty on the canal and training that included exercises up to the battalion and brigade levels. Based on interviews with men in various positions in the battalions, brigades, and division headquarters, the consensus is that RSOs did not detract from war preparations. The IAF's encounter with SAMs and antiaircraft fire in the War of Attrition was estimated to be similar to what it would face in the next war. Force design focused on increasing the number of armored formations. Designated units were set up for RSOs, in addition to the Egoz Unit, which was responsible for defending the northern border before the Six-Day War. These newly formed units were Haruv (in the Jordan Valley), Shaked (originally set up by Southern Command in the 1950s for security in the Negev and, after the Six-Day War, for operations in the canal sector), and Rimon (for Gaza Strip counterguerrilla operations). Special equipment was developed for daily security activities, such as night-vision optics, explosive devices, mines, and AFVs, but attention remained focused on the development and acquisition of weapons for war. Combat doctrine was the only part of force design where the focus shifted from war to RSOs.

Shai's study on mission command found that insufficient attention was given to the fact that the daily security battlefield is essentially different from the wartime battlefield. Because of this, battle procedures, organization, and C2, all of which were created to solve the special problems of RSOs, gradually transitioned from an "oral doctrine" to an "ad hoc necessity" and then to bona fide "doctrines." These doctrines eventually replaced the IDF's original doctrine, which was designed for war and was based on a mission-oriented command philosophy.[60]

The Agranat Commission found: "Parallel to the written doctrine in the IDF's basic instructional literature, which remained unaltered since the early 1960s, an oral doctrine developed . . . that provided ad hoc answers to problems that the IDF faced at various levels. The nature of an oral doctrine is less binding than a written doctrine since it allows more room for interpretation and is thus translated in different ways. Its validity is limited to time and place. . . . When consensus is reached, those advantages vanish . . . and the [oral] doctrine is left with its drawbacks."[61]

Shai notes that after 1967, GHQ dealt with RSOs on a regular basis and served, in effect, as the IDF's ground forces headquarters. GHQ had to divert most of its attention to this activity instead of concentrating on force design, as it had before the Six-Day War; thus, it neglected the preparation of doctrinal infrastructure. Routine security activity took its toll on the development of the pillars of doctrine in various areas, such as "the absence of doctrinal material on the use of operational level combat formations" and "replacing the combat doctrine in instructional manuals with solutions to concrete operational problems."[62]

Shai also points out that after 1967, the IDF ceased to update and complete the basic doctrinal tenets it had initiated in the 1950s. Instead of formulating basic comprehensive doctrines, it printed "professional manuals" that focused on concrete solutions to the operational problems in each period. For example, the pre-1973 period was rich in manuals on crossing a wide water obstacle. When crossing the Jordan seemed a realistic possibility, manuals were printed on crossing a narrow water obstacle. The changes in Syrian obstacles after 1973 led to manuals on how to break through and capture a Syrian volcanic hilltop. These concise manuals were easy to digest, memorize, and even carry during training, but they offered formulaic responses rather than doctrines and sometimes even contradicted basic doctrines (such as instructions for training infantry battalions). This eventually led to a disregard for learning and the use of doctrinal literature, including basic operational field manuals.[63]

It is difficult to quantify the effect of doctrinal stagnation on the IDF's performance in the Yom Kippur War, but it undoubtedly had an impact, even on training for war.

Impact of 1995–2006 RSOs on the Second Lebanon War

For more than two decades (the interval between the First and Second Lebanon Wars), the IDF was occupied primarily with routine security activity on the northern border—the Israeli security zone in Lebanon (and later along the international border)—and in Judea, Samaria, and the Gaza Strip. These two decades amplified the slippery effect of long periods of RSOs on war preparations. Two facets are discussed here: the adoption of RSO norms, and the loss of war capabilities due to cutbacks in resources, with a focus on solutions to daily security challenges.

The Second Lebanon War began with the abduction of three Israeli soldiers by Hezbollah on July 12, 2006, and lasted for thirty-four days, until August 14. During that time, IDF ground forces were suddenly employed in a manner that came close to major combat operations (combined-arms task forces, massive fire assets, division-sized structures). This was markedly different from their experiences during two decades of RSOs.

Routine Security Norms

Twenty years of daily security efforts had a powerful effect on the norms of military activity, such as C2 philosophy and devotion to mission accomplishment versus minimal casualty rate. Most of the eighteen years of fighting in the Israeli security zone in Lebanon, as well as the intensive action against the Palestinian uprising (intifada) and terror between 1987 and 1993 and the Second Intifada between 2000 and 2005, were characterized by the following features:

- A large force with superior weapons compared to terrorist squads and suspects.
- A high level of preparation for actions conducted as special operations by experienced regulars operating in the same sector for a long period.
- A relatively small number of offensive operations (compared with large-scale war) that enabled much greater investment in planning.
- Ongoing operational activities (patrols, escorts, ambushes, guard duty) that exhausted most units.
- Low tolerance for casualties.

Centralized C2 in RSO Periods

Two basic C2 issues seem to be by-products of RSOs: detailed C2 and the physical location of commanders. The Winograd Commission examined the relatively detailed management of the Second Lebanon War and found that in Operation Change of Direction (a full-scale military operation), war planning suffered from daily security management characteristics that were lopsided in the areas of peacetime approval procedures for cross-border operations and sorties, safety constraints, prohibition on the use of AFVs and weapons under certain conditions, and prohibition on the advancement of logistical units and forward command posts close to the fighting forces.[64] The basic problem was that the attempt to prevent casualties influenced the value placed on devotion to mission accomplishment (see later). The Winograd Commission also cited the pejorative influence of RSOs on initiative, boldness, and creativity.[65] According to another source:

> In the struggle against terrorists and guerilla forces, like the one that was fought in the security zone, the situation was completely different. The limited scope of the fighting events and the interval between them frequently allowed senior commanders to be involved in battle management of their units sometimes to the point of neutralizing

> the independence of the field commanders. The tactical failures, the growing public criticism, and above all the casualty rate put pressure on senior commanders and forced them to be involved to an even greater extent in tactical operations. Thus, a centralized, rigid system developed in Northern Command that suppressed initiative and creativity in the operational units. This was the result of the unwillingness to incur error. Ironically, in fighting an irregular enemy, where cognitive flexibility and freedom of movement in the lower echelons are required, we missed the opportunity to exploit the IDF's greatest advantage in every type of encounter—the quality of the field commanders.[66]

Mission-oriented command was crippled during the years of RSOs. The article by Uzi Ben-Shalom and Eitan Shamir points to the factors that muffled the IDF's mission command, such as superior commanders' overriding concern about mistakes made by subordinate commanders in daily security actions and field commanders' reluctance to assume responsibility because of the price (public criticism, pressure from superiors) of making such a mistake.[67]

The Winograd Commission also examined the commanders' physical location during the war and concluded that some of the recent changes in the army, together with routine security procedures, the IDF's ability to maintain remote C2, and the limitations placed on commanders' movement in Lebanon, produced the phenomenon of senior commanders who were situated inside Israeli territory, "accompanying" their fighting forces in the field from afar.[68] "Again it is reasonable to assume that this was the result of general changes in the army and its modi operandi. However the fact remains that the IDF did not employ large-scale ground forces in combined arms operations and that the convention of commanders of large formations going into the field with their forces eroded."[69]

The commission also found that the lapse in these norms was probably the result of technological means that enabled effective remote C2 and the fact that the IDF entered the Second Lebanon War after a long period with no large-scale combat, and no such scenario was envisioned. Thus, there were no exercises that included the use of large formations or demanded intensive fighting to capture grueling objectives that exceeded short-term raids or pinpoint operations.[70]

Devotion to Mission versus Protection of Troops

The Winograd Commission found that "the general RSO attitude contributed to the general approach of some commanders to the main goal in their command period which was 'to get things done' without incident, without encountering the enemy, and without incurring casualties. This approach creates a distinct vulnerability in wartime where initiative, boldness, and creativity are needed."[71]

Gal Hirsch, commander of the 91st Division in the Second Lebanon War, had previously served in various positions in the Judea and Samaria Division. He describes the difficulty of shifting from routine security norms to wartime norm with regard to mission accomplishment versus casualties: "Over the years the slogan of many commanders in the Judea and Samaria Division was 'better 1:0 than 3:1.' When it came to carrying out a mission the first thing we had to do was check military value versus risks. Chief of Staff Mofaz determined the norm, and the same norm was upheld when he became defense minister later in the battles against terror in the territories [Judea, Samaria, and Gaza]. In other words, we had to evaluate an action if it was important enough to incur casualties."[72]

Moshe Tamir best describes the evolution of this phenomenon, observing that one of the issues field commanders in Lebanon had to deal with was cost. Officers and men had been trained to adhere to the army's basic values in combat, such as devotion to mission accomplishment, evacuation of the wounded, and prevention of equipment falling into enemy hands. All these tasks are difficult in any battle. When the cost issue is factored in, mission completion becomes all but impossible. Although it was never specifically stated during the fighting in the security zone in Lebanon, the idea that nothing was more important than avoiding casualties slowly penetrated all the echelons of command. Public pressure against remaining in Lebanon had an impact on the army; this pressure trickled down to lower levels and became entrenched in the phenomenon of surrendering values because of the fear of casualties. "I viewed this phenomenon as catastrophic," writes Tamir.[73]

The Technical Side of RSOs: Readiness, Protection, and Intelligence

During the IDF's long stay in Lebanon, Judea, Samaria, and Gaza, certain norms took root: debriefings with superior echelons of command before an operation, senior-level approval for pinpoint operations and convoy movement to strongholds, the cancellation of operations if the force was not sufficiently prepared, and higher-quality equipment for the operation than for war. For example, AFVs were mostly upgraded tanks with special protection, and armored personnel carriers (APCs) were part of the equipment designated for routine security sectors. The emphasis on readiness and protection arose from the need to limit the number the casualties.

Asael Lubotzky, a platoon leader in the Golani Infantry Brigade's 51st Battalion, was surprised at the poor quality of the intelligence aids in the Second Lebanon War compared with those available during limited operations in Gaza:

> "What happened to the quality of the air photo," Ahikam asked?
>
> "A black and white photo?" Getta, disappointed, wanted to know. "In Gaza everything was easy to identify because it was in color."
>
> An armor officer who happened to be listening joined in, "Do you know when these maps are from? They look like they're from the War of Independence or maybe the First Lebanon War."
>
> I checked the corner of the photo. The date was 2002. God knows how many changes had been made in the area since then. The intelligence aids were definitely obsolete and obviously hadn't been updated. We'd grown accustomed to high quality aids in Gaza and were shocked by their shoddy quality in Lebanon.[74]

In my view, a four-year-old air photo in wartime is reasonable. The problem is that the Israeli forces expected the war in Lebanon to be like an RSO.

AFV Protection

Beginning with the attack on the Kalkiliya police station in October 1956 and extending through the battle over water resources in the north (1965–1967), the Battle of Samu in Jordan (November 1966), the War of Attrition, and the Yom Kippur War, the IDF employed tanks and APCs without special protection for border defense and offensive operations (Operations Kalachat and Kiton). But since the First Lebanon War, an entire field of protection had been developed for tanks and APCs because of the need to keep casualties to a minimum. Specially armored ("up-armored") AFVs carried out limited offensive operations, and the higher standards of AFV protection prioritized the use of up-armored vehicles over models without advanced protective systems. This phenomenon had two dimensions:

1. The formation of up-armored first-echelon units led to a feeling of inferiority among unprotected second-echelon units (recall Spector's sense of inferiority in the War of Attrition).
2. The up-armored norm became a condition for deployment, even though its relevance for war was relatively low.

Amira Shachar studied the Merkava Mark II and III with up-armor in RSOs and found that Merkava tanks in the Israeli security zone in Lebanon were hit by scores of antitank missiles between 1985 and 1997. Following serious clashes in Lebanon in 1997, the armor protection of the Merkavas in the 7th Brigade (regulars) was upgraded for operational duty. This required changing the Mark IIB tank's protective system, which was more sophisticated, especially in the hull and turret, than the one on the standard Mark II. According to Shachar, General Amos Malka, commander of Ground Forces Command, was against up-armoring the tanks. As Malka explained to Israel Tal (assistant defense minister for the Merkava project), a change in the operational approach, rather than added armor protection, would lower the casualty rate. Despite the ground forces' rejection of a limited number of upgraded tanks for RSOs because of cost, Tal planned for additional protection for the Merkava Mark II, up to the approval stage. By mid-October, more Merkavas were hit, and Israeli casualties rose. On October 22 the chief of staff approved armor protection kits adapted to Lebanese conditions as an urgent operational necessity. Work had to be completed by March 1998, before the 7th Brigade replaced the 188th in Lebanon. An advanced protection kit was also prepared for the Mark III, and because its protection was based on the principle of modular armor, the Mark III was easier to upgrade. Eventually, dozens of Mark IIs and IIIs underwent up-armoring. At the same time, Tal suggested upgrading the up-armored protection of the tanks already engaged in RSOs in Lebanon so they could cope with the new antitank missiles. The 7th Brigade was scheduled to begin operational duty in March 2000, and Tal wanted to complete the work before that date. As it turned out, the IDF withdrew from Lebanon later in 2000.[75]

These cases illustrate how armor protection became the norm in RSOs and the sine qua non for units' entry onto the line. The main problem was the expectation of similar protection in wartime.

After tank underbellies were hit by improvised explosive devices (IEDs) during RSOs in southern Lebanon in 1988, the chief of armor doctrine, Colonel Gidi Levanon, recommended protecting the Merkavas. The chief of armor, Brigadier General Yossi Ben Hanan, conveyed his agreement to Tal. Thus a special effort was made to protect the tanks' underbellies from large IEDs. Because the protection system was modular, it could be mounted and unmounted, depending on circumstances. When mounted, it narrowed underbelly clearance and added extra tons that limited mobility. Dismantling the system restored the tank's former mobility. Given the crucial need for armor protection, the project circumvented the regular bureaucratic channels and came under the supervision of Tal and the ordnance branch. Dozens of Merkavas, Centurions (Shots), and M60 Pattons (Magach) had to be up-armored.[76]

A recent example of an active protection system for tanks is the Trophy system. Immediately after a Kornet missile struck a tank in early December 2010 in Gaza, the first Trophy-mounted tank battalion entered operational duty. In March 2011, after the system's first successful performance in the Gaza Strip, the 9th Battalion, the only up-armored battalion, was ordered to remain on the line until another battalion could be up-armored.

Keeping "War Secrets" during RSOs

Some of the equipment used in the Second Lebanon War is still classified. However, one example we can discuss is the Nakpadon heavy APC that was developed specifically for RSOs. The Nakpadon was equipped with state-of-the-art integrated protection. On September 22, 2008, a Nakpadon fell into a ravine that feeds into the Litani River in Lebanon, and the air force had to destroy the vehicle. On the night of May 23–24, 2000, during Israel's withdrawal from Lebanon, a Nakpadon in the Golani 13th Battalion experienced a technical breakdown. Having no alternative, the Nakpadon was left on a bridge, and the air force annihilated it to prevent the vehicle from falling into enemy hands.[77]

Another example is the Tamuz missile, which saw action in Gaza in 2011, despite the risk of the enemy getting ahold of it. Until then, it had been kept secret since the 1980s.

Force Design for War during Extended RSOs

Loss of Knowledge and Combat Proficiency Due to Training Cutbacks

The Winograd Commission's investigation of the Second Lebanon War reveals a comprehensive picture of the loss of skills due to training cutbacks:

> If somebody thought that the IDF could go to war unprepared, the Second Lebanon War proved him wrong. The IDF entered the war barely ready. Let us recall, the "great" IDF and especially the ground force reservists had not fought a major war for many years. On the one hand this was a blessing but at the same time combat skills based on operational experience atrophied, therefore the substitute should have been effective training suited for the designated fighting theater. We wish to re-emphasize, significant results were attained when early preparation was implemented. The most telling example of this is the air operations in the opening days of the war. This success teaches what was done wrong. In the years preceding the war, IDF ground forces had been bogged down in endless, exhausting combat duty against Palestinian terror. This was the main reason why the army failed to receive training and the preparation that it desperately needed. The results spoke for themselves.[78]

Cutbacks in training were not accidental. Concentration of activity in the Palestinian theater and the enormous burden on regulars and reservists in that theater resulted in neglect—in both practice and theory—of the fundamentals of force employment in a "classic" wartime scenario or even against a paramilitary nonstate group like Hezbollah. Both scenarios were significantly different from the conflict in the Palestinian theater.[79]

Regarding training, the Winograd Commission reported that 2000–2006 was characterized by a continuous decline in training periods and in the number of exercises and combined-arms maneuvers. This phenomenon deteriorated the ability of the troops in general and of commanders at the battalion, brigade, and division levels in particular because training and exercises at those levels were repeatedly dismissed.[80]

The 162nd Division suffered, as did all regular units, from a decline in the scope of training. The commission's report emphasized that the armored units, the division's main force, conducted no exercises. Tank crews underwent training only at the basic proficiency level (and this too was curtailed, making mastery of combat skills impossible). Certain topics were removed from training programs because of a lack of resources or a resetting of priorities at even the most basic level. In addition, formation maneuvers and combined and joint exercises with the infantry, artillery, air force, and others were scrapped. In this new situation, division headquarters planned and drilled operations on the basis of war games, while the rest of its forces had no training and were thus unprepared to carry out the planned missions. In effect, the headquarters drilled alone, without its units. As a result, the starting point for wartime missions was the operational plan that headquarters alone had exercised, while scenarios that approximated reality (usually through brigade and battalion exercises) were left untested. The division's armored units did not train as units. All the commanders and staffs, from company commanders up, were replaced in 2005–2006 and underwent no training with their units. The only training they did receive was essentially infantry activity and occasional crew- and platoon-level refresher drills, but nothing higher. Crew exercises were conducted at the basic level. Although plans were afoot to complete the training, nothing came of them. Essential organizational readjustments, such as changes in the logistical layout, battle techniques for use of a tank company, and deployment of reconnaissance and intelligence units according to the operational concepts of Northern Command's 91st Division, were neither tested nor drilled in the units.[81]

According to Israeli officer and researcher Ron Tira, the reserve units did not train in large formations for four to six years. Interestingly, this lack of training was not the result of neglect or omission; rather, it was intentional policy. Under the IDF's new doctrine, the corps formation was eliminated, and plans were in the works to abolish the division as well when war erupted in 2006. Chief of staff Halutz and the disciples of Shimon Naveh's systemic operational design "did not see a role for land formations larger than a brigade. . . . The important point is that they failed to perceive training above brigade level as important and therefore did not invest in it."[82]

Yonatan Cohen, a tank commander in the 9th Battalion, 401st Brigade, 162nd Division, recalled the armored forces' proficiency during the war:

> It's weird. I'm a tanker. A year and nine months in the army, and the last time I trained on a tank was a few months ago. And then too it was for only three days when I stood in the commander's post. The truth is, since graduating the tank commander course nine months ago and arriving in the operational company, only once did I train on the tank. That's kind of unbelievable when you think about it. The whole time I was in an operational company I trained on a tank only once! So what did I do? Lots of roadblocks, lots of guard duty, lots of RSO. . . .
>
> . . . The automatic gear system conked out. . . . The transmission gave out . . . and I had to shift to manual gear! . . . This stick was frozen, I realized that no one had ever used it. . . . We never used manual gears in training. If the automatic gears get stuck, everything stops. We'd call the maintenance team and they'd come and fix it and we'd continue on our way. But now it's different. Here our lives are on the line. The maintenance crew isn't going to hop over. Forget about the maintenance crew. It's only you now, you alone, Yonatan, I whispered to myself. That's when I really regretted that we, especially me, hadn't received more training on these tanks. I hadn't been in the [tank commander's] post for nearly a year.[83]

The widest gap between readiness for war and the skills needed in a limited conflict seemed to be in the artillery. (Tanks were used occasionally in RSOs, but the artillery never was.) The need to integrate artillery units into RSOs led to major changes in training—rifle marksmanship, roadblocks, patrols, urban warfare, and the operation of newly acquired light weapons—all of which detracted from the time allotted to artillery training. The solution was supposed to be artillery training at a basic level; then, when a concrete situation estimate deemed it necessary, a higher degree of proficiency could quickly be attained through intensive training within the framework of the IDF's war preparation plans. Thus, the units could maintain a minimal level of proficiency for artillery missions, while other skills could be taught and maintained for more pressing and relevant needs in the conflict with the Palestinians.[84]

However, sending the regulars to intensive training in the artillery professions proved more difficult in practice than in theory. Compounding the problem, when the partially trained artillerymen became reservists, their ability to complete professional training was even more limited.

Platoon commander Lubotzky described his men's proficiency level in hand-grenade throwing: "I saw that some of the soldiers hesitated when I mentioned the hand grenade. I asked them about this and they said they felt nervous about practicing hand grenade throwing. . . . They'd all tossed live hand grenades in basic training, but afterwards they'd practiced only with dummies. The reason seems to have been the profusion of accidents, therefore live grenade throwing exercises were kept to a minimum. . . . Of course training accidents must be avoided as much as possible, but a soldier going into battle has to have the required operational skills."[85] The level of training in most of the reserve units was even worse. According to the Winograd Commission: "As regards the [Mapatz Armor Division's] readiness for combat, the situation was abysmal. The division's infantry and armor units had not trained for four or five years before the war."[86]

A concrete example of the loss of professional knowledge involved close air support for ground troops. Benjamin Lambeth's study of the air force's performance in the Second Lebanon War and Operation Cast Lead received generous assistance from the IAF and was published by the Rand Corporation. He found that the IDF entered the Second Lebanon War with a weak liaison officer layout and that it lacked experience in combined-arms training, professional familiarity, and a common language.[87] Lambeth noted that the major improvements introduced after the war proved themselves in Operation Cast Lead (2008–2009).

Unit Structure and Organization

The IDF's traditional approach to solving new but limited challenges was to establish designated units, as it did between the Six-Day War and the Yom Kippur War. This trend continued with the formation of two units—Shimshon and Duvdevan—for operations in Judea, Samaria, and the Gaza Strip and the revival of the Egoz Unit for duty in the Israeli security zone in Lebanon. Boaz Zalmanovitch found this solution to be tactically successful but also damaging to the army's structure and organization.[88] In these and many other cases, the solution was relatively local and did not divert organizational attention from war preparations. The period between 1995 and 2006 witnessed both a deviation from this model and an increase in RSOs' influence on the organization of regular units for a war scenario, as well as the establishment of a large number of new-type RSO units. Between 1995 and 2001 the IDF established a new type of infantry unit designated for RSOs: low-intensity conflict (LIC) light infantry. These new units were:

- The Duchifat Antitank Battalion, converted to a mechanized infantry battalion in 1992 and, since 1995, operating in the Jordan Valley, subordinated to the Binyamin Brigade (Ramallah sector).
- The Haruv Battalion, established in 1995 for operations in the Nablus sector.
- The Shimshon Battalion, established in 1997 and named after the Mistaravim, a former undercover counterterrorism unit. First active in the Bethlehem sector and later in Gaza until the 2005 disengagement, it is currently operating in the Bethlehem sector.
- The Nachshon Battalion, established in late 1998 and initially operating in the Efraim Brigade sector.
- The Nachal Haredi (Netzach Israel) Battalion, established in 1999–2002 for operations in the Jordan Valley and the Samaria mountain ridge.
- The Lavi Battalion, established in 2001–2002 for operations in the Hebron sector.

In 2005 a brigade-sized framework, the 900th Force Buildup Center, was established. In addition to force building, it engaged in LIC operations in Judea and Samaria.[89] After the Second Lebanon War, the IDF diverted the force design of these units to war preparation in their training scenarios and established the 900th Brigade Headquarters as a standard infantry brigade.

Zalmanovitch notes the direction of force design between September 2000—the start of the Palestinian riots—and the outbreak of the Second Lebanon War in 2006 and the various adjustments made in the ground forces. "For example, armor and artillery units had to perform infantry tasks that entailed altering their training. Marksmanship received higher priority than their designated professions."[90]

In late 2001 the chief infantry headquarters concluded its study of the new infantry unit concept and focused on RSOs. Because of the need to set up battalion headquarters for fighting in the West Bank and the Gaza Strip, Chief of Staff Mofaz ordered the infantry brigades (regulars and reserves) to consolidate the brigades' reconnaissance, antitank, and demolition companies into a brigade reconnaissance battalion.[91] Many problems related to the use of regular forces in LIC assignments led to another idea that was tested in the Givati Brigade's reconnaissance battalion, which had been reinforced with new technologies and was operating successfully in RSOs. According to this concept, the infantry brigades' reconnaissance battalions, which had originally been established to meet RSO needs, would be converted into special units designated solely for LIC. In other words, multitask regular infantry units would be transformed into units unsuited for large-scale war. Zalmanovitch claims that the terms "special forces" and "reconnaissance unit" (instead of reconnaissance battalion and reconnaissance company) injected confusion into the discussion of the "specific abilities needed in the current fighting in the West Bank and Gaza Strip and the tactical abilities needed for fighting in a divisional sector in Syria or elsewhere."[92]

In the years leading up to the Second Lebanon War, the Ground Forces Command expended a great deal of effort to convert the brigade into the basic ground formation for a war scenario. However, as the preceding examples illustrate, attention was being diverted to RSOs.

Development of Combat Doctrine

Erez Weiner claims that after failing to develop a doctrinal answer to the LIC challenge between 1996 and late 2002, a significant awakening took place between 2003 and 2006.[93] It was fully understood that fighting in an LIC without a doctrine was a problem that had to be resolved. It can be stated unequivocally that the limited number of doctrinal writers who produced books on urban warfare (2004), counterinsurgency in LIC (2005), the defense of security borders (2007), and a wide range of guidelines on low-level tactics and the use of weapons almost completely ceased their professional work related to a large-scale war scenario. No doctrinal material on a war scenario was written or circulated during this period. However, after the Second Lebanon War, doctrinal writers resumed writing about war.

The period between 1995 and 2006 witnessed the integration of two trends discussed earlier in this chapter: the growing dominance of routine security norms, together with a force design that limited the resources allocated to training for war; and the diversion of attention of doctrine and organizational efforts from HIC to LIC. Taken together, these trends created gaps in land warfare in the Second Lebanon War.

It should be noted that RSOs can also have a positive effect on the doctrine and techniques of large-scale warfare. For example, the actions of Unit 101 and the paratroopers before the Sinai Campaign (1956) led to greater competency in laying ambushes and capturing fortified objectives.

* * *

Long periods of routine (but intense) security activity can lead to accumulated damage by weakening wartime norms and diverting organizational attention from war preparations to RSOs. This phenomenon has a simple psychological explanation: success in RSOs results in an immediate gain, whereas failure generally exacts a high price and demands an immediate explanation. The success of force design for war is often demonstrated after many years and is the result of a cumulative effort on the part of many individuals.

Each of the periods examined in this study is unique: routine security norms had an overarching effect on the IDF before the Yom Kippur War, but force design was concentrated on large-scale maneuvers in a wartime scenario. The long period between the First Lebanon War in 1982 and the Second Lebanon War in 2006, and especially the decade between 1995 and 2006, witnessed the crystallization of two trends: the impact of years of RSOs and the shift away from force design for war toward daily security demands.

Even if the IDF is aware of the danger inherent in these trends, it is still at a higher risk than other armies because of the permanent state of RSOs, even as it plans for the next war. The solution lies in the following recommendations:

- Develop a historical awareness (the primary goal of this chapter).
- Emphasize training in order to create a counterweight to routine security norms. For example, if routine security is performed at a very high level of certainty, training needs to simulate extreme uncertainty in battle.
- Ensure that attention is focused on force design for war, even during periods of RSOs.
- Inculcate devotion to mission-oriented command norms in training and RSOs; otherwise, it will be absent in wartime.
- Guarantee that the norms, principles, and values of war, such as devotion to mission accomplishment, are maintained in RSOs.
- Adhere to the procedures and language used for war when conducting RSOs (for example, using the term "reserve" instead of "extraction/backup force").
- Set up units specializing in policing activity to ease the burden on IDF ground forces. When forming and employing elite units and special forces for offensive action, ensure that the regular units' level of proficiency, and especially their confidence in their abilities, is not impaired.
- Take extra precaution in the use of state-of-the-art weapons, lest their capabilities be exposed.

3

The Outbreak of War during Conceptual or Doctrinal Change

An army is a huge, complex organization that must be constantly updated for a variety of reasons: changes in the enemy, new operating methods versus new operational problems, the replacement of outdated weapons, and so forth. According to a former IDF chief of staff: "The world is changing at a mind-boggling pace. I remind my subordinates that the only permanent thing in our age is change. . . . The challenge is enormous when you have to transform and adapt to changes, when units under your command are organized and trained for certain threats, and the changing threats call for new solutions—changes in doctrine, structure, organization, combat techniques, exercises and weapons."[1]

"Operational concepts are the stuff on which armies feed and nurture themselves. And so a dialogue about them is essential to the Army's well-being."[2] As a consequence, at the start of a war, the army is likely to be in the midst of some kind of change process. Risk management's aim in this case is to minimize the transition period between concepts and the assimilation of doctrinal, organizational, and technological changes. Conflict occurs at various levels, such as conceptual disagreements over the basic approach to the use of forces at the strategic level, doctrinal disagreements on how best to employ forces at the operational level, and the absence of a common language at the tactical level, which can lead to misunderstandings on the battlefield. The danger is the impairment of military effectiveness in wartime.

Two examples are reviewed in this chapter: the defensive concept on the Suez Canal in the Yom Kippur War, and the concept behind the use of the IDF in the Second Lebanon War. Both cases represent a situation in which war broke out either during an unresolved conceptual debate or after the debate was resolved but before the concept had been assimilated.[3]

A concept describes the general approach (or idea) for obtaining a military goal and is the theoretical basis for everything the army does. An operational concept (sometimes called a concept of operations) defines the underlying approach of an operational headquarters in fulfilling its main mission or missions.[4] It stems from the requirement to solve a problem (a specific threat). An operational concept defines the manner of force employment. Operational concepts can be strategic, operational, or tactical. The operational concepts analyzed in this chapter can be defined in today's terms as GHQ concepts from which tactical-level concepts are derived.

An operational concept is essentially a basic choice: from a wide range of options, there is one optimal method for achieving success.[5] Conceptual clarity is essential. Certain flaws are apparent in the two cases examined here:

- In the Yom Kippur War, no choice was made between two concepts; in the Second Lebanon War, a conceptual choice was made, but it was not assimilated through organization and procedures.
- In the Yom Kippur War, there was ambiguity and indecision regarding alternatives; in the Second Lebanon War, some of the ideas in the concept were obfuscated, as was the terminology to a certain degree.

It is not my intent to justify or criticize any concept but to analyze risk management when there is an absence of agreement over the concept itself or over changes stemming from its implementation.

Unlike an operational concept, an operating concept describes how an organization works—how it conducts learning processes and decision making, who is responsible for what tasks—and defines a common language for internal use. The case of the Second Lebanon War deals with both the operating concept of the IDF, GHQ, and regional commands and the operational concept that focuses on a future war against Hezbollah.

Defense on the Suez Canal before the Yom Kippur War

The debate over the optimal defensive system on the Suez Canal line began four years before the war. Discussions officially started in GHQ on November 21, 1968, and the decision was left pending. During the bitter fighting in the war, appalling issues arose regarding the function and evacuation of strongholds (in Hebrew, *maozim*). The concept developed in three stages:

1. Late 1968 to early 1970: The "static defense" concept, based on a series of fortified strongholds on the waterline, was crystallized, along with their role in the event of war. The decision was made to build the strongholds.
2. Early 1970 to the spring of 1973: The commander of Southern Command, Major General Ariel Sharon, took a combination of approaches: fortifying the strongholds after the War of Attrition and then closing some of them and reducing the manpower in others. The static defense

concept was eclipsed by a new "mobile defense" approach and the construction of a rear line of fortifications and a network of north-south and lateral roads. There was, however, no official alteration of the original concept.

3. July–September 1973 to the Yom Kippur War: Major General Shmuel Gonen, the new commander of Southern Command, reinstated the static defense concept without working out the physical gaps left by Sharon's concept.

The static defense method was designed to prevent the enemy from gaining any ground, whereas the mobile defense method presumed that any ground ceded could be retaken in mobile fighting. The IDF's 1965 lexicon defined the terms:

> Static defense: a method of defense based on the application of the primary force in static defensive arrays and positions that are protected by a network of obstacles, and where a relatively small part of the force—namely armor—is positioned in reserve.
>
> Mobile defense: an active defense system based on the application of covering forces with a mobile force in reserve. Only a relatively small part of the force holds the strongholds and static positions.[6]

Conceptual Discussions

Three discussions were held during the first stage; the first was at a GHQ plenum on November 21, 1968, and the next two took place at the GHQ operations branch on December 19 and 26. The GHQ plenum debate pitted the supporters of static defense—Brigadier General Avraham Adan, head of the team assigned to recommend IDF deployment in Sinai; Major General Yeshiyahu Gavish, commander of Southern Command; and Lieutenant General Haim Bar-Lev, the chief of staff—against the advocates of mobile defense—Major General Israel Tal, the armored corps commander, and Major General Ariel Sharon, head of IDF's instruction branch (a kind of GHQ TRADOC). The discussion revolved around the strongholds' role in wartime. Gavish envisioned fighting on two static defense lines: on the canal and in the mountain passes, with mobile battles being fought between them. The strongholds would prevent the enemy from crossing in their vicinity and alert the mobile forces in areas where the strongholds had no direct control.[7] The chief of staff summed up the discussion by saying that static defense had to be based on the strongholds. According to Bar-Lev's biographer, he also stated, "The defense line has to be based on a ground force strongly entrenched in the right place, significant armor forces capable of reaching any point within two to three hours, and, of course, the air force."[8]

In the December 19 discussion, Adan and his team presented their recommendations. Adan's stronghold model was built on his experience in the War of Independence. The stronghold's task was to warn of a crossing and protect those inside the stronghold. "The main effort in a defensive battle goes to the armor forces that are assisted by infantry, artillery, and the air force."[9] Adan proposed paving a road so that the artillery could move rapidly along the canal (Artillery Road) and a second road (Lateral Road) about thirty kilometers to the east for the movement of large armored forces and logistical supplies. His plan contained other defensive elements: setting up a permanent division HQ in Sinai, dividing the canal line into sectors, and establishing the order of battle in them. Gavish approved the plan, adding strongholds in sensitive places. Bar-Lev ordered additional strongholds at the perimeters. Adan recalled, "No one disagreed with the main idea of integrating two defense systems and building a rigid defense on the water line."[10] His concept emphasized that the strongholds' function "was not the Bar-Lev Line nor the Maginot Line but only a chain of warning points."[11]

Leading the camp of opponents was Tal, who argued that "defense on the water line doesn't mean bringing all the forces to the water line. I'd deploy only those that guaranteed complete control over the water line, and the main force I'd position in the rear."[12] Sharon thought the strongholds would be useless in a full-scale attack. "As I see it the stronghold layout is a secondary warning system. Tank concentrations will smash an all-out offensive."[13] Tal proposed cutting back investments "to the minimum for the strongholds' tasks and functions," trimming the number of strongholds by half, and extending the gap between them.[14] General Ezer Weizman, GHQ's J3, enthusiastically supported Adan's model, and Bar-Lev authorized it.

On December 26 the generals repeated their arguments. Sharon contended that "what we're building today is better suited for peacetime. Their [the strongholds'] value in wartime will be zero. Only tanks and planes will break an effort to cross the canal." Tal stressed that "the troops manning the strongholds on the canal will be useless. . . . Not a single bullet will be fired from the strongholds once the crossing begins because Egyptian artillery concentrations will destroy them."[15]

After the general staff approved the strongholds plan, Adan put it into action between November 1968 and March 1969. This was an enormous fortification enterprise that employed thousands of soldiers and civilians. "The operation was almost completed when the Egyptians began interfering with sniper fire."[16] In March 1969 most of the fortifications were in place, except for three: opposite the Chinese Farm, Tusan, and El-Balah Island in the south.[17]

Dayan stayed out of the debate, although he took part in the GHQ discussions. According to his account: "The strongholds were built during the ceasefire between November 1968 and March 1969. The fortification layout—the second line on the hills about ten kilometers from strongholds line—was established in the spring of 1971. Thus the two defense concepts that GHQ members held were both realized."[18]

Ariel Sharon as Commander of Southern Command

As the commander of Southern Command, Sharon was ordered to uphold a concept that he believed was fatally flawed. Given his views on static defense, he was asked whether he intended to resign. He answered that he preferred to fight for his opinions within the military. After his position was rebuffed at another meeting in early June 1970, the commanders and Dayan inspected one of the strongholds. After weathering a barrage, Dayan told Sharon that he had to convince the chief of staff that a conceptual change was needed.[19]

At the end of the War of Attrition (August 1970), the debate over the defense of Sinai flared up again between Sharon and the rest of the general staff. Dayan still refused to take sides, which explains why a compromise between the two approaches was reached. The Bar-Lev Line, which had been heavily damaged by Egyptian shelling, would be rebuilt but would not be equipped or fully manned. Over the next three years, Sharon closed fourteen strongholds, blocking their access with sand. At the same time, work began on a line of fortifications in the hills dominating the canal at a distance of ten kilometers. This line consisted of observation posts, underground bunkers, reserve unit bases, artillery positions, and a logistical center for forward tank companies. A road network was constructed consisting of two roads parallel to the canal (Artillery Road and Lateral Road) and interconnecting roads to the line of strongholds.[20]

Tal had his own ideas for a warning system on the waterline. It was based on mechanized infantry in AFVs and two armored brigades to hold the line; both the mechanized infantry and the armored companies would operate on twenty-four-hour shifts. The plan's drawback was the need to double the regulars' tank forces, which would increase the cost of maintaining the line, especially in terms of material fatigue of the tanks. These added expenses would eat into the budget intended for force design and acquisitions. Another disadvantage was the enemy's expected familiarity with the new system.[21] According to Adan: "The fact that the strongholds line was a series of warning points that was called the 'Bar-Lev Line' did not transform it into a fortified defense line. Just as Tal's proposal to deploy dozens of tanks on the line did not turn it into a mobile defense system. . . . The difference between them was that Tal's plan called for the deployment of an armored mobile warning screen whereas the current system was based on the strongholds as the warning screen."[22]

Adan commanded the 162nd Division in the war. After the cease-fire, he testified before the blue-ribbon Agranat Commission:

> Chairman [Shimon] Agranat: Was their [the strongholds'] purpose limited to hanging on for a few days? Weren't they supposed to do something more than this?
>
> Adan: I don't think that we ever thought they'd have to hold out for a few days, at the most a few hours.[23]

After visiting the canal front in early 1972, chief of staff David Elazar called a meeting at GHQ to discuss "Sinai's defense concept." At the end of the meeting he stated: "We'll remain in the strongholds. But if the situation becomes intolerable, they'll be evacuated. The Arabs don't appreciate the idea of holding on (to the strongholds). In a worst case scenario, before we take out their missiles and artillery, and given the meagerly fortified condition of the strongholds, we'll evacuate them before they're overrun. This isn't rigid defense. Rigid defense is a defensive line where a battle is waged and held at all costs."[24]

Elazar was not against Sharon's proposal to close some of the strongholds, reduce the number of troops, and remove some of the weapons. He approved the closure of five strongholds in July 1972, followed by three more in October. Sharon kept pressing, and after another visit to the canal in November, Elazar approved the closure of three more strongholds and a manpower reduction in others. "Thus, by one step at a time, fourteen of the original thirty strongholds were either closed or pared down by spring 1973."[25] According to Sharon, Elazar agreed at a 1972 meeting that if war broke out, the troops would be ordered to vacate the strongholds immediately. "Thus, I considered the matter settled, but five months later when the attack came, nobody ordered an evacuation."[26]

On May 1, 1973, at a special meeting between Elazar and Tal on the defense of Sinai, the Dovecote Plan was defined in detail: infantry reservists would be replaced by regulars; the armored division would operate on three lines with eight platoons on the stronghold line, eight companies on the fortification line, and three battalions concentrated in the three sectors (north, central, and south) on Lateral Road; and a full brigade would reinforce the rear as a division reserve. Sharon described the plan's aim as being to "prevent a surprise. Concentrated forces will stay close to the areas of action, and our forces will be waiting for the enemy, not the opposite. Dovecote's purpose isn't to evacuate the strongholds or aid them but to conduct a battle in the strip between the canal and Lateral Road."[27] Be that as it may, Dovecote was a deployment plan and not a defense plan, as the following evidence shows.

Called before the Agranat Commission, Colonel Dan Shomron, commander of the 401st Brigade, clarified Sharon's prewar stronghold concept:

> SHOMRON: Sharon was under the impression that the strongholds would be evacuated and their usefulness ended as soon as they warned of the attack. Since he didn't want to hold onto them, he saw no need for them. But if they were there, then their job was over once they sounded the alarm. This was why there were vehicles in the strongholds—AFVs and others—to get out with. . . .
>
> CHAIRMAN AGRANAT: What was his concept, that when war erupted [the strongholds] would be evacuated? Was there a war plan?
>
> SHOMRON: Do you mean a written order?
>
> [COMMISSION MEMBER YIGAEL] YADIN: For example, was anything mentioned about this in January's documents . . .?
>
> SHOMRON: I know that they ramrodded the strongholds down his throat. Maybe there was an order that he didn't want put on paper. It was probably a kind of "oral doctrine" that would be decided the moment it was needed.[28]

In his study on the use of the regulars in the first days of the Yom Kippur War, Emanuel Sakal states, "The compromise on the Bar-Lev Line ran counter to military logic, and the line's raison d'être (as a warning system or defensive line capable of blocking an enemy attack) gradually became blurred. The IDF would pay an exorbitant price in men and equipment for this ambiguity in the first two days of the Yom Kippur War."[29]

Shmuel Gonen as Commander of Southern Command

Gonen replaced Sharon as commander of Southern Command in July 1973. In his previous role as head of the instruction branch, he had participated in the discussions headed by Tal on the Sinai defense concept and the future of the Bar-Lev Line and the strongholds. At the time, he favored the mobile defense proposed by Generals Tal and Sharon, but he was not convinced that all the strongholds had to be shut down. He therefore submitted an alternative: set up "defense triangles," with the strongholds at the apex and the tanks in the rear.[30]

Upon assuming command, Gonen learned that Sharon had closed fourteen strongholds, destroying some and blocking others. According to Gonen's own account, he wanted to reopen all the strongholds and get rid of the canal's large embankment because it would hamper operations against Egyptians attempting to ford the canal. He set to work on a second line of three-sided dirt embankment positions, termed "fins," to the rear of the strongholds, where Israeli tanks could pick off the enemy without exposure to Egyptian fire. He also requested permission to return troops to the fourteen closed strongholds and was allowed to reopen some of them.[31] Elazar's biographer states that Gonen submitted his request one month before the war.[32]

It should be noted that the public was aware of the debate over the defense system before the war. Sharon expressed his views on the subject to newspaper editors in late 1970.[33] The American journal the *New Republic* published two articles on the polemic over the defense of Sinai in October 1970.[34]

Sakal states, "The strongholds line was defined as the forward line, but was never officially defined as the rear defensive line where the Egyptians would be held to the last bullet. Nevertheless, the understanding, agreements, and often vague statements by Bar-Lev and his successor, Elazar, created (whether intentionally or not) a situation in which the canal's eastern bank became the de facto rear defensive line."[35]

In his study on force design between the Six-Day War and the Yom Kippur War, Major General Haim Nadal found that after the Six-Day War, the IDF invested enormous resources in regular operational duties, RSOs, and day-to-day readiness, sometimes at the expense of preparations for a future war. The IDF deployed in a static (rigid) defense system, keeping part of its forces (mainly mobile units) in reserve rather than having them serve as key agents in the mobile defense system that Tal and Sharon favored. The IDF regarded the Bar-Lev Line not as a defensive line but as a routine security line whose chief purpose was to block the Egyptian forces at the waterline and serve as observation posts. Nadal writes, "The upshot is that neither of the two interwar chiefs of staff considered the Bar-Lev Line a defense line, but neither did they decide where the defense line should be and where engineering preparations should be carried out. Thus, military exercises were not held on a different defense line in Sinai, and the Bar-Lev Line, which was originally designed for routine security activity, became ingrained in the minds of the commanders and men as the canal's defense line, with all that that implied."[36] It should be noted that "defense line" is not a doctrinal term, and in this case, the term can be interpreted to mean the canal line or a line at a certain depth. This is not to refute Nadal's conclusion that, in the absence of another plan that defined a different rear defensive line (the line in the command's defense area that, if broken, spelled failure), the stronghold line became embedded in the collective military mind, even if the chief of staff intended something different.

The Strongholds in the Yom Kippur War

When war broke out, sixteen of the original thirty strongholds were manned (three in the south with Nachal infantry, and the rest with reservists of the

68th Battalion, 16th Brigade). Within the rotation system of the armored brigade (regulars), the 14th Armored Brigade was on the line, and the 401st Brigade was training in the rear. On October 6 three of the 14th Brigade's battalions were deployed on the canal line (the 9th in the north, the 184th in the center, and the 52nd in the south). Most of the strongholds came under immediate attack, and in most cases, bitter fighting ensued. Only a few lasted more than two days. Of the sixteen, two fell or were evacuated immediately. The remaining fourteen held through the first day of fighting, but seven fell or were abandoned between noon and midnight on October 7. On October 8 troops in five more strongholds either fled or raised the white flag. On October 13 the Hamezach stronghold surrendered. Only Budapest hung on until the end of the war.[37]

Dovecote divided the tank force on the line, as well as the brigades that came to reinforce it. Tank platoons and companies encountered a mass of antitank weapons, RPG launchers, and mines. Most of the Sinai Division was exhausted in the first day of fighting.

Since the War of Attrition, Israeli tanks had been trained to rush to the assistance of a stronghold under attack. Adan observed, "Now when war broke out they responded with a conditioned reflex. A stronghold radioed for help, the tanks scrambled to reach them! This time, however, it wasn't just one stronghold crying for help; this time all of the strongholds were screaming for assistance, which immediately split up the first echelon tanks waiting in the rear. The sense pervaded that we were too late in deploying the forces in the right places, and as a result the strongholds' situation was untenable. To improve the situation second echelon tanks were sent, but were also dispersed in too many directions."[38]

The consequences of the prewar indecision about the strongholds' purpose were illustrated by Southern Command's gnawing dilemma over their evacuation during the war. This dilemma bedeviled commanders at all levels, from the defense minister, chief of staff, and commander of Southern Command to division, brigade, and battalion commanders and down to the stronghold commanders themselves. After realizing the critical situation on the morning of October 7, Elazar granted Gonen permission to evacuate the strongholds "if the pressure becomes unbearable."[39] The chief of staff was unaware that the strongholds were already surrounded. Dayan arrived in Southern Command's war room that afternoon. Later he penned: "I said that a supreme effort had to be made to evacuate the strongholds . . . I emphasized to the general [Gonen] that I didn't think we could hold the water line therefore we had to get the men out of the strongholds any way possible and the sooner the better."[40]

According to Adan, "The [defense] minister failed to comprehend why the strongholds hadn't been evacuated the night before since they couldn't have prevented, and weren't designed to prevent, the crossing."[41] In a meeting with the prime minister at 15:00 that day, Dayan proposed abandoning the canal line and redeploying at the Mitla-Gidi Passes.[42]

That evening, Chief of Staff Elazar and the division commanders, in Sharon's absence, planned the next day's counterattack. After much consideration, Adan recommended leaving the strongholds to their fate and waiting to amass strength and apply it in a concentrated effort. In short, the chief of staff stressed that "we wouldn't attack near the canal . . . let alone go to the strongholds and try to cross [the canal]."[43] Elazar ordered Gonen to use all means necessary to evacuate the strongholds. To save time, Adan instructed his deputy "to order the evacuation of the strongholds a second time and plan a diversionary attack towards Kantara, so that the troops in the Milano stronghold could try to escape and link up with our forces."[44] After the planning group dispersed and the chief of staff issued his instructions, Sharon arrived and was flabbergasted to learn that no one had given the order to evacuate the strongholds when the war broke out (as he had previously instructed).[45] He continued to pressure Gonen to vacate the strongholds until the latter finally relented. Sharon's division would extricate the stronghold troops and, upon completion of that task, would move to the rear and clear the way for Adan's counterattack. The orders that night shifted the responsibility for evacuating the strongholds from Adan's division (order issued at 03:54) to Sharon's (order issued at 04:13). Later, Southern Command ordered both divisions to prepare to evacuate the strongholds, depending on the enemy's situation.[46]

Sharon returned from the planning group believing that his division would attack toward the strongholds at dawn. Based on orders issued at 02:00, he was prepared to take personal command of getting the men out of Hizayon, Purkan, and Matsmed. In the morning he was surprised to receive the order not to attack.[47] Adan, in contrast, viewed the evacuation as a possible course of action rather than an order, so he made no plans to execute it.[48]

Shomron, the brigade commander responsible for the southern sector of the 252nd Division when the war broke, testified before the Agranat Commission, pointing out the inherent contradiction in the concept:

> SHOMRON: "Little Dovecote," as I understood it, was better suited for beefing up the line in a conflict the size of the War of Attrition. It wasn't a solution for a massive crossing.
>
> YADIN: In other words this puts the contradiction into even sharper focus that Mandler [the 252nd Division commander] felt that this was the case of all-out war but gave orders relevant for a War of Attrition scenario.
>
> SHOMRON: Correct. This was the contradiction. . . .

SHOMRON: In my opinion, the defense concept based on strongholds contained a logical flaw and we missed it. The same night that we reached the strongholds, we also reached the canal and prevented the landing of bridging equipment. But the brigade was at the point of total exhaustion from maneuvering between the hordes of enemy infantry and the strongholds and protecting them, at the same time it was searching for the areas where the bridging equipment was being laid. . . . I want to emphasize that we reached our limit because of the concept.

[COMMISSION MEMBER JUDGE MOSHE] LANDAU: Does this "concept" refer to the defense of the strongholds or to their evacuation? . . .

SHOMRON: Around two in the morning I contacted the division commander and told him a decision had to be made immediately. I'm protecting the strongholds and on the line the brigade is being chewed up. In a few more hours I'll have to abort the mission. I request a decision or we'll evacuate the strongholds. . . .

CHAIRMAN AGRANAT: What would have happened in the "few more hours" that you just mentioned?

SHOMRON: I couldn't hang onto the line and the strongholds any longer. I requested evacuation of the strongholds immediately—I was in radio contact with all of them. By the way, the whole day we took out their dead and wounded. A fresh force was needed to reinforce the strongholds . . . so they wouldn't be so dependent on me and I could concentrate on blocking the crossing . . . with my mobile forces. I also suggested exactly how this could be done. This was the real dilemma of the first night—not the time needed to reach both the canal and the strongholds—but how to hold [the line]. There was still no decision at this point. [Mandler's] answer was: "permission to abandon strongholds denied."[49]

In reply to former chief of staff Haim Laskov's question whether the brigade could have prevented the crossing had it been deployed on the canal at the beginning of the war, Shomron said: "There was a chance. But what I believe clinched the matter was the rigid concept of holding onto the strongholds. I'm certain that this is what sealed their fate. I still believe that I could have blocked the crossing in the southern sector if I hadn't been responsible for protecting the strongholds, yet without being allowed to evacuate them."[50]

Asked about his departure from the strongholds, Shomron said: "At this point [the morning of October 7] I contacted the division commander a second time and told him 'This is final. My situation is either I link up with the strongholds and stay with them till the bitter end or I block the Egyptian forces from entering Sinai with a mobile defensive maneuver. A decision has to be made right now!' [Mandler] said, 'forget about the strongholds.' That was one of the worst moments I remember."[51] The order was immediately retracted. Shomron "called division headquarters and got the division's deputy commander, Baruch Harel, not Mandler. I told the deputy: 'This stronghold is worthless; I request permission to surrender it.' Harel's answer: 'They'll fight to the last man. Do not surrender.'"[52]

> Yadin: When you were in the GHQ operations branch, was there a debate on the concept of strongholds and tanks?
>
> Shomron: Yes, in fact there was a bitter debate.
>
> Yadin: A bitter debate. What was your position, do you remember?
>
> Shomron: The irony is—and I thought about this during the fighting—here I am, losing the brigade over a concept that I argued was unsuited for just this situation. That's what there was.
>
> Chairman Agranat: Were you against the concept of the strongholds?
>
> Shomron: Very much so. It was unsuited even for the War of Attrition, and definitely not for [a full-scale] war.
>
> Yadin: In other words, you were of the same opinion as Generals Tal and Sharon?
>
> Shomron: I am saying it was not [the right concept] for all-out war. Not even for a war of attrition. . . . There's an internal contradiction between the concentration of forces for blocking an attack and dispersing everything you've got on the canal along the whole width of the front.[53]

Later, Shomron explained that the strongholds were solely for observation, yet observation was possible with a tank or a long-range observation tower. "All of the strongholds were superfluous if their purpose was not to fight. . . . They were a liability and obstruction in time of war."[54]

A different view was held by the commander of the 14th Brigade, Colonel Amnon Reshef, who was responsible for the central sector. Reshef claimed that the concept was clear-cut. "The defense concept, as it was written, was to destroy the enemy on the water line. There was no question of allowing the enemy to penetrate inland."[55]

> Laskov: From what I've heard about the strongholds in this sector it seems that the commanders and the men inside the strongholds were somewhat confused about their main purpose?
>
> Reshef: The Bar-Lev Line wasn't just about the strongholds. It was about the strongholds and the fortifications and the artillery and

the roads and the water and the mail and the ordnance and the medical units and everything else. It wasn't only about the strongholds line but about the whole system up to Refidim. The strongholds' purpose was observation and demonstrating our presence on the water line. . . .

YADIN: You said it was no secret that there were different schools of thought within the IDF regarding the strongholds . . . but in retrospect, as a result of the disagreement over these concepts, would you say that what happened in the war was a compromise between two concepts. Would this be a correct appraisal?

RESHEF: To a minor degree yes, but only to a certain and minor degree. . . .

CHAIRMAN AGRANAT: In line with these questions, was there a concept before the war of the possibility of an Egyptian attack and attempt at a canal crossing, etc.? Was there any discussion on the conditions or the earliest time necessary for evacuating the strongholds? Was such a possibility ever broached?

RESHEF: I'll explain. The defense concept, as it was formulated, was about the existence of the strongholds. The combat doctrine said nothing about evacuating them. But evacuating all the troops from the strongholds went against the operational concept and was only part of battle management decisions.[56]

In other words, the order meant that some strongholds had to be strengthened with more troops, and the thinly manned strongholds with just three soldiers had to be abandoned. As for vacating the strongholds while in the midst of battle management, the 14th Brigade report states: "On October 7, 1973, I looked into the possibility of evacuating the strongholds. . . . It was obvious that Hizayon and Purkan could not be evacuated."[57]

According to one account of events, on the afternoon of October 7, "The brigade commander [Reshef] took the initiative of evacuating the strongholds in his sector. The men in Lakekan were able to get out on their own. But the roads to Hizayon and Purkan were blocked to the brigade's armor and the commander of the Matsmed resisted the brigade commander's pleas to extricate his men without assistance. In the end they were captured."[58] Later, when the sector came under Sharon's command, he devised a plan to send armored forces to the strongholds to bring the men out, but Southern Command vetoed the plan.[59]

The battalion commanders on the front received no explicit orders before the war regarding the strongholds' role in the event of hostilities. The only defense plan the brigade and battalion commanders possessed was the Dovecote deployment.

None of the commanders (Lieutenant Colonel Yom Tov Tamir, 9th Battalion; Lieutenant Colonel Emmanuel Sakal, 52nd Battalion; and Colonel Amnon Reshef, 14th Brigade) received the Sela (Rock) Plan before the war.[60] According to Eitan Haber and Ze'ev Schiff, authors of *Lexicon of the Yom Kippur War*, the defense plans had their shortcomings. The defensive layout in Sinai was planned only at the tactical level; limited defensive battles were planned for the sectors and for small- to medium-level formations, while nothing was planned for a major battle. Nor had a defense plan been drafted at the operational level. The planning assumed that the tactical defensive battle on the way to and on the waterline would develop into major combat on an operational level only when the IDF shifted to the attack. This would happen after the reservists, who had been called up under the guise of a defensive battle, reinforced the regulars engaged in the blocking battle.[61] Although the commanders knew of no defense plan other than Dovecote and realized that the strongholds had to be evacuated in the present situation, convincing their superiors proved to be a formidable task.

Sakal's battalion held the southernmost sector of the canal at the beginning of the war. He regretted "not being able to get the troops out of the thinly manned strongholds before one o'clock [in the afternoon] on Saturday though there was an explicit order to do so. By one o'clock it was no longer possible."[62] He also describes how, on the night of October 6–7, his battalion reached Mefatseyach and Lituf and evacuated a wounded soldier from Hakfar. "I'm sure if we'd been given the order—and I know the brigade requested as such—we could've gotten the guys out of Lituf, Mefatseyach and Hakfar."[63]

After Hamezach's commanders consulted with 401st Brigade headquarters, the 252nd Division, and Southern Command, they surrendered after seven days of bitter fighting.[64] Israeli tanks reached the Hakfar stronghold in the northern part of the Bay of Suez on the night of October 6 and evacuated a wounded soldier and those killed in action. The Egyptians surrounded Hakfar during the night, and the stronghold capitulated on October 9.

The forces of Lieutenant Colonel Amir Reuveni, commander of the 68th Battalion, 16th Brigade, were manning the strongholds. Reuveni reached Baluza Camp on October 7 and walked into the office of Major General Kalman Magen, who was responsible for the northern sector of the Suez Canal. Reuveni requested permission to evacuate the strongholds immediately. "The battalion commander reminded the general of the large exercise in mid-1971 at the end of which Sharon, then commander of Southern Command, had said that in a war situation the strongholds would have to be immediately vacated."[65] Magen initially thought the battalion commander was exaggerating; however, he quickly grasped the situation and told Reuveni that he agreed with him, but first he had to get permission from the top brass.[66]

The 184th Battalion, 14th Brigade, under the command of Shaul Shalev, held the central sector with two tank companies and a mechanized infantry company. Shalev's battalion was responsible for the Lakekan, Matsmed, Purkan, and Hizayon strongholds. According to the brigade's defense plan, the canal line was the rear defensive line. "The strongholds served as part of the defense layout on the line and in the event of war [the troops inside] were supposed to stay put."[67]

The commander of Purkan, Major Meir Wiesel (68th Battalion, 16th Brigade), requested permission to evacuate on Tuesday morning (October 8) and received a negative response. Later that day, brigade headquarters granted permission. The task was initially assigned to the 421st Brigade, which was in the area, but the 14th Brigade commander, in whose sector the stronghold was located, requested that his brigade carry out the mission, and the task was transferred to him. That night, a force set out on foot from the stronghold and was evacuated in the morning by the commander of the 184th Tank Battalion. Gonen, it will be recalled, had vetoed Sharon's plan to attack with a battalion and extricate the troops. In the end, the evacuation operation was carried out by a limited force under the personal leadership of the 14th Brigade commander, using his own tank plus two command tanks from the 184th Battalion (those belonging to the battalion commander and the artillery support officer), along with four mechanized infantry APCs.[68]

Lieutenant Colonel Tamir's 9th Battalion was spread out in the northern sector, but it linked up to rescue the survivors at Mifreket. Upon entering the stronghold, Tamir found that only five of the sixteen men were not wounded. "His request to evacuate them was met with Magen's refusal."[69] (Magen had assumed command of the 252nd Division after Major General Avraham Mandler was killed.) The wounded were evacuated to the rear, and further attempts to reach the stronghold in daylight failed. On the night of October 7–8 the strongholds in the northern sector were ordered to evacuate east on their own. Only five of the men in Mifreket managed to reach friendly lines; the rest were either killed or captured.[70]

Colonel Gabi Amir, commander of the 460th Brigade, received command of the northern sector on the night of October 6. The commander of the 198th Battalion, Lieutenant Colonel Amir Yaffe, reinforced the sector and arrived at Mifreket. He requested permission to evacuate the strongholds and withdraw his tanks to the rear because of Egyptian fire from across the canal and the eastern bank. Permission was denied.[71]

"Enormous efforts were made in planning and implementing the rescue of the strongholds. But these efforts, which exacted so heavy a price in lives, failed to offset the feeling of many in the strongholds that the IDF had abandoned them and done too little to save them."[72] It should be noted that the 252nd

Division's deputy commander and operations officer believed that the strongholds were of great importance in relaying a picture of the enemy's crossing.[73]

Regardless of whether the strongholds should have been evacuated, this example illustrates what can happen when war breaks out while the army is locked in disagreement or indecision over a method of fighting. On the battlefield, this translates to a lack of conceptual coherence, which in turn reduces the force's combat effectiveness. Although this situation is hardly a rare occurrence, military commanders must manage the risk, come to final decisions, and swiftly convey those decision to their forces.

A chapter in the book by Major General Eli Ze'ira, the head of military intelligence before and during the war, is entitled "Defense of the Sinai Peninsula—Two Doctrines." He writes about "the blunder of evading a decision. In 1972 when the new chief of staff was appointed, the commander of Southern Command (Sharon) demanded a change in the defense concept for the canal. But again no serious steps were taken, and those responsible for protecting the country—the defense minister and chief of staff—let the situation decline." He observes, "Nothing is more dangerous than an ambiguous strategic concept. The primary duty of the heads of Israeli security forces is to reach a clear decision among the various strategic concepts and ensure that the operational plans are derived from the chosen concept. In this area, the heads of the defense ministry fell short."[74]

One solution in the absence of a decision is to prepare an alternative defense plan and assimilate and exercise that plan (in the Yom Kippur War, establishing a defense while withdrawing from the waterline and pursuing regular activity on the basis of Dovecote). Such a plan did not exist in 1973. Sakal argues that although the Rock Plan was called a defense plan, in practice, it was a plan for force amassment rather than defensive battle. It contained no details on the method of conducting a defensive battle or the location of rear defensive lines, immediate lines for delay and withdrawal, killing zones, counterattack routes, fire support, and so forth. In essence, Rock was only a schematic outline of force concentration.[75] In an interview, Gonen emphasized: "Southern Command was without a defense plan. . . . Vital areas, defense lines, force concentration—nothing was defined. Everything was scattered. . . . The basic assumption was that the Egyptians were incapable of carrying out a hasty attack that couldn't be quickly dislodged. . . . [Unlike Northern Command, where a detailed defense plan had been drawn up, Southern Command] had no defined and organized plan where to fight and for what. Everything was in the spirit of 'we'll deal with it as it comes.'"[76]

The commanders who were interviewed for this chapter (commanders of the 14th Brigade and 9th and 52nd Battalions) admitted that even though they had heard of the Rock Plan, they never received it. In light of Sakal's study, it is clear why. An alternative to the Dovecote Plan would have given the commanders an indispensable tool for decision making as the situation fluctuated.

The Second Lebanon War

The Second Lebanon War (2006) provides another example of a war erupting during unresolved conceptual debates. Here, gaps appeared at multiple echelons and in multiple domains. The debates involved the IDF's basic operating concept for the conduct of operations, the operational concept for the northern theater of war, and the resulting tactical disagreements over the application of tanks and logistics. The piecemeal assimilation of new, overly laundered strategic and operational ideas and abstruse language made matters worse.

The IDF's 2006 Operating Concept

At the most basic level, on the eve of the war the IDF was in the midst of crystallizing and assimilating a new operating concept. In other words, when war broke out, the concept was incomplete and had been applied only intermittently. The GHQ completed the work and published the operating concept in April 2006 as a binding IDF document, even though some senior commanders found it unclear due to major lacunae in its infrastructure and flaws in its content, language, and degree of absorption. Although chief of staff Dan Halutz lent his signature to the document, disagreement over the concept was rife in the IDF. Moreover, nonstandard terms in the document had not been translated into common professional language, and some of the principles were obscure in the extreme. Certain ideas and understandings contained in the concept (such as prioritizing fire over large-scale ground maneuvering) were hazy and ambiguous. There was no real connection, at least in the Lebanese theater, between the new operating concept and its binding translation in operational plans and orders.[77]

After the war, the Winograd Commission put its finger on the main lesson to be learned:

> Indeed, it is unwise to authorize an operating concept that the IDF is unable to maintain without leaving a complete set of transitionary instructions in force in case of an emergency. This was the main shortcoming of the Second Lebanon War. The war was not forced on Israel when it wasn't ready, and the IDF wasn't caught by surprise in the middle of a transition period. Israel went to war on its own initiative. It could have—and should have—taken into account the lack

> of a comprehensive operating concept and its carefully arranged translation into an operational plan that was updated for the Lebanese theater.[78]

It should be noted at the outset that this lesson is problematic. What complicates the discussion on the assimilation of the operating concept is that the IDF did not operate in a wartime mode of action but in an RSO mode during most of the operation (see chapter 4).

The operating concept was the product of a long process that began a decade before its publication. This process was led mainly by Major General Moshe Ya'alon, beginning with his posting as commander of Central Command, then deputy chief of staff, and later chief of staff. Some of the people involved in developing the concept and making it a binding document—Brigadier General Meir Klifi, head of the IDF's doctrine and instruction branch (J7), and Brigadier General Dov Tamari, head of the Operational Theory Research Institute (OTRI), which was part of the J7—wrote about the challenge of assimilating the concept. They claim that the J7 set up work teams and held discussions with the Ground Forces Command, air and naval services, GHQ branches, regional commands, and so forth. According to Tamari and Klifi:

> There was nothing in the operating concept that had not been discussed with these commanders, as well as the chief of staff, and senior staff officers in ad hoc meetings. For example, the discussion on the term "decisive victory" lasted seven hours. During the talks, and especially after the publication of the operating concept, differences of opinion arose as the result of the new conceptual ideas. . . . Two schools of thought divided the senior officers. One, which the generals supported, held that the IDF's universal knowledge is adapted for every war and conflict so that new thinking patterns are superfluous. They also claimed that the current language of military terms answered all the needs and had to be absolutely clear "from sergeants to the chief of staff." The other approach contended that new terms were required and, above all, in a theoretical platform that enabled critical inquiry into the IDF's past so that the present could be understood and the future prepared for.[79]

The development of the operating concept and the process of integrating it into the IDF were intertwined and inseparable. First, this was not a phased process of development and integration but a bilateral process of development, examination, and assimilation of various components that took place over two years. This process included experimentation by the general staff with multiple subcomponents of the concept, which was part of the integration. Second, knowledge development was not executed by a small group of experts and later distributed to a wide and unknowledgeable audience; rather, knowledge was developed through the relatively broad participation of the target audience. Dado Center researcher Dana Preisler writes that the development process lasted more than two years and required the efforts of separate teams working with a central body in the general staff's J3. The teams examined the existing data, studied foreign doctrines, and conducted a series of multiechelon meetings with various commands and services and with the chief of staff. Throughout the process, a number of general staff and regional command exercises were conducted that tested the concept. Feedback was provided by the brigadier generals' forums, an internal forum of Israel's security leaders, the National Defense College, and general staff discussions, forums, and workshops. Every group played an important role in the enrichment of the process and provided important criticism and observations. Preisler writes that, "in some ways, the integration of the concept began even as it was being written and developed."[80]

In light of the above, Lieutenant General Halutz's statement that the IDF's performance during the Second Lebanon War was not based on this concept is only partially true.[81] In his book *Eye to Eye,* Halutz testifies that, as air force commander (April 2000–April 2004), he took steps to strengthen the centrality of the air force in the IDF's concept. He states, "The ideas that were developed in the IAF were practiced and tweaked. After reaching a sufficient performance level, the ideas were presented to the general staff, including the chief of staff, and began to be embedded in the operating concept that was being written simultaneously."[82] The draft of the first operating concept was written in 2005 and was finally published in 2006, just prior to the Second Lebanon War. Halutz, who had been chief of staff for a year, signed it after a brief round of discussions in GHQ.

What Halutz, Klifi, and Tamari missed is that the main problem lay between the poles of assimilating and not assimilating and was much more complex than they realized. Itai Brun was the commander of the Dado Center (which replaced OTRI) after the war and led the investigation of the operating concept.[83] Both Brun and Preisler claim that in order to understand the difficulties of developing and integrating the concept, one must understand the attempt to include a wide range of components in it. Every component was at a different stage of development and testing, as detailed below.

The three most complicated issues were closely connected: systemic design planning, effect-based operations (EBOs), and regional command's role as the "operator" responsible for implementing the campaign plan resulting from the first two components. At the time the document was written, each of these components was at a different stage of development and maturation, which caused the document to be muddled and the concept difficult to implement. This was probably the main reason for the IDF's difficulties in assimilating the concept and for its failure to employ the concept in the Second Lebanon War.

Another challenge was resistance within the IDF to various elements in the concept. Ephraim Segoli, a former researcher at the Dado Center, studied knowledge development in the northern theater before the Second Lebanon War and found that the learning process—the assimilation and integration of the operating concept and other ideas developed during this period—led to the formation of three groups:[84]

- The disciples: those who devoted themselves to the process and enthusiastically took part in it. It is important to note that among the disciples were some individuals who devoted themselves to the process without fully understanding it or its concepts.
- The coerced: those who understood the process and participated in it, following their commanders' lead.
- The opponents: those who harbored doubts about the process or openly objected to it.

The formation of such groups is natural (for example, similar groups formed over the defense of Sinai before the Yom Kippur War). The challenge is to manage the process so that in the end, and despite objections, the army will be equipped with clear ideas and relevant concepts. The doctrine and instruction branch tried to bridge the gaps in content and deal with the challenges that arose (some of which were common knowledge, while others were withheld).

One of the three major changes arising from the new concept was the regional commander's role as "operator" in the theater of operations. The Winograd Commission's report stated that, according to the new operating concept, on the eve of the war priority was given to operational-level commanders charged with force employment. But this priority was not accompanied by a suitable mechanism for force employment and C2. For example, the C2 approach assumed that the commander of Northern Command would lead the operation in the north, which included the entire theater of operations in Lebanon and Syria, even though the strategic depth area exceeded the regional command's capabilities as defined by the old operating concept. In other words, on the eve of the Second Lebanon War, the organizational aspect of the new operating concept was incomplete and had not been exercised or assimilated. Furthermore, significant gaps still existed that precluded a practical reliance on the new concept in terms of organization.[85] The Winograd Commission seems to have erred with regard to Northern Command's scope of authority, as the Syrian and Lebanese depths were not included.[86] Nevertheless, even without responsibility for the strategic depth, this signaled a major change in the command's realm of authority.

The northern theater of operations was parceled into sectors: up to the Litani River was Northern Command's responsibility, north of the Litani was the IAF's responsibility, and the maritime theater was the navy's responsibility. Researcher Gabi Siboni from the Institute for National Security Studies claims that the IAF failed in its role as headquarters of the operational theater. As for Northern Command, he found that, "at first glance, the command found it difficult to integrate and synchronize all of its efforts to a genuine, all-encompassing achievement. Implementing the concept demanded adaption, training, and exercise by command headquarters. These were missing. Even before the war it was known that several years of organization would be needed before full and exhaustive use of the concept could be made."[87]

The Winograd Commission states that the new operating concept envisioned the regional commands (as well as the air force and the navy) functioning as commanders of theaters of operations and GHQ functioning as commander of the theater of war. In practice, however, Northern Command and the IAF commanded parts of the area of operations, while GHQ served as commander of the entire theater of operations. The Winograd Commission concludes:

> On this point the new operating concept does not seem to have had a direct influence on war management mainly because it was not used, due to the lack of new procedures and measures. The misunderstanding regarding the areas of responsibility and the division of labor may have had a negative influence on the organizational interface and discourse between GHQ and the Northern Command since the concept itself and the initial order created an expectation in the Northern Command that it would operate as a commander of the entire theater of operations and have greater independence in the management of the war in its area of responsibility.[88]

Operational Concept for the Northern Theater

Before the war, there were both obvious and hidden conceptual gaps between Major General Udi Adam and chief of staff Halutz. Discord developed between Halutz and Adam concerning war plans for Lebanon. Major General Benny

Gantz, commander of Northern Command before the war, during the time the Syrians were in Lebanon, recognized the need for a relatively broad maneuver in Lebanon, contrary to the opinion of the chief of staff. However, the newly appointed Adam, like the chief of staff, viewed an operation in Lebanon after Syria's departure as occurring in stages.[89] The Winograd Commission and Halutz described these stages as (1) "Icebreaker," based on powerful standoff fire and special forces raids (both under the direct command of the general staff), as well as a limited maneuver aimed at capturing areas near the security fence to improve defense, and (2) a broader maneuver called "Mei Marom" (High Water).[90] The disagreements between Halutz and Adam remained largely below the surface and unobserved, as their differences had developed well before the war, when Northern Command proposed integrating the general staff into the Icebreaker stage by conducting brigade-sized raids several kilometers from the border. Northern Command's proposal was not discussed in depth. At any rate, it was not approved before the war and remained a factor in the interechelon conceptual rift. Sources show that before the war, both Northern Command and the chief of staff viewed Mei Marom as a last resort.[91]

During the war, the conceptual gap between Adam and Halutz reared its head. Adam considered the ground maneuver an integral part of the multistage plan; he saw it as a realistic possibility that might be required, even if on a relatively limited scale. Halutz, despite approving the multistage plan before the war, did not visualize a real need for a limited ground operation and therefore did not study the option thoroughly (nor did the political echelon).

The two sides were at odds with the basic logic of the plan that was being developed and institutionalized through formal J3 channels, whereby the failure of Icebreaker demanded the activation of Mei Marom—not in the intermediate stage of the plan, but as a broad maneuver that included the encirclement of southern Lebanon. Because the diverse opinions regarding the necessity of maneuver and its nature were not clarified before the war through discussions, exercises, and war games, additional issues, such as the disparity between controlling and capturing territory, were murky and remained unresolved well into the war.

In June 2006, during Northern Command's combined-arms exercise that practiced the Lebanon scenario, the focus was on experimenting with the new operating concept that dealt with establishing the regional command as the campaign operator. The operational concept for fighting Hezbollah was not the focus.[92]

With these rifts still open, the chief of staff, the general staff, and Northern Command entered the confrontation that would later be called the Second Lebanon War. Immediately after Prime Minister Olmert vetoed Halutz's proposal to bomb Lebanese dual-purpose (civilian-military) targets, the need for ground action grew. The tension between Halutz and Northern Command soared to the breaking point, leading to a loss of confidence in Adam.

To sum up the issues at the strategic-operational level, the crux of the matter was the attempt to implement three significant, closely linked changes simultaneously. The integration of the EBO concept, a component that included new terms, was at an advanced stage when the war erupted. As for the systemic design of the campaign, which had been devised by various senior commanders in the years preceding the war, especially by Ya'alon and Gantz and, to a lesser extent, by Halutz and Adam, training for this approach had yet to commence. The third component—changes in the general staff and organizational adjustments at regional command headquarters so that it could function as the campaign operator—was still in its infancy. The lack of synchronization among these three components, which were extremely interdependent, seems to be a major reason why the IDF did not adhere to the concept's principles. An additional factor was Halutz's lack of attention to the northern theater (because of his preoccupation with disengagement from Gaza in August 2005) and his bias toward firepower over maneuver. The main lesson is that change must be applied in a measured manner, in stages that can be digested in a relatively short period; only then can the next component of change be embarked on. Another lesson is that an attempt to introduce change through language and concepts, without making the requisite organizational adjustments, is doomed to fail.

The Tactical Level

The problem of failure to use a common language, which slowly entered the tactical level from the strategic-operational level of knowledge development, was evident in the area of logistics. In this case, the use of all but meaningless new terms (such as "combat logistics") hampered communication between regular and reserve units. In a survey of logistics troops who participated in the war, only 13 percent were familiar with the new terms, and only 40 percent were somewhat acquainted with them.[93]

A new concept that has not been assimilated, and developing knowledge that has not been integrated into the combat doctrine in the form of lucid directives, can affect the common language in its technical context. As the Winograd Commission pointed out, the merging of obscure language with ambiguity of purpose (with regard to thought and planning) exacerbated an already dubious situation. For commanders, the blurring of discourse on the operation's objectives was aggravated by the use of ill-defined jargon. The commission's report emphasized the importance of having a common language between planners and operators to create a shared and agreed-on basis for connecting an idea and its execution. The report referred to the town of Bint Jbeil as an example where language was not only unfamiliar but also incomprehensible and damaging. The chief of staff noted "the problematical nature that was rife in the dialogue between GHQ and Northern Command over the definition of the term 'capture' in the case of Bint Jbeil. To sum up: an essential understanding and agreement was absent on what was supposed to take place in Bint Jbeil in the first round of the fighting." He continued: "Here I refer to the fact that the initial fuzziness regarding the goals and missions multiplied because of lack of common understanding and precise terminology in expressions such as 'capture,' 'attack,' 'gaining control of' and 'encompassing.' I also note the proliferation of ambiguity because of the Palestinian context where raids of limited duration were most common. 'Capture' generally means gaining control for an unlimited time and mopping up. With reference to raids, 'capture' can mean something else."[94]

The report continued, detailing the lack of clarity in the military discourse among senior commanders and upper-level headquarters: "We cannot ignore the novel terminology of the [91st] division commander [Brigadier General Gal Hirsch]." The report provided two examples of language that was designed to clarify the division commander's intent: "an operational demonstration in the town Bint Jbeil while neutralizing, enmeshing, and occluding the area, and its systematic anatomization via a synchronic, swarming, multi-dimensional onslaught," and "wide-scale infiltration in low signature (wasp cloud) incursion plus the rapid stabilization of dominating areas while precipitating lethal contact with urban areas (swarms) and engendering systematic shock and awe to the enemy." The report observed, "No one will deny that the division commander adopted creative vocabulary, which some even described as poetic. In part this was the logorrheic language that entered the concept of operations and the new operating concept. Some of [the division commander's] subordinates were comfortable with the semantics and understood them perfectly; others had not been under his command before the war. Small wonder that they and their troops struggled to interpret the terminology and translate it into operable language."[95]

Hirsch expressed his apprehensions about a common language at the tactical level before the war: "I'm concerned about not having enough time to train the troops. Even though I invested in 'centers of gravity'—officers at the Command and Staff College, instructors of battalion and company commanders courses, and the staff at the Tze'elim Reservists Training Center—I was worried that this wasn't enough and that time was too short to assimilate all of the material. . . . I did everything possible to prepare the entire army—not only my own division, though naturally this was the division that I focused on." He acknowledged: "I know that Amnon (7th Brigade commander) and Hagai (Paratrooper Brigade commander) never trained with my division. They didn't breathe the same language, which is always a problem between units and the reason why we always strive for integration, language uniformity, and simplicity. . . . It's an inherent gap that has to be bridged because new ideas are always developing. We have to keep one step ahead, be relevant and situated at the cutting edge."[96]

The problem from the strategic, operational, and tactical points of view can be summed up as follows: The operating concept was validated and apparently became the basis for Northern Command's combined-arms exercise in June 2006, but when the war broke out, the concept was incomplete and had not been assimilated; therefore, it was incapable of establishing a common infrastructure. The attempt to apply the concept was a failure and resulted in ambiguity and frustrated expectations.[97]

As noted, the concept reflected a long-running debate in the IDF over several issues. Some of these issues concerned content, such as regional command's role as campaign commander; others dealt with cognitive tools and language. Some of the participants claimed that new phenomena demanded new conceptualizations, while others countered that the current military language was sufficient (and solved certain problems by stretching familiar terms to encompass the new phenomena). As this chapter has shown, the proposed conceptual change was deep and multifaceted; therefore, the challenge to assimilate it was urgent. Even though the war, which began as a routine security operation, was not executed according to the new operating concept, it revealed the risks involved in such a broad change and the need for the proper tools to manage it.

* * *

In the Yom Kippur War, long-term conceptual ambiguity revealed a gap in common understanding at the moment of truth. In the Second Lebanon War, hostilities broke out while an in-depth conceptual change was just starting to be assimilated, and the effect was felt at all levels.

The lesson is that when a conceptual change is deemed necessary, the new concept must be assimilated swiftly so that new ideas and new terminology will become integrated as soon as possible. All commanders involved in the change must undergo a special study program that defines and explains the new concept, followed by exercises that are repeated until the concept has been completely absorbed. IDF ground forces are relatively large, and the time required to train them is long, but given Israel's small size, commanders can be assembled relatively quickly so that they can at least be made aware of the change.

The IDF does not properly distinguish between exercises for headquarters and units and experiments that examine new concepts, organizational changes, and the integration of new weapons. The typical formula tests future concepts and capabilities in an exercise with a standard unit. This can create situations in which you feel that you are on target when, in reality, you are way off center. This phenomenon was manifest in the Second Lebanon War at the regional command level, which ran the combined-arms exercise nearly one month before the war and served as headquarters for the theater of operations without altering the organization and supporting processes. The same was true at the brigade level of the 91st Division, which exercised combat logistics even though the IDF had not yet procured the requisite amount of suitable equipment.

Given the risk that war will erupt while changes (conceptual, doctrinal, organizational, technological, and so forth) are being introduced, all new concepts, organizations, and weapons have to tested before the binding concept or doctrine is published. The shift from the old system to the new one should be made only after most of the relevant changes have been completed. For example:

- Organizational change—using the Second Lebanon War as an example: The regional command's ability to command a theater of operations should be drilled to the point of implementation. Only then should the new lines of responsibility between GHQ and the regional command be officially defined.
- Conceptual change resulting from a change in weapons—again using the case of the Second Lebanon War: The method of employing logistics can be changed only after the last mobile equipment has arrived and the forces have been trained in its use.

Sometimes the changes are too deep to be assimilated quickly. Under these circumstances, the solution seems to be a slower pace and smaller increments of change. To avoid what happened with the operating concept before the Second Lebanon War, learning patterns have to be developed that enable continuous change, and the operational-strategic echelons have to be trained to manage the state of constant transition.

4

From Routine Security Operations to War

Identifying, Assimilating, and Implementing Change

In wartime, the need to transition from one situation to another is a common enough event, though it is generally difficult to do. There is very little theoretical foundation for making such a transition, and the historical research is minimal. Three basic elements are involved: identifying the change in the situation and making the decision to recalibrate operations accordingly; assimilating the change into units, as well as among superiors and peers; and taking practical steps to shift to the new situation.

There are various types of transitions. Some are classic-universal, such as the transition between types of battle or combat (e.g., offense to defense) or from fighting a regular army to engaging in counterguerrilla warfare (e.g., the Roman army after the conquest of Gaul, the IDF upon completion of maneuvers in the First Lebanon War, the US Army in the Iraq War in 2003). Others are relatively rare but are characteristic of the IDF, such as the transition from routine security operations (RSOs) to full-scale war, reserve units' transition from peacetime duties as civilians to emergency activities, or the rapid transition between theaters of operations within the theater of war.

The commander has to identify certain changes, such as the transition from RSOs to a battle day (a concentrated clash lasting a few hours) or war or the transition between types of battles. In other cases, such as the transition from one theater of operations to another, the challenge lies not in identifying the change but in implementing it. In some cases, commanders have a relatively long time (days to weeks) to make the transition, as in the above-mentioned cases. In other scenarios, such as the Israeli transition from RSOs to major combat operations, the time might be measured in hours. In a transition situation, "a soldier, a unit, and a system can be prepared for the transition from routine operations to combat . . . [but] the heart of the matter depends on the resilience of the units and the troops since resilience is the key element in dealing with the shock of surprise."[1]

Conceptual Framework

The aim of this chapter is to enhance the ability to deal with transition by presenting a theoretical infrastructure for identifying change in a situation and for transitioning between combat situations once a decision has been made. The focus here is on the transition from RSOs to war, and for purposes of this chapter, RSOs include the following:

- Defending the borders against enemy penetration and preventing the abduction of IDF personnel.
- Policing or stabilization missions in captured or occupied territories.
- Static battle days on the ground (tank and artillery fire) and in the air—lasting for one day or less and with a relatively limited order of battle on both sides.

Identifying a Change in Reality

The difficulty of identifying a change against the background of an existing concept has been discussed at length from a psychological point of view in the context of a surprise attack, but it also applies in the case of transitioning from RSOs to war. The desire to maintain contact with some concept of reality is a basic human need. A concept provides the link between an action and its result; it enables one to respond to change, serves as a common language between echelons, and so forth. Certain parameters enable one to classify changing combat situations according to the type of transition. For example, when an army conducts offensive operations in order to occupy an area, it has to identify the nature of the surviving resistance elements—generally, guerrilla activity—and adapt its forces and activities to the new type of resistance.

In the transition from RSOs to battle day or from RSOs or battle day to war—the focus of this chapter—the following evidentiary indicators are present:

- Change in the intensity of enemy activity: the size of the force and volume of fire being applied, the type of activity conducted by the enemy (fire from static positions or an offensive), the type of weapons used by the enemy.
- Change in friendly forces: a deliberate order to execute the prewar plan, a situation in which the number of casualties is greater than expected, the unsuitability of physical deployment in the new situation, the unsuitability of the C2 layout due to the volume of data processed in a given time, the type of decision making required by various echelons in the new situation.

Research has found that the main variable that influences the ability to identify change is past experience. If a commander or soldier is a war veteran, he has a fairly clear reference point, even if the nature of the previous war was basically different from the present one and unsuitable for comparison (e.g., the Yom Kippur War compared with the War of Attrition). Because this chapter focuses on the transition from RSOs to war, it deals with combat units consisting of regulars who are relatively new to the military and unlikely to have fought in a war (regulars serve three-year stints, and the interval between wars in Israel has always been more than three years). In general, soldiers seem to regard casualties in their own units as the most significant sign of change in a situation. Death is quite rare during RSOs (including battle days), but among company and battalion commanders who have lost subordinates and comrades, the combination of increased enemy strength or determination and rising number of in-unit casualties is the most recognizable sign of change. At the lower command echelon, another factor that hampers the identification of change is the absence of situational awareness within the whole sector. When war erupts, the commander of a stronghold under attack is totally focused on defending his perimeter and sees the attack in terms of RSOs rather than as part of the enemy's wider operation.

Introducing the Change to Subordinates and Convincing Superiors

This is a crucial challenge because even if a commander or staff officer realizes that the situation has changed, his subordinates and superiors must be made aware. Informing subordinates is easily accomplished, but its relevance is negligible if the second element—convincing superiors—does not take place, since a military unit's effectiveness at any level requires the superior echelon and the neighboring units to act in unison. Issuing an order that changes the mindset of its recipient is not as simple as it seems. As this study shows, declarations that "Tomorrow is war" or "This is it, we're at war" are often ineffective, for the following reasons:

- Some individuals might ignore these declarations because commanders often make such statements to heighten the troops' level of readiness.
- Because most of the men in the units (all the regulars and noncommissioned officers and the majority of junior officers) have never fought in a war, there is a dissonance between what is said and what is absorbed. A commander who announces that war is imminent bases it on his experience, whereas the soldiers have no experience of war.
- Even if some individuals have experienced war, it is usually only partially comparable to the new situation.

This study also shows that the transition from RSOs to a war footing must be multidimensional and should include the following elements:

- Assigning a code name to the order for the new situation, such as issuing an order to transition to a plan with a different code name.
- Introducing changes in RSO instructions: rules of engagement, delegation of more authority to junior levels, approval for the use of weapons and activities forbidden in the previous situation (e.g., tank fire, AFV movement on roads, access to emergency storerooms).
- Changing units' subordination relative to the situation prior to the change (according to the plan for the new situation).
- Revising maps and communications regulations to reflect wartime conditions.

Senior commanders need to be out in front at this critical stage to be absolutely sure of the change. This is crucial because of the difficulty of determining that war has indeed broken out and the drawbacks in decision making based on reports alone. The higher the echelon, the harder it is to decide to shift to war due to its wider consequences.

Transitioning from One Mode of Action to Another

Identifying, announcing, and inculcating the need for change in relevant units cannot guarantee that the transition to the new situation will be successful. The challenges involved in ensuring that a military unit operates effectively in the new situation include the following:

- Reorganizing the C2 layout (e.g., changes in subordination, redistribution of sectors, entry of an additional command echelon).
- Moving to a new position.
- Altering task forces.
- Changing the method of fighting (form of battle, warfare or battle technique).
- Revising C2 measures (e.g., maps, communications codes).

The cases analyzed here to test the proposed theory are outlined in the accompanying table. Because the focus is on the outbreak of war, this chapter examines the functioning of the regular units deployed on the line at the time of the event.

Table 1. Test Cases

Case	Type of Transition	Conceptual Reference for Identifying Change	Challenge of Identifying Change	Challenge of Convincing Superiors	Challenge of Implementing Transition
Golan front in Yom Kippur War	From RSOs to all-out war (188th Brigade vs. 7th Brigade)	"Capital" battle day in the Golan	Intermediate	Relatively easy	Substantial–during intense combat
Suez Canal front in Yom Kippur War	From RSOs to all-out war (252nd Division)	War of Attrition on the canal	Intermediate	Relatively easy	Substantial—during intense combat
Air force in Yom Kippur War	From peacetime to war	War of Attrition	Early identification by chief of air force	Intermediate	Relatively easy
IDF GHQ in Second Lebanon War	From RSOs to war (GHQ)	Previous abduction attempts	Substantial	Substantial	Intermediate
91st (Galilee) Division in Second Lebanon War	From RSOs to war	Previous abduction attempts	Substantial	Substantial	Intermediate—light enemy pressure

The Golan Front in the Yom Kippur War: From Battle Day to War

Identifying the Change

The difficulty of identifying a change in the situation is closely linked to the existing conceptual reference. The degree of difficulty in this case differed from unit to unit and in the various echelons.

For the 188th Brigade—the armored brigade (regulars) operating on the Golan Heights—the years before the Yom Kippur War were characterized by battle days; thus, the battle day was the conceptual reference with which the brigade's men and officers were familiar. The brigade was involved in two battle days (code-named Capital B and Capital D, which took place on November 21, 1972, and January 8, 1973, respectively); they consisted of static fighting during which a number of Syrian tanks were destroyed.[2] The forces' training focused on the Capital Plan, which was the master plan for the battle days and required expertise in precision tank fire. The tank crews became adept at reaching their positions in daylight and darkness and practiced daytime and nighttime linkups with the strongholds.[3]

According to Aviram Barkai, who researched the 188th Brigade, the tankers got used to the following routine:

> Most of the incidents on the Northern Command front were battle days with familiar patterns of action. In the morning the Syrians would initiate an artillery attack on a wide front. Simultaneously, with the sun in the enemy's eyes, the tanks of the line brigades would sally forth and direct their fire on Israeli armor that was waiting for them in their positions.
>
> Even before the sun had set and the cannon din abated and the forces separated, the end result could be predicted. Hurt and licking their wounds, the Syrians would withdraw their guns, while on the other side of the purple line [the 1967 cease-fire line] the men of the 188th Brigade inflated their chests with brassy pride, celebrating their professional superiority with victory parties awash in champagne.[4]

When the Syrian fire that initiated the Yom Kippur War started at noon on October 6, 1973, the 188th's commander, Colonel Yitzhak Ben Shoham, realized that this would be an expanded battle day. He ordered the execution of the Capital Plan and instructed the commander of the 74th Battalion in the northern sector, Lieutenant Colonel Yair Nafshi, to implement it. In addition to deployment of the forces on tank ramps (enabling better observation and firing zones), the length of the battle day's fighting, which was limited to the daylight hours, played a significant part in the prewar mindset. Thus, the battalion commander left the night-vision equipment, the light mortars, and the antiglare equipment (a countermeasure for the rising sun in the Golan Heights) in the garrison.[5]

How did the 188th Brigade commanders and men realize that this was not the usual battle day? A platoon commander of C Company, 53rd Battalion, observed the damaged tanks and the casualties and noted that the tanks' withdrawal to the rear-area workshop in Nafach for repairs was no longer relevant.[6]

The tank force in the southern sector—Stronghold 116—incurred no casualties, but there was an indication that something had changed: a number of Syrian tanks were crossing into Israeli territory. "The platoon sergeant, Atir, recalled that it was only in the morning that Tsurich, the brigade intelligence officer, came and tried to calm us by saying: 'This is just a battle day against static predetermined targets. Don't worry about the growing Syrian force out there.' But Yoav Yakir, Nir Atir and Yair Waxman looked out and wondered if the wave of tanks approaching was the static targets that the intelligence officer had talked about and whether there really was nothing to worry about."[7]

One of the survivors of the battle on the Tel Saki stronghold told Lieutenant General Haim Laskov (retired) and journalist Aryeh Arad:

> At first there was nothing particularly threatening. Some shelling—big deal! The truth is that spirits were rather high until the evening. We heard champagne bottles popping open whenever the tankers ignited a Syrian tank. . . . Actually, until Saturday evening we were sure that this was just another battle day—the Syrians shell us, our tanks clobber them, and everything returns to normal. A heavy sense began to creep in when the first wounded guys arrived. One was a pilot whose plane had been shot down and the other an armor officer with a bad head wound. Only after we saw the first casualties did it dawn on us that this was serious business.

> LASKOV: You were prepared for shelling or a battle day, as Northern Command called it, and suddenly it turns out that this is war. How long did it take you to realize this?
>
> ANSWER: After I listened to the news a few times, I understood that this was something bigger than an ordinary battle day. But the next morning when we left for Tel Saki and later when we got blasted at the entrance I still believed that this was a battle day.[8]

The commander of an artillery battalion that fought on the Golan Heights also answered questions posed by the former general and the journalist:

> LASKOV: So what you're saying is that you deployed for regular security activity.
>
> ANSWER: That's right. We prepared for RSOs with the drills that we'd gone over hundreds of times.
>
> ARAD: For a battle day?
>
> ANSWER: For a serious battle day or something larger that might develop. . . .

Laskov: At what point did you decide that this wasn't just another battle day, that this was war?

Answer: Around six in the evening the guys who'd been on leave returned and told us there's a war in the south. At first we thought that this was a battle that would begin in the morning and at ten or eleven that night we'd clean the cannon barrels and go to bed. But they [the men who had come back from leave] told of battles on the Egyptian front. This was something different.

Around 22:00 I realized that this wasn't an ordinary battle day but something far more serious than what we'd seen in the sector up till now. When I learned the size of the Syrian penetration, I understood that we'd have to perform maneuvers that went beyond the bounds of previous battle days.[9]

The penny finally dropped at around 22:30, when four Syrian tanks reached the battalion's deployment area. At the company commander level, there were various signs that something had changed. After the war, Emmy Kochav, commander of H Company, 77th Battalion, was questioned by his commander, Avigdor Kahalani:

Kahalani: Emmy, on Yom Kippur, when did you realize that this was war and not a battle day?

Emmy: On the way to the ramps, when I asked questions and realized that I had to make decisions that were different from the answers I'd been given. . . .

At first everything seemed well organized. The collapse came at night when I realized that we really didn't have a clue to what was going on. That what I know is what I'm seeing. . . .

Also, when I requested basic assistance, like illumination, and realized there was no chance of getting any.[10]

The 13th Battalion, Golani Brigade, commanded by Lieutenant Colonel Ze'ev Oren, was responsible for the northern section of the Golan Heights strongholds, from Stronghold 116 to Mount Hermon. Oren testified before the Agranat Commission:

Laskov: Please go on. You said it was as if you were told to prepare for a battle day.

Oren: Yes. . . . Battle day is the term for an action that includes enemy artillery activity and our artillery redeployment—what you might call a large incident.[11]

Regarding his growing awareness that this was more than another battle day, Oren stated:

Chairman Agranat: [Do you mean] Syrian tanks and infantry?

Oren: Yes. That's when I realized that this was somewhat more than a battle day, bigger than a large incident. We turned on the [three o'clock] news and head marching music and Hebrew songs. We knew that something was up. . . .

[We heard] on the radio that the Egyptians had opened artillery fire the entire length of the front. I immediately said: "Guys, this is war. . . ." Nobody told me, I just knew it.[12]

The identification of a change in the situation was different at other military echelons. The senior commanders, with their wartime experience, needed a trigger to make it clear that the new situation was unlike anything they had seen in the past. Major General Uri Simchoni, operations officer of Northern Command during the war, wrote:

> Even on October 6, when we already knew that war would break out in the afternoon and we'd already started calling up reserves, I still didn't really get—and I'm sure that others didn't either—the type of war that was about to erupt. It was unlike anything any of us had ever been through. In our minds a war was like the ones that we'd experienced—the Six-Day War, the Sinai War. But this was a war with a different rate of fire, a different speed of movement, a different size of forces, clashes at a different intensity, a different number of casualties, a different kind of danger. The Yom Kippur War was unlike anything that any of the participants had ever gone through. You have to understand what intensity is. All the fire of both intifadas and both wars in Lebanon lumped together can't compare with the intensity of the artillery barrage that fell on us in one hour on the first day of the Yom Kippur War. The whole Golan Heights shook. For three days dust clouds hung in the air.[13]

In the staff officer's case, the trigger was the intensity of the artillery barrage that opened the war.

Assimilating the Change

At Northern Command headquarters, the situation was evident as soon as war broke out. Nevertheless, the regional command found it difficult to convince the chief of staff. GHQ's October 1 situation estimate forecast a limited Syrian offensive action, so the chief of staff ordered reinforcements sent to the Golan Heights. On

October 2 Northern Command's intelligence staff and GHQ's intelligence branch disagreed over the interpretation of the signs of war. "The command's intelligence officer closed the meeting, saying 'indications that Syria is ready for an attack are all there, I mean we don't need any more signs to prove that the Syrian army has finalized its war plans.'"[14] At 10:00 on October 6 the commander of Northern Command, Major General Yitzhak Hofi, summoned an orders group and stated that a full-scale Egyptian-Syrian war was about to be launched against Israel. He ordered the evacuation of women and children from the Golan Heights; in addition, he ordered that the strongholds be bolstered and Mount Hermon reinforced. Various steps were taken at the regional command level for the approaching war, especially regarding the threat of territorial capture by the Syrians. These steps bore no resemblance to those taken previously to prepare for a static-fire battle day.

In contrast to Hofi, who talked about war, the 188th Brigade commander briefed his battalion commanders for an "expanded" battle day. He maintained that view even after receiving Hofi's order and after his own intelligence officer, Major Moshe Tsurich, informed him at 11:00 that the intelligence branch was warning that war—not a battle day—was about to break out.[15] After the war, the battalion commanders testified before the Agranat Commission that, based on the brigade commander's briefing, they had understood that a battle day was approaching. Yair Nafshi, commander of the 74th Battalion, stated, "I announced 'Capital' to everyone, the code for entering positions for the start of a battle day. Who could have guessed that this was all-out war? How was I supposed to know?" Lieutenant Colonel Shraga Ben Zvi, commander of the 55th Artillery Battalion, testified, "The last time we were updated was in the forward command post at Nafach on Friday. We expected a large-scale battle day the following day during which the Syrians would probably try to grab a stronghold. Nothing was mentioned of a full-scale war." Lieutenant Colonel Oded Erez, commander of the 53rd Battalion, told the commission, "Something was expected that day . . . so we elevated the anti-aircraft alert . . . but no one said anything about a war."[16]

Unlike the 188th's commander Ben Shoham, the 7th Brigade's commander, Avigdor Ben Gal (Yanush), convened his battalion commanders for a briefing, presented the H-hour, and ordered them to carry out final preparations for the battle: deployment, camouflage, and an antiaircraft alert. Two of the battalion commanders testified before the Agranat Commission that the brigade commander had mentioned "war." But the alert level was raised not only because of Ben Gal's intuition that this was a full-scale war, based on intelligence reports. The 7th Brigade was new to the Golan Heights, having recently been brought up from the Suez Canal as one of the measures taken to increase the level of alert. Thus, the 7th Brigade may have found it easier to adapt to the new situation than did the 188th, where the mindset was fixed on a battle day.

Although the 7th Brigade commander and the battalion commanders understood how events were unfolding, the testimony of Danny Levin, commander of B Company, 82nd Battalion, shows that a dramatic announcement by the commander is not always helpful:

> I returned to the company and called a meeting. I briefed the men on the coming war and told them to carry out all of Yanush's orders. The battalion commander and I, together with the B Company's deputy commander, Jack Cohen, reconnoitered the area to familiarize ourselves with the sector. . . . When I came back around 13:00 I summoned all of the commanders and told them what I thought of the battle, if it took place. The truth is that I didn't think anything would happen even though I'd been told to expect war. I was still thinking in terms of a battle day— perhaps a larger one than usual.[17]

Kahalani's description of the prewar hours best illustrates the chasm in the understanding between senior commanders and the troops, as well as how difficult it is to get the message across, beyond saying, "There's going to be a war":

> [Kahalani:] At 10:00 Yanush told me: "We're at war today!" I went to the battalion, straight to the synagogue . . . tapped the rabbi on the shoulder and told him to "stop the prayers. . . . We're at war." I said that "I don't know exactly when, but be ready by 12:00 with all the gear strapped secure on the tanks and stay under the camouflage nets."
>
> [Interviewer Yom Tov Tamir, commander of the 9th Battalion in the canal sector:] And what did you see in front of you when you told the men "today is war"? You knew exactly what you were saying. Did the soldiers also understand?
>
> [Kahalani:] No, they didn't get it. They were excited, but the meaning of what I said didn't register.
>
> [Tamir:] They may have thought that the battalion commander was "trying to pull one over on us"?
>
> [Kahalani:] No, not that. They became a bit uptight. Maybe they thought it would be a kind of battle day or large-scale exercise. Nobody imagined what was in store for us and the sights we were about to see. . . . But first of all, and because of my familiarity with the religious guys in the battalion, I said, "Just a second, before you get the gear ready—grab something to eat."
>
> I looked at the religious soldiers with the skullcaps smiling at each other and poking their buddies in the ribs. Their eyes said it all: What an order! Whoever heard of such an order!

> I had an apple in my pocket. I took it out and said: "Look at me! I've fasted [on Yom Kippur] since the age of ten; I've prayed all my life. If I eat something—you can too. Go and get something to eat otherwise you won't be able to load the tank shells, rotate the turrets, and operate the tanks. I seriously doubt there's going to be anything to eat later. I'm telling you this because I know." And I bit into the apple in front of all of them.[18]

In his book on the 188th Brigade, Barkai raised the question why there was no open announcement: "This is war." This study claims that such an announcement would have been of little use. "I can't explain why most of the commanders planned for a battle day," Hofi told the Agranat Commission. "It would be irresponsible if I stated with certainty that the last soldier knew that war was about to erupt, but the brigade commanders had personally received the order."[19]

When the fighting began, Northern Command had to convince GHQ that it was war and not a limited event. As Simchoni, the regional command's operations officer, recalled:

> When fire began and the horizon blackened with smoke, I phoned GHQ and asked to speak with the general (Hofi). They told me he was with the chief of staff and couldn't be disturbed.
>
> "Then I wish to speak with the chief of staff," I said. "It's urgent."
>
> The chief of staff (Elazar) came on the line.
>
> "War's broken out," I reported.
>
> "How do you know this is war?" he asked.
>
> "I can see it," I said. And that was the end of the conversation.[20]

If the transition from RSOs to war had been announced, it might have significantly contributed to the absorption of the change, but this did not happen.

On the canal front, the commanders had no knowledge of any plan except for the Dovecote Plan (for RSOs and a battle day). In contrast, war plans existed in Northern Command and theoretically could have facilitated the shift from RSOs or a battle day to war. The Capital Plan consisted of tank deployment on the line (while maintaining battalion-level reserves in the rear) and advancing artillery batteries. In all of Northern Command's defense plans, the forward line on the Golan Heights was divided between two brigades: the 820th (regional) or 179th (armor reservists) in the north, and the 188th in the south. The Hol Yam (Sea Sand) Plan, which was designed to block a limited Syrian offensive or territory grab, was based on the regulars' order of battle. The Geer (Chalk) Plan, which was based on reinforcing the regulars with two reserve brigades and artillery, included deployment on the line and two reduced brigades in reserve in the rear. Chalk was a minimalist plan for defending the Golan Heights against a Syrian attack. The Sela (Rock) Plan included Northern Command's entire order of battle and enabled defense of the Golan Heights and a rapid transition from defense to offense.[21] According to Yehuda Wagman, a reservist battalion commander:

> The explicit warning for war did not bring the senior headquarters to act accordingly or the general staff to take the trouble to check whether they were deployed as ordered. As a matter of fact, there was no order to change the force deployment for a battle day and shift to the defense according to the Chalk plan. The three brigades remained deployed for a battle day. . . . For all practical purposes the Golan Heights had an order of battle similar to what the Northern Command's Chalk defense plan called for which was derived from the Rock plan. But no one took the trouble to order Chalk and switch to defense mode that was essentially different from an RSO situation.[22]

Despite the existence of alternative plans and the opening of Syrian fire at 14:00, the Capital Plan went into effect for several hours. Even after its irrelevance was recognized, no one ordered a transition to Chalk, which likely would have led to an understanding that the situation had changed.

Applying the Change

A key issue in transitioning from RSOs to full-scale war is the reorganization of the C2 layout, including the distribution of sectors among units and the subsequent changes in subordination and command throughout the sector. The first reason for changing the C2 layout is the increased volume of information flowing into the system in wartime as compared with RSOs. The second reason is the need for a crystal-clear definition of command subordination between headquarters and units, which, in most cases, is different in war than in RSOs.

From 1967 to 1973, the line on the Golan Heights was held by a single armored battalion. On the Jewish New Year in September 1973, the sector was divided for the first time between two battalions: the 53rd, under the command of Oded Erez, in the south, and the 74th, under the command of Yair Nafshi, in the north. Because the situation was still considered a limited Syrian action, some of the 74th Battalion's platoons had not yet been moved to the northern sector but remained in their original sector in the south, under the command of the 53rd Battalion's companies. "This resulted in a battalion anomaly in which each battalion commander had an organic company in his sector and two companies under his command that were attached to the second battalion. . . . Furthermore, G Company, a company on the line in the central sector, had to be divided between the two battalion commanders."[23] In addition, the whole sector was split between the battalion commander and his deputy. This kind of C2 organization obviously created problems in the transition to war.

Another problem was the split between the strongholds' command (the 820th Brigade) and the tank battalions (the 188th Brigade). This ambiguity in the RSO layout impeded effective functioning in the war.

According to Wagman, "The C2 system also prepared for a battle day that headquarters had micro-planned down to the minutest detail according to standing operating procedures for local events. This method of command created a situation in which all the information from all the forces in contact with the enemy flowed into the Nafach headquarters which crashed almost immediately due to data overflow, and thus failed to translate the data into knowledge, understandings, and a comprehensive situation picture."[24]

The next change was the split-up of the entire sector between two brigades—the 188th and the 7th—while the regional brigade (the 820th) continued to have overall responsibility for the strongholds. In the first two hours of the war, the 188th Brigade's commander directed his forces (as well as Northern Command's forward command post) from a bunker in Nafach, alongside the commander of the 820th Brigade and the Northern Command staff. Later, at approximately 16:00, the commander of Northern Command returned from GHQ, assumed responsibility for the entire sector, and divided it between the two brigades.[25]

The third change came at midnight, when command of the Golan Heights was transferred to 36th Division's headquarters. According to the division commander, Brigadier General Rafael Eitan, he took full advantage of the remaining hours of darkness "to organize the headquarters for control of the entire Golan Heights."[26] On October 8 the Golan Heights was redistributed between two divisions.

The changes in the command organization of the Golan Heights in the Yom Kippur War illustrate the inherent problems in transitioning from RSOs to all-out war.

The Suez Canal Front in the Yom Kippur War: From a "Little War of Attrition" to Full-Scale War

Identifying the Change

In a postwar interview, Amnon Reshef, commander of the 14th Brigade, said, "We maintained a military alert in the field but we weren't on a psychological alert for war."[27] After the Egyptian air strike and massive artillery bombardment, he immediately realized that Israel was at war.[28]

Lieutenant Colonel Gideon Avidor, the 252nd (Sinai) Division's operations officer, recalled: "Southern Command issued no order stating 'this is war.' There was an order to prepare to cross the canal the next morning [October 7]. . . . The opening round of fire on the whole length of the front, the Egyptian air attack, and the infantry canal crossing left no doubt that we were facing an all-out war."[29]

For the relatively senior commanders who had fought in the Six-Day War, the intensity of enemy fire helped them grasp the new situation (as indicated by the testimony of Northern Command's operations officer). The 9th Battalion, 14th Armored Brigade (regulars), was operating in the canal's northern sector. According to its history: "The battalion commander [Lieutenant Colonel Yom Tov Tamir] said we can expect 'a little war of attrition' in the sector, which meant implementing Dovecote exactly as the battalion had practiced it dozens of times. . . . The company commanders looked apathetically at the battalion commander; once every two weeks they'd drilled the Dovecote ride in APCs and were sick of it. . . . As for the question, 'What's "a little war of attrition"?' the answer was 'attrition, like three years ago—a little artillery, maybe some tank fire.'"[30]

The battalion commander had fought in the War of Attrition as the 14th Brigade's operations officer, and the company commanders had been platoon commanders in the War of Attrition, but the platoon commanders and soldiers had not experienced war firsthand. This fact complicated the issue whether the term "a little war of attrition" served as a reference point in the battalion. The battalion operated according to the Dovecote order, and most of it was hit when it linked up with the strongholds and fought from inside them.

Laskov and Arad asked the regulars who had fought in the canal sector at what point they realized this was not a routine security event and they were involved in a major war. Here is a sampling of the interviewees' replies:

- "I began to feel that this was war the minute I heard about the dead, including guys that I knew in other units."
- "When we approached the canal we saw—even though the sun was blinding—our planes diving towards the canal. Diving and falling. We stopped at one of the crossroads for a break and somebody turned on the radio and heard them speaking about war in the north [Golan Heights]. That's when we became pretty certain that this was it."
- "The war caught me on special leave. I contacted the base and asked if our unit had been called up. They told me that our unit no longer existed. I didn't take this seriously but felt that I was missing my unit in a war and

> that I'd have to fight while attached to another unit, and this really bothered me. This is what happened in the first days of the war."[31]

A tank gunner recalled:

> I didn't think this was war. I thought it might be an "incident," an action that would be over in a couple of hours. Everything my tank commander said had the word "incident" in it. At first he repeated that the "incident" would be over in a minute, and that every enemy tank that we knock out, the crew gets Coca Cola in the PX. . . . The first time I felt that I was in a war was when the company commander radioed the battalion to ask if he was permitted to open fire. That's when it hit me that this was more than just another "incident" and from that moment on the rules of the game changed.

Laskov asked him, "What did the ground events tell you about the enemy? That this is war?" The tank gunner realized it was war, he replied, "when I first saw tanks that I could definitely identify as enemy armor."[32]

Another soldier said: "I came across a tank—not from our company—that had been hit. Two wounded soldiers were lying on the side of the road and an officer was with them who had once been in our company. The tank was on the side, damaged, the driver inside was dead. This encounter with the damaged tank, the dead soldier and the wounded who I knew left no doubt in my mind that this was war, and a bitter one at that."[33]

In response to Laskov's question, "When did you finally decide that this was war?" one commander (of a company or battalion) said: "Toward Sunday morning . . . it became clear that we'd taken a lot of casualties, that there was no end to the enemy, and that this was a case of full-scale war and not a limited action."[34]

Emanuel Sakal claims that the standard C2 system in effect during RSOs and battle days had a major impact on the difficulty of transitioning from a routine security situation to war. The fact that unit commanders at all levels remained in the tactical operations centers was largely responsible for the unacceptable amount of time it took to perceive the enemy's modus operandi and battlefield gains and to comprehend that this was all-out war.[35]

The Agranat Commission reported that the habits commanders had developed during RSOs in and after the War of Attrition were not suited to the circumstances present at the outbreak of war. It took time for the commanders to adapt to the differences. In the meantime, the picture was as described by Colonel Granit: "I met the brigade commander, Dan Shomron, who was sitting in the 'pit' in the Mitle Pass. He was directing combined battles with some of the strongholds. . . . I reached the 'pit' in Tasa where Amnon [Reshef] was. The whole staff was seated in the tactical operations center. Everything was like it was in the War of Attrition, communication by telephone. Nobody went out with the forces."[36]

There is substance to the claim that the forward location of the senior commanders is crucial in achieving the early identification of a change in the situation.

Understanding and Assimilating the Change

The challenges of adapting to change are illustrated by the following recollections:

> Around four o'clock, when I reached the battalion from home, I ran to the tank. You can imagine the surprise that Yom Kippur afternoon by the response of the guys who remained in the battalion. For example, the communications platoon made me sign for the equipment that I received as though there was no war going on outside. The order was still in effect in Sinai that tanks were not to travel on the road, only on the side of the road. When we moved out towards the canal beyond the Gidi Pass I was careful at first to travel on the side of the road and not on the road. As we approached the canal I heard on the radio what was happening and only then did priorities change.[37]

The mechanized infantry company (regulars) of the 184th Battalion, 14th Brigade, under the command of Lieutenant Colonel Shaul Shalev, was operating in the central sector. One of its members recalled:

> The company commander, Shlomo Levin, assembled his men in the mess and told them to get ready. There might be a war. "We don't know what will be," he said. "Maybe when the air force comes in. . . ." When the company was ordered to arm the APCs, Vasserman (the squad leader) prodded Salman (a soldier): "Let's go, we have to move out and organize, a war's about to erupt." And Uri said, "Hey, give me a break. There's not gonna be any war." . . .
>
> It finally dawned on Koby Ravid (a soldier) that this was war only after Sharoni (platoon commander?) yelled "open fire." Other than Yigal and Roni, none of the guys knew what was going on. When Roni shouted "commence fire!" only then did we get it into our heads that it's us or the Egyptians. Nobody could have guessed what we were getting into.[38]

Pini Paz, a company commander from the 196th Reinforcement Battalion, related the details of his encounter with an intelligence officer from the 184th Battalion: He said, "'Hi, I'm Ze'evik, I'm the intelligence officer of the 184th, looks like it's going to be another battle day. The Egyptians opened fire in a lot of places it seems, and here and there some boats are trying to get cross the canal. We'll go down to the canal and fling 'em back.' That's how things were before we realized what was happening at 16:00."[39]

Lieutenant Colonel Avidor believes that the problems related to implementing change occurred at two levels:

1. Recognizing the shift to a war situation was not a problem at the fighters' level. The problem was that Southern Command and the chief of staff failed to understand that the IDF was neither prepared nor organized to defend the waterline and that Six-Day War–type plans were immaterial.
2. A similar problem in transitioning from routine security combat techniques to wartime fighting techniques occurred at the tactical level. This transition took about two days—and it was the number of casualties and the Egyptians' hold on the canal line that caused the reality to hit home.[40]

The absence of an alternative order for Dovecote stymied the possibility of dealing with the change in the situation by switching to a different order. According to Dovecote, the 14th Brigade's tanks were supposed to link up with the strongholds, assist them in the fighting, and evacuate the wounded. Another brigade—the 401st, in this case—would relieve the southern sector (in the event of a "two in front" deployment) or concentrate in the rear and wait for the counterattack. The third brigade—the 460th—would act in a concentrated manner in the northern sector. It should be noted that the Dovecote deployment was the brigade and battalion commanders' only defense plan. As noted in chapter 3, the commanders interviewed for this study—Reshef, Sakal, and Tamir—said that although they had heard of the Rock Plan, they were never issued such an order. In light of what Sakal wrote (about the lack of major features of a defense plan), it is clear why. Had there been an alternative to Dovecote, it would have provided the commanders with an important aid for both the mental and the physical shift required to face the new situation. A derivative of this could have been replacement of the Sirius RSO code maps with other maps designed for such a contingency. But this step was not taken.

Implementing the Change

C2 Organization

The canal front, like the Golan Heights, underwent a redistribution of sectors and subordination. The 252nd (Sinai) Division's sector, which had been split between the northern regional brigade and the southern tank brigade (regulars) during RSOs, was divided twice in short succession. At 17:55, four hours after the war began, the 14th Brigade's commander transferred the southern sector to the commander of the 401st Brigade, and the 52nd Battalion, which had engaged the enemy on the line, came under the 401st's command. Later, with the arrival of reservists, the sector was divided again between them and the 252nd Division.

Another difficulty in C2 was the transition from a centralized to a decentralized modus operandi. As Sakal points out, "In RSOs centralization of authority is the norm. In wartime, however, delegating authority is a vital aspect of command because of the inevitable influx of problems. . . . Southern Command attempted to control both the fighting on the contact line and the flow of reservists, creating a situation in which both suffered."[41]

Tank Employment

In the absence of an alternative order the forces were familiar with (such as Rock), the trigger for the change from RSOs to full-scale war was, to a large degree, the transition in the use of tanks. Their employment shifted from small formations that linked up with the strongholds to battalion-sized (or larger) formations that opposed the Egyptian concentrations crossing the canal. "As aptly described by Brigadier General Baruch Harel, deputy commander of the 252nd Division: 'On the first two days of the war and during the whole first week we misused our armor force, we took our tanks and turned them into bunkers that moved between 500 meters to a kilometer. This is not the way to apply armor.' Finally, late Sunday morning, the headquarters woke up to the need to change the manner and direction of operational thinking."[42]

The book *Stouthearted Men,* which details the actions of the 184th Battalion, 14th Brigade, in the war, states that on the night of Sunday, October 7, the deputy battalion commander assembled the remaining tanks into a battalion force after thirty hours of fighting according to the Dovecote concept. "The decision to fight as a united battalion force was a basic change from the previous concept that tank platoons had to rush to the waterline at the start of hostile fire."[43] Benny Taran, the deputy battalion commander, described the situation: "The blow came on the night between Yom Kippur [Saturday] and Sunday in Pearl's company/79th Battalion when I heard the missile flying straight at us and the screams over the radio. At that moment you don't know what to do. You lose control in these vast spaces. This was the first time I realized that what was happening was apparently not what I thought would happen, what in effect we all thought would happen. And at this point I knew that I had to protect the force and not split it up. And that was how we worked."[44]

According to Avidor (252nd Division J3): "As long as the strongholds could be reached and as long as they were fighting for their lives, the battle continued according to RSO techniques. Only after the strongholds fell [October 7–9] did the rest of the battalions and brigades assemble into a [small] concentrated force. The arrival of the reservist brigades in the sector and the redistribution of the sectors created a situation in which the division was deployed defensively in brigade concentrations along Artillery Road."[45]

The following exchange describes the shift in the tanks' operating concept as a trigger (and answer) to the surprise:

> Arad: We were talking about the surprise. When was the surprise over?
>
> Answer: The surprise ended on October 7 the moment the battalion and the rest of the forces in the area entered into a concentrated formation and began operating according to tactics derived from the situation. Also, by breaking off contact with the strongholds, we adapted ourselves, in effect, to the existing situation. . . .
>
> Arad: What characterized the shift from "Dovecote," successful or not, to real war?
>
> Answer: In the drills the forces were dispersed—a platoon here, a platoon there; one company here, another there. And this was how we operated at first, like robots, and I saw this as a good work. . . . The situation changed 180 degrees the minute the battalion, no matter how reduced it was, took casualties, dead and wounded. That's when we became a unified formation.[46]

The Air Force in the Yom Kippur War

The IAF entered the Yom Kippur War mobilized and prepared. Its main challenge, in the context of this study, was not understanding the change in the situation but assimilating that understanding as it was formulated by the commander and officially announced at all echelons and in all formations one day before the outbreak of the war.

The Assimilation Challenge

In the book *30 Hours in October*, Shmuel Gordon describes the challenge from different points of view. Lieutenant Colonel Avihu Ben-Nun, head of the attack branch at IAF headquarters, testified: "The air force was ready on Rosh Hashanah [the Jewish High Holiday ten days before the war] when we elevated the level of alert and called up 1400 reservists. Benny Peled [the IAF commander] insisted that we 'ignore them [the intelligence branch]. This time there'll be war.' He said this in the general staff forum, in the IAF forum, and in the commanders' forum. We weren't able to inculcate it in the bases and squadrons and get them to realize that war was imminent, [because of] the divided opinions in IAF headquarters."[47] Ben-Nun was referring to the differences between Peled, the IAF commander, and Rafi Harlev, the commander of IAF intelligence.

Colonel Oded Merom, commander of the Tactical Air Support Center that was responsible for the air force's participation in ground combat, recalled, "A few days before the war we realized, logically speaking, there was going to be a war, but mentally the reality didn't register."[48]

In an interview with Gordon, Peled said: "At 14:00, Friday, October 5, exactly twenty-four hours before war broke out . . . I spoke in the forum: 'Gentlemen, I believe we're facing a war. I can't say whether it's tomorrow or Sunday, but for us this is war. . . .' Did anyone really think that we were on the verge of war? Nobody! This was because of the distorted terms. When even the War of Attrition is war, then it's obvious why my meaning didn't get through."[49]

After the meeting: "Colonel Ran Ronen (Pekker), the commander of the Tel Nof Airbase, flew back from a briefing at the Sde Dov Airbase . . . . Pekker convenes an orders group, a strange name for a meeting of squadron and unit commanders on the base. The protocol of the meeting states that 'tomorrow will be a war' and the commanders had to prepare everything as required, but nobody seems to have internalized the meaning of the orders. All the senior commanders on the base were engaged in 'social games' until four in the morning, October 6."[50] At the Ramat David Airbase, the 69th Phantom Squadron's log notes: "At 15:00, Friday October 5, when an alert was announced, no one in the squadron took it seriously. This was just another routine alert on a holiday evening that would end as usual with all the crews being sent home."[51]

The realization that a preemptive strike could not be carried out should have spurred the commanders' awareness. Peled wrote in his memoirs:

> It was clear to me and the other commanders that we'd be fighting in opening conditions far different and much harder than our plans had assumed. Some of the men needed a whole day to wake up to the

new reality. This was felt in the first two days of the fighting. It was hard for the combat echelon to adapt quickly to the realization that:

- This was real war and not an RSO action, in which we operated according to "soft" criteria, like risk versus the chance of losing an aircraft and/or pilot.
- The enemy was the initiating party, and despite our operational superiority we would have to fight according to the script that the enemy had written for the most part at least until we neutralized his initiative and dictated our own script.

Other statements corroborate the lack of awareness that Israel was at war. Lieutenant Magen, a reservist flight leader in the 109th Squadron, stated during an after-action review: "Until Sunday evening I still believed this was another battle day with the Syrians and not a real war." Colonel Iftach Spector, commander of the 107th Squadron, criticized "the IAF headquarters' lack of awareness that the squadrons were not a hundred percent ready. It too didn't realize that this was not one of our initiated battle days where we could postpone its start until the 'squadrons were a hundred percent ready.'"[52]

Gordon concludes that a high state of alert and readiness cannot offset the numbing surprise at the outbreak of war. Despite Peled's explicit warning, the commanders, soldiers, and officers at IAF headquarters could not accept the fact that war was about to erupt. "Scores of testimonies refer to the expectation that this was just another state of alert that would soon be over. Many stories testify to the ongoing refusal to recognize that we were in a war. The surprise is not in the operational readiness domain but in the mental one."[53]

The C2 Challenge

Unlike the ground forces, which operated according to battle-day orders (Dovecote and Capital) and did not convert to war orders or war plans that would have helped reorganize the C2 layout more quickly, the IAF issued orders designed for war from the outset. Gordon claims that the IAF erred when it used a plan as complex as Dugman, which was still incomplete when the war broke out. (Gordon is somewhat mistaken, as the problem with the plan was not its prewar incompleteness but the fact that the SAM-6 mobile batteries had moved west.) Instead, it should have employed a preexisting plan in every unit that would have enabled a more rapid, smoother, and more efficient application than drafting a new plan or issuing partial ones. Gordon asks: "Why then didn't the IAF issue such an order? This is exactly what Motti Hod, the former commander of the IAF, asked. The main advantage of Hod's plan was the use of a prearranged plan that included most of the combat aircraft. The Sreeta (Scratch) plan was intended to disperse the fog of battle and make sense of the enormous friction at the start of a surprise war as happened a few minutes to two in the afternoon. The war plan is a common denominator for all IAF units."[54]

Another issue was the decentralized control demanded by the war situation. Chapter 2 describes Gordon's explanation of the basic difference between the detailed planning conducted by IAF headquarters during the War of Attrition, which resulted in very little room for decision making by flight leaders, and the urgent need for decentralized control and freedom of action at the lower echelons when the Yom Kippur War broke out. Gordon's quotation of Ben-Nun is worth repeating:

> Given the combination of the central command's inability to control all the forces and the expendability of such control, the flight leaders suddenly have freedom of action and decision-making that they are unaccustomed to. They are unprepared for responsibility and authority so unlike the patterns of conduct they had grown used to in the long period of limited warfare. Lieutenant Colonel Ben-Nun, the commander of the IAF planning branch for most of the offensive operations in the year before the Yom Kippur War, describes the situation: "In RSO we reviewed every order that the squadrons had to carry out down to the last detail. The squadrons became accustomed to receiving everything spoon-fed and neatly packaged. Everything was elaborated even for the smallest operation. During the [Yom Kippur] war I saw how we had failed to prepare the squadrons to act independently. The shift from RSO to wartime conditions became a cognitive issue."[55]

The Second Lebanon War

On the IDF's transition from RSOs to war, the Winograd Commission stated:

> We are investigating the conduct of a war that Israel ended without a definitive victory, even according to the military leaders who led it. A major reason for this was that up until the very end of the conflict, and even afterwards, no explicit statement was made and internalized by all levels of command that this was indeed a state of war. Therefore, it was not clear to the commanders that other rules applied, different from those of high-intensity RSO, or even from an

> operation. Failure on the part of the military and political levels to grasp the situation precipitated a chain of errors in the conduct of various command echelons that contributed to the outcome of the war. The opinion that the IDF was at war had been voiced from the beginning of the hostilities, but because these voices did not constitute the basis for clear instruction and appropriate action, the ambiguity continued.[56]

Here I focus on two command echelons: the strategic level—the IDF's GHQ, headed by Halutz; and the tactical level—the 91st Division, commanded by Hirsch. The operational echelon, the Northern Command headed by Adam, appears in both descriptions.

IDF's General Headquarters

In this case, the chief of staff tried to define the conflict as a war from the start, but for various reasons, such as his personal conduct, he failed to do so.

In his book *Eye to Eye,* Halutz describes his growing awareness of the situation and his attempts to ensure that this realization trickled down the chain of command. I perused the transcripts of his meetings and found his accounts to be unfailingly accurate. On July 12, 2006, at the beginning of the war, Halutz came to the unequivocal conclusion that the campaign was going to be fundamentally different from what the IDF was used to, but this understanding was not translated into specific measures: "I couldn't say how long the campaign would last, though I intuitively felt it would be a long drawn out affair. This is the message that I relayed to the general staff and Northern Command. The word 'war' came to mind, and I asked myself how to convey to the forces the need for a mindset switch from RSO to a state of war. The mental transition was imperative. It was an operational game-changer, both for our forces and the enemy."[57] On the afternoon of July 12, in consultation with senior officers, he said:

> When the military thinks routine security, it thinks in terms of targeted killing, safety measures, things that are irrelevant in this war in Lebanon. We're fighting a war in Lebanon! I tell you [Eliezer] Shkedi [the IAF commander], Gadi [Eizenkot, the J3], . . . make no doubt about it we have to get out of [this RSO mindset]. The generation doing the staff work today is a generation that has never fought anywhere. They're used to Gaza and Judea and Samaria, their entire military experience amounts to just that . . . they think this is routine security—a paradigm shift is needed.[58]

During a situation assessment on July 13, Halutz emphasized the definition of the new state of affairs:

> "Routine security terminology is still being used as if this were a mere incident along the security fence. Gentlemen, this was not a border incident, this is war in Lebanon. This situation must be internalized. Perhaps our troops will finally 'get it' when a pair of surface-to-surface rockets slams into Haifa, and then everything will become clear. . . ." This statement indicates that the chief of staff understood this incident to be fundamentally different from RSO. Like the J2, who criticized the persistent use of RSO thinking patterns, Halutz believed that the current mindset had to be replaced with wartime terminology and thinking. In response to another comment, Halutz declared: "We're not fighting a battle on the southern front, or in central Israel, we're engaged in an all-out war. This is how I define it and these are the rules we'll be working by."[59]

As for changes in thinking and work patterns that had to be made, the J3 noted that "operations and sorties approvals," a weekly GHQ procedure during RSOs, were now being handled on a daily basis by the defense minister. Furthermore, Halutz announced that only he and his deputy would participate in forums with the defense minister. He concluded by saying that the IDF's mental state had to change: "We have to get out of the RSO mode that waits to see which window a missile will sail through."[60] In his opinion, the sea change in awareness would come about when massive volleys of missiles landed in Israel's rear.

Having witnessed the chief of staff's anger over the RSO mentality, the head of the operations division (within the J3) during the war, Brigadier General Shlomo (Sami) Turgeman, decided to take an unorthodox step for someone in his position. On the night of July 14 he flew to Northern Command and convened a meeting of the command's intelligence officer, artillery commander, tactical air control commander, and other relevant officers. He tried to determine why the general staff's conduct was preventing missions and fire support plans from being implemented while Israel was in a state of war. According to Turgeman, after that meeting, he became fully aware of the gravity of the IDF's situation.[61]

During a situation assessment on the evening of July 15, the chief of staff used the Israeli naval corvette *Hanit,* which had been struck the day before by an antiship missile, as an example of IDF units that were still following RSO protocols.[62] He stated, "When the most advanced ship in the world, equipped with all the systems designed to handle this type of threat, exits Israel's territorial waters with its switches off and the crew thinks they're on a pleasure cruise, this is not a war." Halutz claims that despite his best efforts to instill the understanding that this was war, the IDF was incapable of making the mental transition from routine security principles to wartime operational patterns.[63]

No doubt it was very difficult to shift the mindset of an entire organization as large as the IDF. The aftereffect of so many years of RSOs, during which the IDF was engaged mainly in military policing, left its mark. The incident involving the *Hanit* was tangible proof of this residue. The crew's flawed operational conduct can be blamed on their inability to internalize the change in the theater of operations.

According to Halutz, from the first day of the conflict, the general staff failed to absorb the fact that the IDF was in a state of war. He reached this conclusion after seeing the internal instructions issued by Northern Command, the IAF, and the navy that shackled the forces with restrictions unsuited to the reality of war. "I cannot solely blame the commanders, because over the course of many years we, as an army and society, showed little patience and less absorptive capacity for dealing with casualties. We demanded that commanders maintain a 'zero casualty' policy; devotion to mission accomplishment was no longer the highest value since the loss of human life was above all other considerations. So how can we complain? And yet, dedication to mission completion was not the only value that was jettisoned."[64]

On July 20 he described another incident: "During the situation estimation, the IAF commander, Major General Eliezer Shkedi, said that caution is required during air operations in the presence of ground forces. What he meant was that when employing the air force we have to stick to the routine safety limitations. So I re-emphasized to him, and the others, that our current situation is closer to war than to RSO. Shkedi's reply on the eighth day of the war illustrates best just how difficult it was for the commanders to absorb and adjust to the new situation and abandon their former mindset."[65] As the Winograd Commission report stated, Halutz failed to inculcate his situational perception into the IDF during the war.

The IAF's situation was similar. After the war, the internal investigation of the mental transition from RSOs to war raised issues similar to those in Northern Command. Shaul Yardeni and Gal Oren found that pilots and flight commanders had been ordered to fly at minimum altitude, execute flights in accordance with routine security border regulations, maintain the nonwar state of alert, and so on. An analysis of various issues showed that the IAF command had never really transitioned from a routine security mode to a state of war; therefore, neither did the air force. As in Northern Command, the problem was the absence of a uniform perception among the various echelons. Whereas the strategic and operational command levels viewed the situation as a large-scale routine security incident, at the level of pilots and crews, the need for change was painfully obvious, and the tension between the official IDF approach and actual activity on the ground increased. Yardeni and Oren also note that the inconsistencies in defining the situation led to further rifts among the general staff; for example, the logistics and communications branches continued to operate in a peacetime mode for a relatively long time. The peacetime routine persisted with regard to officer availability, hours of operation, and protocol.[66]

What caused the chief of staff's repeated statements to go unheeded? Why did he fail to declare a state of war? It seems that Halutz's announcements from the second day of the conflict were misunderstood. His exhortations were interpreted as authoritative reprimands, not as literal commands, possibly due to the discrepancies between his statements and his conduct as commander of the IDF. One act that contributed to this misinterpretation was his decision to operate partially from the Supreme Command Post (code-named Mitzpe) but to manage situation assessments from the chief of staff's office.[67] Another inconsistency was his decision to retain the approval procedure for operations and sorties, a framework designed for routine operations. This procedure remained in effect until a relatively advanced stage of the conflict, despite the J3's statement on July 13. For example, on July 26 an operation was planned in the Lebanese border village of Kfar Kila. The operation included the destruction of a few houses and was conditioned on the approval of the defense minister.[68] On August 3, while approving plans for the 98th Paratrooper Division, the chief of staff acknowledged that, "essentially, this is just an 'operations and sorties approvals' procedure—but I'm expanding it a little."[69] Also contributing to the confusion was the slow and fragmented recruitment of reserves, which belied the IDF's sense of urgency that Israel was in a state of war, and prohibitions on the use of certain procedures and weapons.

Northern Command shared the last problem related to the use of procedures and weapons. The commander of Northern Command limited the use of armored vehicles to only tanks (not APCs), restricted operations to nighttime, and authorized the intelligence, logistics, fire, and home-front staff branches to continue in the RSO operational mode.[70] The problems caused by this pattern of action filtered down to the battalion and squadron levels.

The 91st (Galilee) Division

Identifying the Change

As we have seen, the regular army's conceptual reference before the Second Lebanon War was RSOs in the West Bank—arrests, roadblocks, curfews, and the like. In addition, some units carried out mechanized raids in the Gaza Strip. The impact of this long COIN period manifested in various ways during the war, such as the balance between devotion to mission completion and treatment of the wounded, the degree of initiative commanders were allowed to take, and the loss of professionalism in many areas because of training cutbacks. Because this subject has already been discussed, the focus here is on the challenges involved in shifting from border defense and prevention of abduction to an expanded military action. Unlike in the Yom Kippur War, identifying the change was thorny because the scope and intensity of the fighting developed gradually, like a frog being slowly boiled. The difficulty of identifying and assimilating the change, especially at higher levels of command, and of convincing senior commanders of the need to redefine the operational situation was significantly greater in 2006 than in the Yom Kippur War, when the intensity of the enemy's offensive made it clear that what was taking place was not a typical battle day.

In the Second Lebanon War, a conceptual gap existed at the different echelons regarding the type of activity being carried out. At Northern Command, the perception seemed to be that of an expanded RSO, with a broad range of limitations on forces and an attitude toward casualties similar to that in RSOs. In contrast, the lower echelons seemed to understand that they were fighting a war.

Assimilating the Change

In his book *A War Story, a Love Story,* 91st Division commander Gal Hirsch describes his experience as he tried to convince his subordinates and superiors of the need to transition from a routine security situation to war. The rift between the division level and Northern Command began with the action in Kfar Ghajar on July 14, two days after the kidnapping that sparked the war. Hirsch saw this event as surpassing the RSO paradigm:

> Despite what was happening in the sector, [our response to it was as] though it were a routine security event that required higher approval of my plans and the operation's presentation in Northern Command. This isn't how things are done in wartime. "You don't present war plans as though you're in a routine security action," I fumed. "That's the way things are done," came the answer. Approval reached all the way up to the chief-of-staff level. We were still bound to the conduct pattern of limited warfare, and remained fettered to the "ritual" of approval for operations and sorties by all levels until the end of the war. . . .
>
> I remembered reading Avigdor Kahalani's book on the Yom Kippur War, *The Heights of Courage: A Tank Leader's War on the Golan,* where he describes his dilemmas at the outset of the fighting:

> whether or not to drive on the roads and ruin them, and whether or not to crush the irrigation lines in the fields. And what if it turns out to be just another battle day . . . [and] not a war? . . .
>
> Since I wanted to bring my men to the mental state that "this is war," I ordered the tanks to move on the main roads whether or not we were at war. When the battles ended we'd repair the damage. [Unfortunately] that was not how things were understood in Northern Command, the general staff and the political level.[71]

After the attack on Maroun al-Ras on the afternoon of July 20, during which five soldiers were killed, the commander of Northern Command, Major General Udi Adam, summoned Hirsch to discuss the casualties: "'Gal,' Udi seethed, 'too many men were hurt in this battle.' Udi seemed to be still digesting the number of casualties and the transition from RSO to war. 'That's not true,' I tried explaining. 'This is a war and there are casualties in a war.'"[72] Hirsch's description of the meeting continued:

> "Listen," he [Udi] exploded, "you can't let this continue! Do this; do that." He spat out his instructions to me. "Udi," I said, trying to calm him down, "you don't understand the situation."
>
> "No," he cut me short. "You are wrong and you'll do what I tell you. You've been racking up too many casualties!" . . .
>
> "Listen," I finally let loose, "and listen hard, this war will cost us 250 dead and 1500 wounded. Get those numbers into your skull, that's the way it is in war. Quit calling me every time a soldier is hit; you're interfering with my fighting; you can't hold a conversation during a war every time a tank track snaps and breaks; I'll stop answering the radio; you're driving me crazy!" I was furious.[73]

That evening, when Hirsch returned to the division's operations center, he said, "We're at war, hang a sign in front of you that says 'WAR' and let it sink in."[74]

In the conclusion to his chapter on the battle, Hirsch writes: "Northern Command wanted raids and dead terrorists. That's all. As I saw it, even at this stage the command's direction had still not transitioned to a wartime footing. Maybe the events were seen as the aggregate of battle days, as a large-scale incident and nothing more. From my point of view this was a war from day one. In such a situation the rationales of the command and the division were completely out of synch, and I found it impossible to integrate them."[75]

The chapter titled "Identification and Definition of the Situation" sums up the key insights of the war:

> The Northern Command staff didn't relate to the war as such and continued to operate according to RSO procedure for quite some time. The division had to pass through a fine mesh of approvals for every action, the opposite of a wartime situation and the acknowledged principles of C2. The transition and development were a conspicuous factor: RSO, battle day, counterattack, defense, first brigade battle, first division battle, a full division campaign, the entire Northern Command campaign. . . .
>
> The main questions in identifying the situation are: Where am I? What's happening? Is this another battle day, a war, an incident? What's going on? What am I allowed to do, what's still taboo, am I restricted to RSO? Do I need approval all the way up to the general staff for every battle according to the peacetime operation and sortie approval procedure as though this is a standalone action? . . .
>
> This was the crux of the tension in the first days of the war and the situation began to change only toward the end of July. . . . Expressions of "generalship," the mobilization of the reserves, and attack orders are in themselves an excellent way to alter awareness, to reset the mental state and recalibrate the situation in the head. But an even better way is to switch to code words and contingency plans drawn up before the war. However this was not done. While the battles were raging we had to invent everything from scratch.[76]

It should be noted that the conceptual gap between Hirsch and Adam may not have been the fault of the commander of Northern Command, who, according to Hirsch, failed to comprehend the situation. It may have been Hirsch himself who failed to comprehend or did not want to carry out the commander's instructions to conduct a limited operation. Be that as it may, the example clearly illustrates the problem of a conceptual gap between the different levels of command in a changing situation.

Major Yaron Sitbon, deputy commander of the paratrooper reconnaissance battalion in the war, provides an example of this dissonance at the battalion level. He quotes his commander, Lieutenant Colonel Nimrod Aloni, describing his method of assimilating the transition from RSOs to war:

> [It involved] forcing himself to speak military language and not RSO language so as to enable the battalion's forces to internalize the fact that they were fighting in a war. The battle page that was published after the war states that "the factor that influences the proper transition from a routine security situation [to war] is the language

> used." As commander I was very careful to change the language from that of LIC to the language of the combat doctrine school lessons and war exercises. . . . This sharp transition includes the use of terms such as: "brief preliminary barrage," "brief concluding barrage," "suppressing force," and "reserve" instead of "relief force." These and other terms bring the commanders back to basics and make it clear that we're speaking about something different from what we'd become used to.[77]

In a lecture at the Command and Staff College after the war, Aloni said: "You toss around these terms and people get a smack in their consciousness: Where did he get this term from? I heard it once! This smack in the consciousness, like an 'attack jump-off line,' or 'attack finish line.'"[78]

It is extremely helpful to explain the situation to soldiers who have never experienced an action more intensive than RSOs, as Aloni found in his conversations before the Maroun al-Ras battle. "The talk raised the soldiers' morale, but I had to tell them the truth that chaos would likely ensue and everyone, including the subordinate echelons, was expected to do their utmost in performance." Sitbon, however, insists that a chasm exists between words and actions when a commander tries to instill in his unit an awareness of the shift from routine security to war:

> In addition to what is said in discussion rooms and in talks with the troops before battle, they [orders] must be relevant to the decisions made following events and developments in the field. Many of the decisions and orders issued during the war hampered the mental transition to war, even though it was frequently declared and written that the IDF was in a war. For example, the decision not to travel on roads after a Merkava tank detonated an explosive charge [on a road] in the beginning of the war, or the order to move only at night after five Egoz commandos were killed during daylight movement. Actions and decisions have a greater impact than the spoken word. . . .
>
> Additional steps have to be taken to distinguish between actions carried out in RSO periods and what needs to be done in wartime. . . . Some examples of change in the commander's duty, which, according to Aloni, had an effect on the troops: dealing with logistics; involvement in the superior level's mission definition and its relations to the unit's mission; interface with neighboring fighting units; and the fire support plan (air, artillery, mortars).[79]

Aloni notes another example of actions that expedited the mental shift from RSOs to war: "Mobilizing the reservists . . . created an entirely different atmosphere. We're not dealing with just another exercise—this is something totally different. The addition of soldiers who recently completed their military service, of freshly discharged age groups . . . to the combat teams added a strong sense that something out of the ordinary was going on."[80]

* * *

The swift transition from RSOs to war is a typical situation for the IDF and has a great effect on the war's outcome. A well-implemented transition facilitates the army's performance in the first stages of the war and significantly reduces the price of its entry. Although this situation is expected in theory, and every war on Israel's borders has begun this way, this is the first time it has been studied in depth.

The three stages of making the transition to war have been outlined: identification of the change, assimilation of the change, and practical implementation of the change. Each echelon or commander goes through the same process. The problem is that, in reality, this process is uncoordinated at the different levels. In many cases, the commander realizes that he is facing a war and immediately begins to assimilate and implement the change, while his junior subordinates are unaware that the situation has altered. Sometimes the opposite happens: the commanders in the field apprehend that the situation has changed, but their commanders do not, so they limit their subordinates' activity to RSO procedures and norms.

Identifying the change requires discarding existing concepts. To improve the ability to identify the change from an RSO or a battle day to war, working assumptions about routine security can be formulated based on various criteria: volume of enemy fire, size of enemy forces, types of weapons employed by friendly forces, volume and rate of information reaching decision makers. When fighting is in progress, the commander should assess the situation based on these criteria; if he sees that a major change has occurred in all or most of them, he should conclude that a transition to war has likely taken place.

The assimilation of change calls for creative illustration adapted to the level where the change is to be assimilated. As this study has shown, the announcement that "this is war" is important, but it is not enough for inexperienced forces facing high-intensity combat. The commander must identify and introduce physical actions that convince his subordinates that the situation has indeed changed, such as issuing an order to switch to a plan with a different code name, shifting from routine security maps to wartime maps, granting permission to fire at will, permitting

AFVs to move on paved roads, opening emergency storerooms or installations, attaching auxiliary reserves to the units, and so forth. As for convincing the superior level, nothing is better than viewing the change with one's own eyes. When a commander identifies a change in the situation but fails to convince his commander, he should insist that the commander come and observe the situation firsthand.

Applying change is not easy. A key component is the alteration in the C2 layout, which consists of two elements. The first is the transition from the relatively centralized and often detailed command approach that characterizes routine security activities to decentralized command. This transition is crucial because of the dramatic increase in data flow to the commander and headquarters when the situation changes. It is impossible to effectively control scores of simultaneous small-scale fighting incidents. Oren Avman suggests carrying out practical exercises in making the transition from centralized to decentralized activities during RSO periods.[81] I agree with this recommendation. The second element is reorganization of the C2 layout based on the entry of new units and new headquarters. The lesson derived from this study is that the C2 layout has to be organized during RSOs in a way that is best suited to war plans, while minimizing the number of changes in the resubordination of units.

5

The American Past, Present Challenges, and Future Lessons

The aim of this chapter is threefold: first, to demonstrate that Israel's experience in shifting to war is a global and enduring phenomenon (as illustrated by anecdotes from American military history); second, to illustrate the challenges the US Army faces and will face in the event of a rapid shift from peace to war; and third, to propose practical suggestions to enhance the US military's ability to surmount these challenges.

Two caveats are in order at the outset. First, although Israel's constant need for a rapid transition to war contrasts with the United States' tradition of deliberate and gradual force deployment in war, I contend that the United States may need to adopt some of Israel's practices if it finds itself back in the days of the Cold War, when American armored forces on the East German–West German border were ready for action within minutes.

Second, differences in the strategic military culture between the two countries may stymie the US Army from adopting recommendations suitable for the IDF. Much has been written on these strategic cultural differences. In his book *The Culture of Military Innovation,* Dima Adamsky describes the American strategic culture as preferring functional and procedural knowledge over theoretical knowledge that emphasizes an understanding of the nature of things.[1] In the book *Transforming Command,* Eitan Shamir defines this cultural aspect as a bias toward managerial knowledge, basing command philosophy on managerial principles that include a risk-avoidance mentality.[2] The IDF strategic culture, in contrast, is defined by improvisation, initiative, and relative independence to act.[3] The main educational inspiration in the IDF is field experience, and risk is accepted as an "inexorable" fact.[4] After almost two decades working with the US Army, I would add that the American military is a strictly hierarchical organization, and challenging superiors is severely frowned upon, whereas in the IDF, almost the opposite is true. Be that as it may, prior to 2006, the IDF suffered (and still suffers) from a deterioration in the mission command approach in RSO assignments, while in recent years the US Army has emphasized mission command. However, the aforementioned general characteristics of the US Army still apply (see, for example, the issue of risk avoidance in the US Army[5] and strict reporting requirements to higher echelons[6]).

These cultural differences may have contradictory effects during a rapid shift to war. On the one hand, the Israeli tendency to thrash out all aspects of an action means that the prewar concept debate will undoubtedly continue into the conflict, while the US Army imposes a simpler standard: the higher echelons issue orders. On the other hand, American commanders' ability to make autonomous decisions during the swift transition to war may be impeded by their procedural and hierarchal bias.

Past Experience

Expediting Force Buildup

Several examples illustrate the challenge of introducing new weapons prior to combat. The Americans' introduction of the bazooka in the Second World War is quite similar to the IDF's introduction of LAW rocket launchers during the Yom Kippur War. In November 1942, as units of the 3rd Infantry Division were on their way to Africa as part of General Patton's Western Task Force, they found crates in the ships' holds with instructions lettered on them. Those instructions told the soldiers not to open the crates until the force was at sea:

> When opened, the crates were found to contain a kind of stovepipe device with ammunition apparently designed to fit. No one aboard the transport had ever seen this equipment, which much later was identified as the 2.36 Rocket Launcher (subsequently commonly known as the "bazooka"). Since it obviously was an ordnance weapon, one deck on the starboard side of the transport was cleared of personnel while two officer volunteers experimented with the new device. After some deductive study, one of the pipes was loaded, aimed at the Atlantic Ocean, and fired. The roar and backblast of the device were entirely unexpected and were followed by prolonged, enthusiastic cheers.[7]

The bazooka was issued to tank-destroyer battalions. "Training in its use started in December 1942. That was too late for the units already overseas, and bazookas were issued to troops already in Tunisia and to soldiers aboard ships. However, no one really knew how to operate and employ them."[8] Colonel Thomas Drake of the 168th Infantry "accepted several truckloads of brand-new bazookas; no one on the hill had ever fired this anti-tank weapon, and Drake planned to figure out how to operate them and to start a training program on February 14. . . . The second part of the Battle of Kasserine Pass started very early on the morning of February 14, before Drake could institute his bazooka-firing training program on Djebel Ksaira."[9]

Another US example is the transformation of the experimental 11th Air Assault Division into the 1st Cavalry Division before its deployment to Vietnam in 1965. The American forces entered the first battle of the Vietnam War in the Ia Drang Valley. The rapidity with which the 1st Cavalry was prepared for deployment left little time for essential specialized training. "It did not get M16s until ten days before departure, permitting no more than hurried instructions in the care and use of the new rifle. The Cav had no experience in jungle warfare or the type of warfare then going on in Vietnam, and it absorbed nothing more than last minute instruction in Viet Cong tactics before leaving the United States."[10]

Other material challenges can accompany the hasty deployment of a newly created unit in a new environment. "Although some of these problems would be fixed, such as the transition of the anti-tank platoons in the infantry battalions to machine gun platoons, the division still found itself in Vietnam with much equipment that it didn't need (camouflage nets being one example) and without much equipment that it did need (more water trucks in the hot, humid, jungle climate)."[11]

Compare the previous examples with a more successful episode in the 1991 Gulf War: "One Marine Corps tank company, which had trained in peacetime on M-60s, managed to retrain for eighteen days after mobilization on very different M-1s, arrive in Saudi Arabia on February 19, 1991, go into battle a mere five days later and perform successfully."[12]

Recognizing the Situation as War

In Korea, Vietnam, the Yom Kippur War, and the Second Lebanon War, the problem was not that war was unrecognizable or that its character was unexpected but that the political and military leadership failed to sustain the force's readiness. Israel's deployment problem in the Second Lebanon War was somewhat similar to that of the 1st Cavalry Division in Vietnam in terms of defining the situation. President Lyndon Johnson, like Prime Minister Olmert in 2006, did not officially declare war. One of the problems in the American case was that the division had been manned with handpicked soldiers during its formation at Fort Benning. Although this benefited the division during the experimentation phase, when it received its marching orders to Vietnam, many of the troops were due to rotate out or leave the service. "Along with the fact that President Johnson did not authorize a call-up of Reserves or a state of national emergency, all soldiers within sixty days of finishing their enlistment were not deployed with the division to Vietnam. The result of this was that the division deployed at seventy percent strength, losing nearly 2700 officers and men, many of them in critical positions such as pilots, crew chiefs, and aviation mechanics."[13]

The impact on the 1st Battalion, 1st Cavalry, can be seen from Lieutenant Colonel Harold Moore's remarks:

> My battalion and every other in the division now began to suffer the consequences of President Johnson's refusal to declare a state of emergency and extend the active-duty tours of draftees and reserve officers. . . . Any soldier who had sixty days or less left to serve on his enlistment as of the date of deployment, August 16, must be left behind. We were sick at heart. We were being shipped off to war sadly under strength, and crippled by the loss of almost a hundred troopers in my battalion alone. The very men who would be the most useful in combat—those who had trained longest in the new techniques of helicopter warfare—were by this order taken away from us. It made no sense then; it makes no sense now.[14]

The United States' painful experiences in Iraq and Afghanistan support the idea that this challenge is more relevant than ever.

Ongoing Conceptual and Doctrinal Debate

The Early-Nineteenth-Century Doctrinal Debate

Theodore Crackel's chapter on the 1812 Battle of Queenston Heights in the book *America's First Battles* is relevant to the issue. He describes a doctrinal debate before the war and its consequences during the fighting.[15]

The American doctrinal debate was waged between two schools. One, a doctrine "suited to the American political temper," was based on the Prussian-like drill laid down and adapted by Baron von Steuben during the American Revolution; it emphasized the militia character of the American army and called for relatively light infantry, cavalry, and artillery elements. This doctrine was championed by William Duane, a journal editor with a military background who was recommissioned in 1808 as assistant inspector general. The second school based its position on recent European wars and argued that against an enemy like the British, only a regular and professional army, with a doctrine derived from the French system, would be able to fight successfully. This school was supported by successive military officers. Discord between two factions in the US Army at that time also contributed to the doctrinal debate. "This general enmity between officers of the two factions," writes Crackel, "manifested itself in every aspect of the army's performance and became linked with the doctrinal debates that were to continue throughout the war."[16] In 1811 a French-based doctrine, written and published by Alexander Smyth, was immediately attacked by Duane and rebutted. The Battle of Queenston Heights (near the southern bank of Lake Ontario) on October 13, 1812, against a combined force of British regulars, Canadian militia, and Indians proved disastrous for the Americans for many reasons, including the doctrinal debate. Undaunted, Duane tried to impose his ideas, and in 1813 his modified "handbook" became the formal doctrine, and the doctrine espoused by Smyth (who had failed as a commander in the battle) was discarded. "Formally adopting a system of discipline, as the Army had done with Duane's Hand Book in 1813 (or Smyth's the year before), and implementing its instruction throughout the Army proved to be entirely different matters. Duane's discipline . . . was so remarkably different in style from anything the Army had previously seen that it was strongly resisted in the field. . . . Early in 1814 a number of senior officers were asked if Duane's Hand Book should be altered or replaced. They overwhelmingly favored replacing it."[17]

The war continued, and so did the debate. Newly appointed Brigadier General Winfield Scott "simply rejected Duane and began immediately to train his troops in the French system. . . . Ignoring the order to use Duane's Hand Book, he drilled his men up to ten hours a day for three months in the French system he preferred. . . . In July, at Chippewa and again at Lundy's Lane, his troops displayed such discipline and skill that they drew praise even from the British commander."[18]

By 1815, most of the incompetent senior commanders had been replaced by junior ones:

> Jacob Brown, for one, looked forward to the next campaign, but he recognized the importance of an immediate solution to the discipline issue. "If you establish a system of tactics . . . and place a copy of the work in the hands of every commissioned officer," he wrote, and if it was made "obligatory upon him to produce the work at every inspection under a penalty of no less than the loss of his commission," it would be worth 5,000 men. It was an essential and hopeful step. It could, he said, "be the means of saving us from the total destruction."
>
> Improved prospects notwithstanding, the situation of the nation, as 1815 approached, was simply too dangerous to allow the conflict over discipline to continue through another campaign. Twice the discipline had been described, and twice the army had refused to follow

> it. Duane had recently completed a new rendering of the French system but was pessimistic about its being greeted with favor. Nonetheless, the realization was dawning that something had to be done.
>
> In November, Congress again inserted itself into the debate. Scott had demonstrated admirably what could be done with disciplined, drilled troops, yet the Army persisted in disorder. John C. Calhoun rose and demanded to know why no one system of discipline was used throughout the Army. "So great was this variance," he reported, "that no large body of our Army, Brown's command perhaps excepted, could be properly exercised together." Was the Army being trained by any one system of discipline? If not, why not? The House wanted to know. The Army confirmed that no uniform system was then being practiced but proposed that a board be formed immediately to recommend such a system. . . . In December, the House agreed with the War Department proposal and directed that a board be convened to establish a system of discipline for the Army. Furthermore, the House specified that the new system be drawn directly from that of the French. The House, which had once promoted Duane, had turned around. Lobbying by the Hampton faction had paid off.
>
> Winfield Scott was chosen to head the board, which began to meet in January 1815. Duane made one last effort to salvage something for his efforts and wrote directly to Scott, but to no avail. Scott's manual, copied from the French system of 1791, became the basis of American drill, but it came too late to influence events in this war.[19]

In his book *U.S. Army Doctrine: From the American Revolution to the War on Terror,* Walter Kretchik summarizes the affair, writing: "The War Department . . . was in disarray doctrinally. The American Army's method for regulating the chaos of war through published doctrine had resulted in three manuals from 1779 to 1813. Although only one doctrinal manual was officially approved for use at any given time, all three, as well as personal copies of the French Règlement, had been consulted by regulars, militia, and volunteer units. Doctrinal dysfunction had not only caused tactical chaos among the army, but nearly caused a national setback in war."[20]

The Late 1970s Debate over the Active-Defense Doctrine

One of the better-documented doctrinal debates is the one over the 1976 edition of *FM 100-5, Operations,* written under the guidelines of the first commander of TRADOC, William E. DePuy. In this case, the debate did not continue during war, but it is still important. Benjamin Jensen, author of *Forging the Sword: Doctrinal Change in the U.S. Army,* provides a detailed account of the development of the active-defense doctrine, emphasizing DePuy's tight control over its writing and his efforts to ensure its acceptance, but Jensen barely touches on the debate that accompanied the process.[21] Robert Doughty, in his short analysis of the development of US Army tactical doctrine, notes that "the 1976 operations manual was one of the most controversial field manuals ever published by the U.S. Army."[22]

According to John Romjue, the manual drew a number of criticisms: (1) an overemphasis on defense and therefore loss of the offensive spirit; (2) a "first battle" orientation, compared with the "extended engagement in which the attacker was continually forced to take high attrition in successive U.S. fire and maneuver actions"; (3) adoption of a Soviet doctrine based on very narrow fronts in great depth, with massed firepower in the breakthrough sector, while the Soviets (learning from the Egyptians' use of antitank guided missiles) were moving away from this concept to "multipronged" attacks by regiments of armor-reinforced infantry fighting vehicles across the entire battlefield, seeking holes and weak spots; (4) the perceived elimination of the tactical reserve "for the fullest application and concentration of the division's maneuver battalions at critical points on the battlefield as the enemy attack unfolded"; (5) adherence to "firepower/attrition doctrine" at the perceived expanse of maneuver; and (6) "concentration tactics"—overorchestrated actions that relied on sensors and communications to locate the enemy's preferred breakthrough sector and the concentration of maneuver units to spot him there. Romjue concluded that "the vigorous doctrinal debate" following publication of the 1976 operations manual "brought the tactics of active defense seriously into question."[23]

Paul Herbert adds to the criticism: "In stressing force ratios and the destruction of enemy forces, the manual ignored the psychological dimension of warfare" and "focused too narrowly on combat in Europe to the exclusion of contingencies elsewhere in the world."[24] Eitan Shamir emphasizes civilian experts' vocal opposition, as expressed by maneuver theorist William Lind.[25]

General Donn Starry, who succeeded DePuy as TRADOC commander in 1977, said, "It's safe to say that no Army manual has ever been so widely commented on, debated, and, to a large extent, misunderstood. It is quite unusual for a field manual to generate such a wide discussion as this one has."[26]

Kretchik writes: "The 1976 doctrine unleashed an intellectual tempest within the Army. . . . Many individuals who had championed the 1976 manual were puzzled by the negative reaction. . . . In seeking to regulate the chaos of war through technology, DePuy's 1976 doctrine tore at the very fabric of the Army's cultural beliefs. By 1981, the strain became readily apparent. Senior officers decided that the 1976 manual had to go."[27]

If war had broken out in Europe at the end of the 1970s, the history books probably would have emphasized the role of the prewar doctrinal debate on the war's outcome.

The Influence of Long-Term COIN and Peace Operations on War Competency

Fortunately for the Americans, they have never had to transition from long-term periods of COIN to a war scenario. Nevertheless, they have been concerned about this issue, as demonstrated by peace operations in the 1990s and COIN operations in Iraq in the first decade of the twenty-first century.

A 1998 Rand study examined the dilemma facing the US Army at the time: "to prepare for and fight the nation's wars (its primary mission) while also preparing for and conducting peace operations."[28] The research included lessons from the US Army's peace operations in Somalia, Haiti, Bosnia, and Macedonia. It is worth noting that the number of troops involved was quite low (5 to 8.5 percent of the total force) relative to the army's total size in those years and compared with the personnel and units deployed in Iraq (after its occupation) and Afghanistan. The key findings were that peace operations reduced the readiness for a major theater war (MTW) among frequently deployed units such as military police and civil affairs, which in turn hampered the collective training of other units preparing for MTW.

Iraq, 2003–2011

The Second Lebanon War reminded Americans of the risk of focusing too heavily on COIN operations in Iraq. Senior Rand researcher David Johnson noted the similarities between the IDF in 2006 and the US joint force in 2011: "After years of protracted irregular warfare in Afghanistan and Iraq, the U.S. military, and particularly the U.S. Army, is stretched to capacity, much like the IDF was during the Second al-Aqsa Intifada. Understandably, the U.S. military is focused on the wars it is currently fighting. U.S. defense officials recognize that preparing for COIN operations has put the force, and particularly the U.S. Army, out of balance."[29] In light of these insights, Johnson recommended that the US Army and US Air Force acknowledge that the skills and processes needed to prevail against hybrid opponents are different in many respects from those required to conduct COIN operations. He also pointed out that these skills and processes require the highly integrated joint, combined-arms fire and maneuver skills used in major combat operations, but at a lower organizational level (brigade combat team), and these capabilities may have atrophied during the United States' protracted COIN operations in Afghanistan and Iraq. Therefore, Johnson asserted, "combat training centers should continue their renewed emphasis on preparing forces for the full range of military operations and should incorporate hybrid operations and hybrid opposing forces into training exercises and experiments."[30]

In a white paper assessing the current state of field artillery, three commanders of brigade combat teams that served in Iraq wrote in 2008:

> With each passing month that we continue to let these perishable skills atrophy and lose our expert practitioners, we are mortgaging not only flexibility in today's fight, but our ability to fight the next war as well. This is similar to what happened to the Israeli Defense Forces. Israel's years of COIN-focused operations in the occupied territories cost them dearly in South Lebanon. When the IDF attempted to return to HIC operations, it found itself unable to plan fires, conduct terminal control or de-conflict airspace. We should consider ourselves fairly warned. We can't afford to lose sight of the critical role artillerymen play in our ability to plan, coordinate, integrate and synchronize our combined arms operation. This is not an artillery issue; this is an Army issue, as the Israelis learned . . . the hard way.[31]

In this respect, it is worth mentioning J. P. Clark's 2016 article, which claims that some members of the "long war generation" who acquired all their battle know-how in Iraq and Afghanistan are convinced that their experience reflects both "war" in general and "the war" they fought in. Clark describes a February 2014 *Washington Post* opinion piece in which a former army captain proposed culling the senior ranks so that outstanding captains, majors, and lieutenant colonels could be promoted directly to brigadier general, based on their superior experience fighting al-Qaeda, Sunni militias, and the Taliban, bypassing old generals "trained to fight World War III against the Soviets."[32]

In his book *Learning to Forget,* which analyzes US Army COIN doctrine and practice from Vietnam to Iraq, David Fitzgerald states that despite the US Army's antipathy toward counterinsurgency (based on the Vietnam experience), it successfully theorized and practiced it in Iraq in 2006–2008. He points out that once the current operational need to conduct counterinsurgency has passed, the army may forget its COIN doctrine and return to its beloved conventional missions.[33] My contention is that the possibility of losing wider-scale war capabilities during long wars is much more substantial.

A non-American example is relevant and worth mentioning: creation of the British Expeditionary Force (BEF)—a rapid reaction force of seven divisions formed prior to World War I. As described in Douglas Macgregor's book *Margin of Victory*, this transformation was led by the secretary of state for war, Sir Richard Haldane, who conceived the BEF as "a force that might make the difference between initial victory and initial defeat." The British Empire formed the BEF even though it had been preoccupied with colonial wars against irregular forces for nearly a century. The Haldane reforms that took place during the lengthy COIN period, under budgetary constraints and against internal opposition, actually saved the day at the Battle of Mons in Belgium (August 22–24, 1914) after only five days of deployment across the English Channel.[34] This is an example of the necessity of preparing for wide-scale conventional war scenarios even during long COIN periods.

Task Force Smith

In the US Army, the phrase "Task Force Smith" came to denote a situation of unreadiness, owing to that unit's failure to stop the North Korean advance south in 1950. A combination of factors—material (qualitative and quantitative), psychological, leadership, and high-level decision making—was behind the Americans' failure in that situation. William Davis focuses on the political and military leadership's role in reducing structure, equipment, and training owing to budget cuts and prioritization of the European theater.[35] Charles Azotea places the blame squarely on operational intelligence.[36] John Garrett writes that the failure was not due to a lack of training, the soldiers' laziness in performing occupation duty, a lack of discipline, or budgetary issues, as previously suggested; rather, the problem was "the lack of any operational plan for the deployment of American troops to the Korean Peninsula with sufficient combat power for the task that was understood to be at hand."[37]

In postwar Japan, US Army occupation forces encountered a major obstacle to preparedness: a lack of training areas where units could fire and maneuver. Japan was simply too populous to set aside precious land for military training, which prevented the American Eighth Army from holding regimental, divisional, and army exercises. Roy Flint writes:

> Smaller areas, such as Mori on Kyushu, permitted limited maneuver of infantry battalions and artillery live fire but not simultaneously. In turn, the lack of training space led to organizational changes. Because it was impossible for infantry regiments stationed in postage-stamp garrisons like Camp Wood to train with their organic tank companies,

> the tanks were eliminated from the tables of organization. . . . At the battalion level, the consequences of lack of training were grave. The 21st Infantry had never maneuvered with live artillery and had no experience with tanks. Tactical training was confined to squad, platoon, and some company exercises in the small training areas beyond the limits of the city of Kumamoto. Even there, Japanese farmers began to encroach on the training reservation. In the 52nd Artillery Battalion the firing batteries were severely limited in live-fire exercises. The battalion could schedule only one trip a year to the Mori training area where it enjoyed sufficient space to shoot its 105-mm howitzers.[38]

Flint also describes a handful of improvisations that were introduced to overcome the problem, but they focused mainly on technical skills rather than combined-arms tactical competencies. "Even in the 21st Infantry, a strong regiment, the inability to practice as battalions was crucially important in the transition to combat virtually overnight. There had been too few opportunities to iron out familiar working relationships, coordination, standard operating procedures, resupply techniques, fire support, ammunition handling, and a myriad of other arrangements that are so important in combat. Many otherwise well-trained soldiers paid a bloody price for their regiments' lost opportunities."[39]

Davis writes that despite General Douglas MacArthur's directive to intensify Eighth Army's training, including battalion-level training by May 1950 and regimental training by July 1950, Smith himself testified that he "did not believe that any live fire training was conducted during the year he was commanding in Japan." Smith also stated that training "was almost nonexistent. We had PT [physical training]. . . . It was PT [in place, not] a three-mile run followed by half a dozen pushups . . . nothing like that."[40]

The US Army is not currently occupied in COIN missions, but considering the geopolitical turmoil in Africa, the Middle East, countries of the former Soviet Union, and Southeast Asia, it could find itself in situations similar to those just described.

Cognitive and Mental Challenges

As noted earlier, US military history is not the best example of this aspect of a fast transition because, in many cases, Americans have deployed for war from the United States. To a limited extent, Task Force Smith exemplifies the cognitive and mental issues that characterize the fast transition from peacetime to war. The American case shares certain characteristics with the IDF's entry into the Yom Kippur and Second Lebanon Wars. According to Flint, "1st Lieutenant Day of C Co l/21st Infantry Battalion felt, as they left Japan, that 'no one believed we were going anywhere to fight.' He changed his mind when he landed amidst the turmoil in Korea. 'My God, I thought, maybe there is a real war going on!' At this point no one was using the term 'police action' and after being strafed and seeing the wounded and untreated ROK soldiers 1st Lieutenant Bill Wyrick stated, 'It affected me when I realized what I was going into.'"[41]

Analyzing war-fighting tactics in the Korean War, Russel Gugeler writes, "The North Korean Army marched. Our leaders met. And Company A, with its peacetime thoughts, unprepared both psychologically and militarily, found itself faced with the stark reality of war."[42]

In his book *This Kind of War: A Study of Unpreparedness*, T. R. Fehrenbach tells of the 1st Battalion, 34th Regiment, which deployed defensively behind Task Force Smith's retreating forces: "The rain continued to fall on the waiting 1st Battalion all night. A few of the men, hearing rumors, grew nervous. They were told emphatically by an officer, 'This is a police action, nothing more!'"[43]

To sum up, the historical anecdotes show that the challenges of making a fast transition to war may be extreme in the Israeli case, but they are also part of US Army history and are therefore fundamental and enduring. Although all the above-mentioned US examples involve expeditionary forces fighting far from home and, in some cases, with no clear time pressure (North Africa and Korea are exceptions), the current situation in Europe seems to resemble the Cold War scenario of facing the threat of a surprise attack.

Present Challenges

The analysis of past experience reveals a pattern. The US Army may fail in its first battles, but in the end it prevails. If this is the case, why bother to plan for a rapid transition to war? I suggest two main reasons. The first is the Russian threat, manifested by both limited-scale direct engagement and "gray zone" conflict in which the Russians (and others) try to achieve goals typically attained through war—such as the capture of territory—while remaining under the threshold of a large-scale armed conflict, which would awaken the American giant. In these scenarios, the US Army (either independently or as part of NATO) may be required to win the first battles and decide the conflict quickly, as failing to do so could drag the United States and NATO into a third world war. Alternatively, the American and NATO decision makers might react too slowly to the urgent need for a shift to war.

The second reason is related to the conceptual revival and the modernization avalanche in the post-Iraq and -Afghanistan era. In this case, if a major war were to erupt during the transformation process, the US Army might find that its systemic capability to fight this kind of war is handicapped.

Before delving into these issues, it should be noted that the need for US forces to rapidly transition to war was recognized by American theorists such as Macgregor, but for different reasons. In 2003 he stressed the need for rapid force employment in unstable areas and in places of emerging terror threats around the globe. US Army forces were required to conduct missions ranging from humanitarian aid to regime change.[44] Macgregor's answer to this challenge lay in organizational changes, C4I (command, control, communications, computers, military intelligence), and improved interservice cooperation, as well as softer aspects such as military training and leadership development (see the conclusions).

The Russian Threat

This section assesses US and NATO forces' ability to rapidly and effectively shift to war against the Russians in Europe, along with the political and strategic issues involved in such a decision. First, however, it should be pointed out that Russia has a rich experience with strategic surprise (Budapest in 1956, Prague in 1968, Crimea in 2014), which may be regarded as one of the pillars of its strategic concept. Stephen Covington describes "decisiveness in the initial period of war" as "the fourth fundamental assumption of Russian strategic military culture." He writes:

> How the Russians think about conflict and war and how they organize themselves in peacetime is set by their strategic assessments of the initial period of a future war. Therefore, the characteristics of the initial period—the geostrategic political situation in a region, military technical capabilities of weapons likely to be employed, and political and military aims of potential opponents—determine how the Russian military postures itself in peacetime, how operational art and tactics are developed, and how forces are orchestrated to achieve military and political objectives in this future war. None of these key elements of Russia's military approach to war are possible without securing control of the strategic initiative in peacetime, in crisis, and in war. In its most basic form, seizing the strategic initiative is achieved through surprise (counter-surprise), suddenness, deception, superiority in military force and firepower, and decisiveness of decision and action.[45]

Covington also writes that although the Russians lack all the modern assets they believe they need to act as rapidly as they would like, and they realize they cannot match the West's advanced technology and weapons, "the requirement to move and strike quickly to not surrender the strategic initiative remains imperative."[46] Henrik Parks claimed in 2015 that although "Russia has refrained from directly challenging the territorial integrity and sovereignty of a NATO member nation . . . it would be a mistake to think that the regime in [the] Kremlin would not be ready to attempt this."[47] Russia is constantly practicing snap exercises that both deter its neighbors and develop its ability to undertake a surprise ground invasion of the Baltic States covered by massive air defenses. Covington notes that "these exercises, which began in 2013, predating Russia's Crimean campaign, raised conventional and nuclear forces to full combat readiness—a readiness level for war—in 24–48 hours. These sudden checks of combat readiness are connected directly to Russia's view of the character of future war and the need to seize or re-seize the strategic initiative in its initial period."[48]

According to a wide range of experts, the US Army and NATO posture against a surprise limited attack is problematic. Although NATO enjoys superiority over the Russians in both total number and quality of forces, the Russians, despite their modernization challenges, have local conventional superiority along the Russian borders, including the fragile Baltic area.[49] War games conducted by Rand during 2014–2015 demonstrated the vulnerabilities of NATO. The games' findings were that, "as currently postured, NATO cannot successfully defend the territory of its most exposed members. Across multiple games using a wide range of expert participants in and out of uniform playing both sides, the longest it has taken Russian forces to reach the outskirts of the Estonian and/or Latvian capitals of Tallinn and Riga, respectively, is 60 hours."[50]

NATO took a few steps to mitigate the problem. For example, after the 2016 Warsaw Summit, it deployed four multinational battalions—the enhanced forward presence (EFP)—to the three Baltic States and Poland. Besides its own limited potential for direct military action, the EFP's purpose is to ensure that as many NATO members as possible will be involved in combat and thus fortify their commitment to declare war. Another step was the creation of eight small headquarters, called NATO force integration units, which are meant to link NATO forces to their national hosts. Under the European deterrence initiative, the United States deployed several units: an armored brigade combat team that rotates through the Baltic States, an aviation brigade in Germany, and a combat sustainment support battalion in Poland.[51] If these limited actions (totaling about 11,000 soldiers) do not deter the Russians from making a lightning move, NATO forces will have to conduct a rapid and effective transition from peacetime to war, similar to the transition Israelis have had to make. In this case, winning the first battle would be crucial for protecting the invaded Baltic State, for bolstering NATO and American deterrence, and for undermining Russia's confidence in its ability to continue.

Land warfare expert David Johnson wrote in 2018 that the answer lies in a more robust deployment of land forces, arguing that even if the deployment of seven brigades (including armored brigades), as proposed by the 2014–2015 Rand war games, is not possible, "making things harder for the Russians is a good first step."[52] NATO's attempt to respond to Rand's assessment and Johnson's suggestion is the 13,000-man Very High Readiness Joint Task Force (VJTF), or Spearhead Force—the most rapidly deployable force of the 40,000-man Enhanced NATO Response Force (eNRF). The deployment time of both elements of the force is a secret that experts estimate to be more than a month.[53] This timetable means that even if everything works perfectly for NATO (i.e., the national armies of the Baltic States and the predeployed forces can delay the Russians long enough), certain challenges will remain, such as integrating the remains of the fighting forces and rushing in fresh forces during battle—challenges from the fields of C2, lesson learning, and assimilation (which the Israelis faced in the Yom Kippur and Second Lebanon Wars).

It is important to note that, according to experts such as Jakub Grygiel and Wess Mitchell, the solution lies not in the overly limited (in their view) efforts already under way or in Rand's high-cost proposals but in a change of strategy. They advocate moving from the current defense-in-depth strategy, which assumes that NATO will counterattack to regain territory lost to the Russians in the initial phase of the war, to a preclusive defense that "assumes that the defender will rarely have the luxury of time to bring reinforcements into play in the critical early phases of the attack. It acknowledges that once lost, it may never be able to regain the territory."[54] The defense-in-depth is relevant, they claim, when the enemy is trying to conquer the entire state. But what if the Russians are satisfied with only limited territorial adjustments? According to Grygiel and Mitchell, the answer is to subsidize the export of advanced offensive armaments to Poland and Romania, which will inflict pain on the aggressor shortly after the onset of hostilities. In this case, the Polish and Romanian armies will have to rapidly transition to war.

It is also important to note that all these force, time, and space factors mean that the US Army might have to rely on partners and must be in tight coordination with them.[55] The US Army's first battle in World War I at Cantigny, when the US 1st Division had to rely on French artillery,[56] and the World War II Battle of Buna in New Guinea, when hastily patched together Australian-American units fought the Japanese,[57] provide lessons to be learned in the context of rapid transition to war.

Before moving on to the challenging political and strategic decision making needed for war against Russia, it is important to note Ulrich Kühn's research on scenarios that may lead to "accidental escalation." Kühn describes the reasons for conventional escalation resulting from the above-mentioned force enhancement steps. These actions, of course, raise the tension and may create a local arms race, but the real issue is that during the time it takes NATO to send the VJTF and the rest of the eNRF, the Russians may make their own early decisions to thwart this development, so the risk of unintended miscalculation grows. Kühn also discusses possible reasons for nuclear or accidental escalation because of an air engagement between Russian and American or NATO pilots (a situation approached in a number of recent incidents), as well as escalation associated with nonkinetic operations, which leads us to political and strategic decision making in gray zone conflicts.

In the Cold War era, readiness for war was a constant concern. The subject is still relevant today, but there is a big difference in the political decision making involved in going to war. During the Cold War, in the event of a Soviet surprise attack, a decision would have been made at the first reports of military acts such as airfield bombings, paratrooper landings, or assaults along the German border. Until now, we assumed that if the transition to HIC was called for, American and NATO decision makers and the public would realize that war was necessary. But when dealing with an actor like Russia that employs a gray zone strategy, these assumptions are far from certain. This, of course, has a significant impact on the ability to make a clear transition to HIC.

What is gray zone warfare? The term has come under scrutiny in contemporary NATO literature and surfaces repeatedly in studies by American and European authors on the current and future challenges emanating from the growing Russian threat. But definitions in these works often conflate gray zone warfare with other types of unconventional warfare, especially hybrid warfare. This reflects a lack of confidence in our understanding of how gray zone warfare is distinct from other strategies employed by substate actors. Therefore, a lucid definition is crucial.

In their 2017 study, IDF Dado Center researchers Lazar Berman and Yaniv Friedman define gray zone strategy as "a strategy by which an actor attempts to change the status quo through means short of conventional military methods, in order to achieve goals typically gained through conventional campaigns. This gradual strategy is chosen in order to avoid provoking a war in which the gray zone actor would be at a disadvantage."[58] One such goal is capturing territory, which is traditionally seized through conventional ground campaigns. For example, China has asserted control over islands in the South China Sea, and Russia took control of the Crimean Peninsula and eastern Ukraine without conventional campaigns and without triggering a broader war (which they want to avoid).

David Barno and Nora Benshael emphasize that the defining characteristic of gray zone conflict is "ambiguity—about the ultimate objectives, the participants, whether international treaties and norms have been violated, and the role that military forces should play in response." This is achieved by a combination of "subversion, destabilizing social media influence, disruptive cyber-attacks and anonymous 'little green men' instead of recognizable armed forces making overt violations of international borders."[59]

In short, the logic of gray zone strategies is to gain significant achievements while not prodding the stronger side to declare war. Although countries like the United States and Israel believe they have laid down clear red lines to deter adversaries, gray zone actors eat away at these red lines, shifting them further back to gain far more freedom of action and to weaken the stronger actor's deterrence ability.

For the United States, facing a gray zone adversary makes it especially difficult to decide on the transition to HIC. With Russia's gradual erosion of red lines, how do American commanders and political leaders decide whether they are really in conflict at all? If Russia quietly urges Russian-speaking populations in eastern European countries—including NATO members—to agitate for autonomy, is that an attack on NATO? If Russian hackers try to influence the US electoral process, is that an act of war?

Beyond the challenge of understanding the state of play with Russia, Russia's gray zone strategy calls into question the legitimacy of the use of military force by the United States and NATO (a problem that has plagued Israel for years). Given the scars of the long wars in Afghanistan and Iraq and the isolationist tendencies of Western electorates, leaders will be hard-pressed to justify the use of military force against Russia if it continues to employ nonmilitary tools. Even when its proxies and private military companies attack NATO countries and partners, an attack on Russian assets—even if that were the strategically prudent course of action—would be extremely difficult to justify.

Despite the United States' influence on the international stage, it faces legitimacy challenges that are only aggravated by gray zone actors. A significant number of countries are looking for opportunities to hobble US efforts, and Washington would find itself on the defensive in both international forums and the press if it used military force to defeat Russian gray zone campaigns. And if the United States decided to go it alone, it would fundamentally undermine NATO's posture, coherence, and legitimacy. Thus, waiting (too long) for a coherent decision by the twenty-nine members of the North Atlantic Council to declare war on Russia and acting much earlier but alone are equally bad options.

Uncertainty about the legitimacy of using force can trickle down to the troops. Trying to get young enlisted soldiers into the right mindset for HIC when there is an undercurrent of opposition to the war becomes even more challenging, as American commanders discovered in Vietnam. Today, when everyone is plugged into social media and its often over-the-top discussions, soldiers are even more susceptible to public opposition to war.

Gray zone actors try to avoid triggering armed conflict against their stronger adversaries, but through their long campaigns, they place themselves in an advantageous position should war eventually break out. They have achieved important goals up to that point, and with the outbreak of armed conflict, the gray zone actor may be a formidable challenger while the United States is transitioning to open warfare. However, the United States still enjoys an advantage in such a situation. Because the gray zone actor—Russia, China, or Iran—is employing that strategy specifically to avoid war, the stronger side can usually decide to move toward war whenever it wants to. This gives the United States time to overcome some of the challenges posed by gray zone adversaries.

The legitimacy challenge is especially problematic for countries that rely on alliances such as NATO. If Russian actions—such as fomenting unrest and sending mercenaries into a NATO country, or accelerating disinformation efforts in the United States—push the Americans to engage in armed conflict, NATO partners may be reluctant to come on board. Activation of NATO's Article 5, under which each member state agrees to consider an armed attack against one member state to be an armed attack against all members, becomes even more challenging in these circumstances. It is already difficult for European countries to invest in defense. How many of them would willingly engage in a potentially bloody war with a peer-plus competitor in response to nonkinetic attacks against the United States or another NATO country? The steps that NATO has taken to fortify member states' coherence in moving toward war were discussed earlier, but in view of the formidable challenges to that coherence and the problematic example of the Second Lebanon War, I believe this issue remains unresolved.

To sum up, the Russian challenge influences the rapid transition from peace to war on two levels: the tactical-operational challenge of the front line and reinforcements, and the political-strategic challenge of US and NATO leadership.

The Multidomain Battle Concept and Weapons Modernization

The coming years will likely be similar to the post-Vietnam era. After more than a decade in Iraq and a decade and a half in Afghanistan, the US Army is now reorienting from COIN and other counterhybrid concepts toward major combat operations against peer or near-peer adversaries—namely, Russia and China.[60] This shift has a sense of urgency because the belief is that the US Army lags behind the Russians in key capabilities such as field artillery, armor protection systems, EWs, and so forth.[61]

Two related topics are relevant to our discussion: concept development and weapons system modernization. Both are being carried out at a magnitude reminiscent of the post-Vietnam era. The conceptual effort is led by TRADOC, which published its "multidomain battle" (MDB) concept in 2017. The concept describes the current and near-future environment in which learning and adaptive adversaries contest the United States not only in the land domain (as today) but also in the air, maritime, space, and cyber domains. "MDB requires the ability to maneuver and deliver effects across all domains in order to develop and exploit battlefield opportunities across a much larger operational framework."[62] It is not my intention to criticize the concept, as others have,[63] but to explain the vulnerabilities if forces are suddenly ordered to shift to war.

TRADOC commander General David Perkins published a trilogy of papers on the concept. The first paper states that, in developing the MDB concept, the army seeks to follow the path blazed by the developers of the air-land battle concept.[64] Perkins explains that both concept development processes are based on proactive choice informed by the threat of failure. Like the air-land battle, MDB will require an intellectual journey aided by simulations, research, and tests. The concept calls for integrating the space and cyberspace domains and the electromagnetic spectrum in the army's new way of fighting. It will also involve the introduction of new technologies such as artificial intelligence and robotics. General Perkins is aware that his long-term vision means that war could break out during the transformation process. He concludes his first paper by stating:

> The Army—along with all the services—has a clear window of opportunity. The security environment is evolving and will continue to change quickly. Our challenges may extend beyond the immediate adversaries on whom we focus. However, by focusing on how to respond to our adversaries' capabilities, the concepts and subsequent doctrine we create will continue to improve our DOTMLPF [doctrine, organization, training, materiel, leadership and education, personnel, and facilities] capabilities in a converged and integrated fashion across warfighting functions, and, hopefully, across joint forces so we can arrive on the future battlefield with convergence and integration—one step further, one step faster, than our enemy. Victory starts here.[65]

In the opening of his second paper, Perkins emphasizes this issue again, while proposing to resolve it through battlefield adaptation and innovation:

> As the pace of change increases, the tension escalates between the need to prepare for future operations and the difficulty of anticipating

> operational environments. Resisting change, however, is not an option; the Army must adapt at least as fast as the Nation's adversaries change their ways of conducting operations. Even though we can anticipate some changes and forecast certain trends, many characteristics of future environments are unknowable. To mitigate this uncertainty, Army forces must be able to constantly adapt and innovate so we can fight and win in the environments we could face—within the next five years, or "tonight"; within the next five to ten years, or "tomorrow"; and in the future beyond 2030. The Army needs to forecast mid- and long-term trends and prepare for them to the best of its ability, but also it needs to develop operational principles that can help guide adaptability and innovation during operations and training today. Multi-domain battle bridges all these requirements.[66]

This paper focuses on the role of *FM 3–0, Operations,* as a bridge between the long-term MDB vision and the current environment's needs.

Two key questions need to be addressed: Is there an identifiable window of opportunity, and if so, how does it relate to the rapidly changing security environment? Can battlefield adaptation cover not-yet-mature institutional peacetime innovations that will evolve as part of the army's transformation?

Instead of focusing on the need to change—which is probably essential—or on the contents of the concept, I want to address the long-term development and implementation processes. I propose that the relatively peaceful era of the US Army's development of the air-land battle—between Vietnam and Desert Storm in 1991—should not be taken as the reference point because a war in the next decade could close the development and implementation "window." The question is: in what state of implementation will the US Army find itself when called to the flag, and how will this affect its systemic effectiveness?

Perkins's last paper in the trilogy illustrates the main capabilities resulting from the vision of MDB, such as long-range precision, cross-domain fire; multipurpose munitions and sensors for long-range precision fire and air-delivered EWs; next-generation combat vehicles that incorporate new weapons with greater range, as well as utility for urban environments; future vertical lifts (for assault, transportation, and medical evacuation); single end-to-end network framework and advanced cyberspace offensive and defensive capabilities; air-missile defense; and enhanced soldier lethality by increasing close- and long-range small-arms accuracy via new fire control systems, munitions, and weapon designs. The introduction of robotics in exoskeleton suits and manned-unmanned teams will improve maneuverability by decreasing the individual soldier's load while increasing small-unit range, coverage, and responsiveness.[67]

From another perspective, the US Army seeks faster development and acquisition processes. US Army chief of staff Mark Milley said, "I am not interested in a linear progression in the force. . . . We believe that we need to significantly reform the way the army does . . . the whole line of modernization."[68] This understanding is shared by Secretary of the Army Mark Esper, who recently announced the establishment of a new "Futures Command" that will ensure the army's "permanent evolution."[69]

Taking all this into account—the introduction of cyberspace and electronic warfare into *FM 3–0* and the army's capabilities, along with new technologies and speedier acquisition led by the new Futures Command—it is clear that orchestrating land warfare is becoming far more complex than in the past. This concern was raised by Colin Gandy from the operational synchronization point of view: "Notably, little has been said on what will be required to optimize the orchestration, synchronization, and decision support functions of headquarters elements and staffs in this environment. [Therefore] a new look at headquarters establishment and employment methods is required to ensure that headquarters structures of the future are optimized for the speed and comprehensive battlefield awareness that the MDB environment will demand."[70]

My concern is similar in nature but occurs at a much earlier stage. Integrating a new weapons system or fire intelligence asset into the complex system of land units will require a better and faster assimilation process; otherwise, units will be caught in an endless loop of change. Past lessons show that when war breaks out, rapid assimilation of the latest weapons systems—specifically, those that are highly integrated with others—is not an easy task. The US Army should deal with this challenge as part of the MDB concept.

Like every conceptual proposition, MDB will precipitate a debate, "a war of ideas," in Jensen's words.[71] Because the formal proposition is only in its infancy, the debate is just warming up. As Johnson wrote, "Without consensus on the specifics of the military problem—including the adversary, his capabilities and weapons that must be countered, and the place where the fight is envisioned to occur—Multi-Domain Battle and other concepts for deterring or defeating peer adversaries (like the third offset) are in jeopardy."[72]

Kevin Woods and Thomas Greenwood recently described the debate from multiple angles. Some have challenged the new terminology, while others argue that "categorization of future war by domain—especially but not limited to the cyber domain—is neither logical nor practical." Meanwhile, cynical critics regard MDB as "a ploy to restore or preserve force structure by returning land power to the tip of the spear in joint operations. . . . Running parallel to the ongoing MDB debate are distinct theater versions of the concept."[73]

It is clear, then, that multiple lenses exist through which the emerging MDB concept can be viewed. Each perspective brings a unique set of operational and institutional contexts to the process of concept development. Expressing a variety of unique perspectives can be a healthy part of a robust debate, but progress requires an agreed-on set of facts or, in the case of an emerging concept, a common basis of evidence. The challenge in concept development is to generate credible evidence that is relevant to decision makers from across the tactical-operational and conceptual-institutional divides. As the process matures and gets into specifics, we can only assume that the debate will heat up, and the risk of entering a war during a conceptual or doctrinal polemic will only increase.

The enduring need to win first battles, the current operational and organizational problems posed by the Russians in Europe, and the upcoming challenge of assimilating changes in concepts and capabilities explain why the US Army should be focused on ensuring the rapid and effective transition from peace to war.

Specific Lessons for the US Army

Universal lessons are outlined in the preceding chapters and in the conclusions, but this section focuses on specific lessons for the US Army.

Force Preparation

The first recommendation is meant to foster the specific kind of adaptation needed for the forces' cognitive and mental transition to war. Much has been written in recent years on the need to enhance battlefield adaptation during education and training. I contend that there is another relevant factor in the fast transition from peace to war. As part of the military education of commanders in Europe, the history of making this transition (works such as *America's First Battles* and this book) should be studied and discussed.

Second, much can be accomplished through training. Surprise exercises that have units moving from one scenario to an entirely different one within hours can prepare commanders to demonstrate the agility needed for a rapid shift to war. For example, a training exercise can open with peacekeeping or border control missions along the Estonian-Russian frontier and suddenly shift into a full-scale engagement with Russian forces. The commander of this unit must transform his unit, serve as NATO's trip wire on the ground, and alert the higher echelons. This kind of exercise is routine in IDF units that operate in the West Bank for months at a time. They are unexpectedly extracted and inserted into a full-scale live-fire exercise that simulates war with Hezbollah. Such training scenarios may be relevant for forces in Europe.

Another part of this equation relates to delegating the authority to change the rules of engagement within the unit and to call for (and receive) higher-echelon assets, such as air support, to lower echelons (e.g., battalion commanders). The MDB concept directly acknowledges the need to "prepare to transition to armed conflict":

> The ability to successfully deter an adversary requires demonstrating the ability to transition immediately to armed conflict and turn denied spaces into contested ones. Without the capability and authorities to respond immediately, the ability to maneuver the Joint Force and challenge the adversary's actions and prevent a fait accompli becomes exponentially more challenging. An immediate response, however, requires extensive preparation. Forward presence and partner forces enable the immediate transition from deterring aggression to armed conflict by conducting ISR [intelligence, surveillance, and reconnaissance] operations and preparation of the environment in all domains and environments during competition.[74]

But ISR operations and preparation of the environment are not enough. Another aspect of authorization must be added, which means, in effect, that a battalion commander will be able to fully engage a Russian attacking force within predetermined but permissive guidelines, without waiting for a specific political decision to go to war. In other words, the political decision is made, ahead of time, to allow the battalion commander and his support system to retaliate strongly against any aggression that crosses the red line specified by higher echelons. To extend the scope of operations with adequate speed, a senior commander has to reach the field and attain a clear strategic understanding of the situation, enabling him to convince the political echelon that this is indeed war. The successful implementation of this suggestion requires massive exercises and war games focused on this type of multiechelon process.

A third consideration is preparation of the public. Historically, there is a pattern of the more powerful side expecting to win a decisive first battle that ends the war—a short, glorious adventure—in one fell swoop. The British in 1775, the Union in 1861, and the Germans and French in World War I all expected to land a knockout punch in the first round, and this was true of Israel in Lebanon and Gaza as well. Even when the stronger side is ready for a high-intensity war, it is often unprepared materially and mentally for a long and bloody slugfest. At present, the situation in Europe is not that tense, but it may be wise to begin rolling the wheel back concerning public opinion. Perhaps the Swedish brochure *If a Crisis or War Comes* should be circulated throughout NATO.[75]

Another part of the solution, which is beyond the scope of this book but should be kept in mind, involves organizational and training cycles to enhance the United States' ability to swiftly amplify its presence in emerging conflict zones.[76]

Risk Management

"You go to war with the army you have, not the army you might want or wish to have at a later time," said Donald Rumsfeld at the end of 2004, speaking about the war in Iraq.[77] Risk management is usually related to weapons systems—their technological and financial aspects, as well as their delivery schedules. Here, I elaborate on this concept in the context of managing risk in scenarios where war breaks out during essential phases of the implementation of new concepts and capabilities. The idea is to constantly monitor and evaluate the systemic and overall effectiveness of the US Army in Europe (or any region where war might break out) during the implementation of new capabilities—specifically, those with a systemic effect, such as networks and fire assets. When there is a possibility that a rise in geopolitical tension could deteriorate into war during an intensive assimilation period, a decision should be made whether to continue the implementation process or suspend it and focus on proficiency with current equipment. To conduct this kind of assessment, two methods are worth mentioning: war games and red teams.

War-gaming the impact of new capabilities—some fully deployed and others still being assimilated—on the capacity to shift rapidly from peace to war can offer important insights into the risks involved. The war games should "hedge" or counterbalance the overly positive view of engineers, who might consider the war games a threat to the project's success. Similarly, due to the obvious positive bias of the generals leading the conceptual transformation process, a sufficiently senior and organizationally independent red team should be created to conduct risk management, especially risks that inform the war games scenario.

Conclusions

Williamson Murray concluded his 2011 book on military adaptation by saying: "At present, the United States confronts the most complex and uncertain international environment in its history. . . . The Middle East is in even greater turmoil than it has been at any time since the collapse of the Ottoman Empire at the end of the First World War."[1] That was before the rise and fall of the so-called Islamic State (ISIS/ISIL), the disintegration of Libya and Syria, and Russia's intervention in Ukraine and Syria.

This book deals with an enduring issue, but when geopolitical uncertainty becomes the rule, the need to frame and portray the challenge of accomplishing the rapid transition from peace to war and to sketch guidelines for meeting that challenge becomes more relevant than ever. This is not because of the greater likelihood of a surprise attack (although a cyberstrike is easier to make than the kinetic attacks carried out at Pearl Harbor or during the Yom Kippur War) but because of the growing importance of swift intervention at the start of a crisis or resolution of a crisis before it spills over into neighboring countries. NATO's need to intervene rapidly to defend the Baltic States in the event of a Russian gambit is only one example.

Chapter 5 detailed the US Army's need to prepare for a fast transition to war in Europe, and before presenting my final recommendations, a note on the IDF's future is in order. Recent strategic, operational, and tactical developments in Israel's northern arena—Syria and Lebanon—including the Iranians' aid to Hezbollah, the Assad regime, and Iranian militias and direct attacks on Israel, increase the chances that Israel will have to make a rapid transition to war. Iranian-backed Hezbollah has very good reasons to respond aggressively to the dozens of Israeli strikes against its weapon transfers via Syria, Israel's destruction of its cross-border tunnels, and attacks against other players with similar incentives. Furthermore, Hezbollah's activity in Syria has been dramatically reduced since ISIS was all but decimated and the civil war in Syria is coming to a close. Even if Hezbollah's response is limited, history shows that the situation can escalate into war, as it did in 2006. At the operational and tactical levels, other factors can thrust the two sides into war. As analysts observed, Hezbollah has accumulated substantial combat experience in Syria, which may encourage its tactical echelons to consider another round of hostilities with the IDF (although the memory of approximately 2,000 killed in action may restrain the upper echelons). As I see it, the most important factor that could suddenly catapult both sides into war is Hezbollah's development of accurate rockets and the limited land attack capabilities in Galilee. The Shiite organization has built "intervention units" for the purpose of "raiding the Galilee,"[2] and it has publicly declared that it will seize Israeli settlements and military posts.[3] In response, Israel has constructed land obstacles, prepared and trained for the evacuation of civilians living near the border, and exercised its Galilee Division in rapid escalation scenarios. "The point of the surprise drill was not to see how Israel would fight a war with Hezbollah, but rather how it would react to the outbreak of one. . . . It's about a rapid transition from routine to a situation that's not routine, where you're preparing for something else."[4] At the start of an escalation, the Israeli "race" to deny and stop Hezbollah land attacks is one of the main reasons for an urgent shift to war. But a shift of this kind will inevitably suffer from traditional Israeli constraints, such as the need to move regular ground forces from the Gaza and West Bank arenas.

Hezbollah is also making rapid progress in its ability to launch precision-guided missiles.[5] The possibility of Hezbollah initiating a surprise, premeditated, high-trajectory fire attack to avoid an Israeli preventive strike (like the one the IAF conducted against the Fajr rockets at the beginning of Second Lebanon War) is another reason for rapid escalation. A sufficiently massive and accurate rocket attack could shut down Israel's energy sources, close its air and sea ports, and cripple its military offensive capability. This is why Israel considers this threat a casus belli.[6] A surprise attack could spur Israel to a fast transition to war to eliminate the threat in the initial stages of a conflict. Israeli military leadership is fully aware of these scenarios, as evidenced by the large-scale exercises it has conducted in recent years.

Practical suggestions for the swift and effective transition from peace to war appear in each of the first four chapters, and specific suggestions for the US Army in Europe appear in chapter 5. Following are some broader recommendations aimed at better preparing the US Army for the future transition to war.

My 2011 book *On Flexibility* focuses on how armies can quickly recover from technological and doctrinal surprises by employing a variety of abilities that come under the rubric of flexibility. Many of the suggestions in that book are also valid here, because every first encounter has the potential to include the same kinds of surprises.

Flexibility contains four strata, the first of which is conceptual and doctrinal. Conceptual and doctrinal flexibility occurs when senior civilian officials and military officers create an organizational atmosphere that encourages lower-ranking commanders to broach ideas that challenge the official doctrine. When officers (and enlisted men) share their original ideas, this expands the number of options, thus enabling an army to modify its doctrine and tactics. A doctrine based on this approach presents a balanced view of all forms of war and reduces the danger of getting stuck in a dogmatic rut. Here, I should emphasize that due to the future battlefield environment envisioned by current Western military concepts, I assume that the US Army or other military force will have to improvise 30 percent of its doctrine in the field because everything it possesses will be contested.

The second stratum is organizational and technological: combined-arms units, redundant capabilities when dealing with major operational challenges, and technological versatility and changeability. The third stratum is flexibility in command and cognitive skills, which is considered of supreme importance in modern military organizations, notwithstanding how difficult it is to implement. Mental flexibility is an acquired cognitive trait of commanders who have learned and operated in an environment that encourages questioning and creativity. In the volatile conditions of the battlefield, it enables commanders to adapt quickly and keep their wits. With flexible command, junior commanders are expected to take the initiative. A wide berth of action should enable them to come up with original solutions in surprise situations and receive their superiors' backing. Conceptual and doctrinal flexibility is sine qua non for the development of this stratum; otherwise, the necessary conditions to cultivate mental elasticity and decentralized C2 methods will be lacking.

The fourth stratum is the mechanism that facilitates fast learning and the rapid circulation of lessons so that the entire military system is updated on and informed of potential surprises and their solutions. This stratum takes into account the need to link past, present, and future and to rely on communications that permit a swift flow of information. The arms industry, for example, can provide swift feedback, enabling recovery from technological surprise. Close working relations between the military and the arms industry can counter surprises by modifying existing equipment even while the battle is still in progress.

Regarding a fast transition from peace to war, I have two major recommendations in the fields of army training, education, and career management. When an army is constantly engaged in COIN, as the IDF is, officers are selected based on their operational performance, even though it may not be relevant in the next war. Nevertheless, they are forced into a friction with reality that enables commanders to observe them in action. In the last decade, this was also true of the American, British, and Australian armies in the dragged-out fighting in Iraq and Afghanistan. When "boots on the ground" is a rare phenomenon and the future area of deployment is uncertain, the challenge of officer selection becomes more crucial than ever. The problem is that in peacetime, managerial issues dominate military life; the need to quickly discern unforeseen situations and respond to them while learning a new adversary or environment is all but absent in garrison life. This issue has already been raised by others. Douglas Macgregor, for instance, notes that in the US Army, like in the IDF, officers are evaluated according to their in-service or branch performance by homogeneous boards that may be biased by personal acquaintance. He recommends rearranging the US Army formations, echelons, and training cycles in a way that enables an officer's career path to contain more military education, interservice positions, and time for self-development. While I absolutely agree with this suggestion, it is based on a much broader analysis and requires a wide transformation that is beyond the scope of this book.[7] Donald Vandergriff recommends that military education pay more attention to the second step of John Boyd's OODA (observe-orient-decide-act) loop: "orientation, where analysis and synthesis of the observations occur. This process consists of taking many disparate nuggets of data and translating them into a mental picture that the decision maker can then use to make a choice."[8] This emphasis is an essential component of the adaptive leaders methodology practiced in the US Army to better prepare soldiers, noncommissioned officers, and commanders for the dynamic challenges of the twenty-first century. Improved orientation capabilities are crucial when faced with the need to identify and assess new situations, which may occur at the onset of war. Some of J. P. Clark's recommendations are also relevant, such as training and education to compensate for the too narrow personal experience of the "long war generation" and to encourage diverse experiences. "Personnel policies, another important tool of institutional control, foster adaptation by making use of the broad base of experience already resident within the institution."[9] Encouraging leaders to take nonconventional development paths (similar to Macgregor's recommendation) will surely promote the army's capability to identify a change early and transition rapidly from peace to war.

My own recommendation for developing counterintuitive measures within military organizations is to create cognitive tests and adaptation-based training scenarios that enable the selection and promotion of individuals who exhibit less classic military attributes and more risk-taking and innovative ones. This is beginning to take place in the IDF.[10] Because the swift and efficient transition from peace to war demands both types of personalities, I suggest that effective command groups comprise both. The challenge will be finding less authoritative leaders who are capable of containing confrontational and annoying subordinates while understanding the crucial need for them.

The process of choosing, promoting, and integrating the right officers and leaders in the right way is part of the answer. Another aspect is developing the cognitive and mental skills they need to perform effectively in the fast transformation from peace to war. Here, the main challenge is gaining the required expertise during field and headquarters exercises that are generally too brief. The demand for greater practical experience in operating the latest C2 systems, sensors, and fire assets and mastery of many other tactical elements all but precludes any chance for mental or cognitive development during large-scale exercises. The only way to overcome this shortcoming is to develop training methodologies that focus on complex cognitive and mental skills such as problem framing, learning while fighting, reflection in action, and so forth. Training scenarios based on these methodologies should be separated, at least at the lower echelons, from the already overloaded regular exercises.

Another recommendation involves the ability to identify a situation that requires a fast transition to war. This is directly related to concepts of war and assumptions about what war looks like. As the Israeli experience in the Yom Kippur War and Second Lebanon War revealed, the first step of the three-stage process described in chapter 4 (identifying the change, assimilating the change, and implementing the change) demands not only the proper cognitive skills but also a multiechelon coherence concerning the situation and its significance. In some cases, the high-echelon commander realizes that he is facing war and immediately moves to assimilate and implement the change, while his subordinates are unaware that the situation has altered. Sometimes the opposite happens: commanders in the field perceive that the situation has changed but their superiors do not, so the subordinates' activity is restricted to peacetime or RSO procedures and norms.

Future American commanders who fought in Iraq and Afghanistan as junior officers carry the burden of the long fight there. Their formative experience in coping with the Taliban, al-Qaeda, and Shiite militias may well shape their expectations of what the next war will look like and how they communicate those expectations to subordinates. The Israeli experience demonstrates that long-term COIN campaigns mold commanders' perceptions of the first event of a war and impede their ability to shift to the proper mode of action. Soldiers probably will not suffer from this problem because they are too young to carry this millstone, but if a high-intensity war erupts in the next decade, American commanders will be prone to this cognitive burden. My recommendation is to take Clark's suggestion to "communicate expectations" among the three generations he describes—the superpower generation, the long war generation, and the nascent generation—and conduct specific war games in which commanders from these generations are required to describe the meaning of the situation they observe, discuss the inevitable differences in those observations, and engage in penetrating discussions of their hidden assumptions based on past experience.[11]

This multigenerational cognitive process will enhance multiechelon coherence because it addresses not only the generation gap but also the conceptual obstacles adversaries will employ to retard US forces' ability to quickly orient themselves and transition to war.

The ability to achieve a rapid and effective transition from peace to war has always been an advantage. In the past, however, it was not such an acute issue. Masses of troops fought in remote war zones, and in many cases, days elapsed before news reached home and affected the public consciousness in a way that drove political decision makers to make a move. Initial failures could be corrected and covered up by later success. Given today's intense media coverage and the relatively small numbers of professional soldiers sent into battle, military intervention is expected to get off on the right foot.

No one wants another full-blown war. As challenging as al-Qaeda, the Taliban, and Hamas are, they are incapable of causing anywhere near the destruction and bloodshed that conventional adversaries can inflict. What is more, we have become adept at fighting terrorist organizations, and we can control the pace, timing, and duration of our operations against them. But signs point to the real possibility of another HIC, and we must not underestimate the challenge of shifting rapidly into a violent reality that none of our soldiers has ever known. This study is an attempt to encourage new thinking on the transition from routine security operations to high-intensity conflict in the hope that it will make our forces better prepared—cognitively, organizationally, and morally—for the fight, if and when it comes. Winning the next war is our only option.

Acknowledgments

I wish to thank the IDF Department of Military History researchers during the years 2007–2014, headed by Professor Alon Kadish of the Hebrew University of Jerusalem, for their review of and advice on chapters 1–4.

I am deeply indebted to my American colleagues Frank Hoffman (National Defense University), David Johnson (Rand), and Colonel (Ret.) Clint Ancker (former director of the Combined Arms Doctrine Directorate, Combined Arms Center, TRADOC) for their contributions to chapter 5 on American military history.

My sincerest appreciation is extended to Dado Center researchers Shmuel Shmuel and Lazar Berman for their unflagging assistance.

Last but not least, many thanks to my stoical translator Moshe Tlamim.

Notes

Most references in chapters 1–4 are in Hebrew; a few are translations of Hebrew or Arabic into English.

Introduction

1. Charles E. Heller and William A. Stofft, eds., *America's First Battles, 1776–1965* (Lawrence: University Press of Kansas, 1986), ix.

2. In this case, although the initial phase of hostilities might seem unimportant from a global perspective, this was not true for the French and Polish people who lost their freedom after Germany invaded their countries during World War II.

3. John Shy, "First Battles in Retrospect," in Heller and Stofft, *America's First Battles*, 328.

4. Ibid.

5. Anwar Sadat, *In Search of Identity: An Autobiography* (New York: Harper and Row, 1978), 244.

6. Headquarters, Department of the Army, *FM 100-5* (Washington, DC, 1976), 1-1.

7. Headquarters, Department of the Army, *FM 100-5* (Washington, DC, 1993), 3-1, 3-3.

8. Headquarters, Department of the Army, *FM 3-0* (Washington, DC, 2008), 1-16.

9. TRADOC, *Multi-Domain Battle: The Evolution of Combined Arms for the 21st Century—2025–2040* (December 2017).

10. Douglas Macgregor, *Transformation under Fire: Revolutionizing How America Fights* (Westport, CT: Praeger, 2003), 96.

11. Douglas Macgregor, *Margin of Victory: Five Battles that Changed the Face of Modern War* (Annapolis, MD: Naval Institute Press, 2016), 174–79.

12. Eliot A. Cohen, *The Big Stick: The Limits of Soft Power and the Necessity of Military Force* (New York: Basic Books, 2016).

13. Ministry of Defense, *Joint Doctrine Publication 04 (JDP 04)—Understanding* (Shrivenham, UK: Development, Concepts and Doctrine Centre, December 2010); Frank Hoffman, "The Principle of Understanding," *Armed Forces Journal International* (February 2012), http://armedforcesjournal.com/in-this-issue-6/.

14. US Joint Chiefs of Staff, *Joint Publication (JP) 5-0: Joint Operation Planning* (2011).

15. "Transitions between phases are designed to be distinct shifts in focus by the joint force, often accompanied by changes in command or support relationships. The need to

move into another phase is normally identified by assessing that a set of objectives are achieved or that the enemy has acted in a manner that requires a major change in focus for the joint force and is therefore usually event driven, not time driven." US Joint Chiefs of Staff, *Joint Publication (JP) 5-0,* xxiii.

16. Chad C. Serena, *A Revolution in Military Adaptation: The U.S. Army in the Iraq War* (Washington, DC: Georgetown University Press, 2011), 58–59.

17. Jeffrey Simon, *NATO–Warsaw Pact Force Mobilization* (Washington, DC: National Defense University Press, 1988).

18. Richard Betts, *Military Readiness* (Washington, DC: Brookings Institution, 1995).

19. Williamson Murray, *Military Adaptation in War, with Fear of Change* (New York: Cambridge University Press, 2011); Meir Finkel, *On Flexibility: Recovery from Technological and Doctrinal Surprise on the Battlefield* (Redwood City, CA: Stanford University Press, 2011).

20. Murray, *Military Adaptation in War,* 1.

21. Serena, *Revolution.*

22. Donn Starry, "FM 100-5 Operations" (seminar, Fort Leavenworth, KS, March 30, 1978), in *Press On: Selected Works of General Donn Starry,* vol. 1, ed. Lewis Sorley (Fort Leavenworth, KS: Combat Studies Institute Press, US Army Combined Arms Center, 2009), 305.

23. Strictly speaking, Israel is not facing an insurgency in the West Bank and Gaza, and it is not carrying out a population-centric COIN campaign. But in broader terms, the challenges it faces and the types of actions it must undertake in these territories are similar to a long-term COIN campaign.

1. Hastening Force Buildup before and during War

1. Unlike situations in which the alert lasted until the outbreak of war, this time the IDF returned to a state of relative quiet (except for a few areas where flaws were discovered during the alert and amended). The return to quiet between late September and early October makes this case conspicuously different from the other two in which the IDF readied itself for war.

2. For example, the Shot tank engine's (105mm L7 Centurion) transition from a manually operated rotating system to a hydraulic one changed the gunners' aiming drill. At first, because of the pressure of wartime conditions, the gunners tended to revert to their old habit of ending elevation by lowering the cannon instead of elevating it. Eado Hecht, private correspondence.

3. Ze'ev Elron, *Bracing for the Second Round: The Development of the IDF and the Change that Never Was in Israel's Strategic Doctrine, 1952—1955* (Tel Aviv: Ma'arachot, Modan, 2016), 79–80, 200–202, 373–75.

4. Amiad Brezner, *Gallant Chargers: The Development and Changes in Israeli Armor from the War of Independence to the Sinai Campaign* (Tel Aviv: Ma'arachot, 1999), 237.

5. Motti Golani, *There Will Be War in the Summer: Israel on the Road to the Sinai Campaign, 1955-1956,* 2 vols. (Tel Aviv: Ma'arachot, 1997), 1:126.

6. Ze'ev Elron, "The Armor Threat (the Anti-tank Formation prior to the Sinai Campaign)," in *When the Engines Roared: 50th Anniversary to Sinai War,* ed. Hagai Golan and Shaul Shai (Tel Aviv: Ma'arachot, 2006), 130.

7. Brezner, *Gallant Chargers,* 235, 225.

8. Ibid., 242.

9. Elron, "Armor Threat," 132.

10. Brezner, *Gallant Chargers,* 386–87.

11. Ibid., 243.

12. Ibid., 161–64. According to Hecht (private correspondence), the French did not view these characteristics as limiting; rather, they were in accordance with the AMX-13's designation as a mobile antitank cannon (tank destroyer) or patrol AFV and armored car on tracks instead of wheels. Thus, the French could sell the AMX-13 to Israel as a defensive rather than offensive weapon.

13. Brezner, *Gallant Chargers,* 220. See also Moshe Givati, *In Their Hands Steel was Forged: The Story of Repair and Maintenance Center 7100, 1948–1996* (Tel Aviv: Ministry of Defense, 1997), 85.

14. Brezner, *Gallant Chargers,* 219–20.

15. Moshe Givati, *On the Path of Desert and Fire: The History of the 9th Armor Battalion, 1948–1984* (Tel Aviv: Ma'arachot, 1994), 325.

16. Ibid., 326.

17. Ibid.

18. Amiad Brezner, *Fire Will Go before Him: Development and Change in Israeli Armor from the End of the Sinai Campaign to the Six-Day War* (Tel Aviv: Modan-Ma'arachot, 2017), 315. The ninety tanks were sold to Singapore. Later, additional tanks were sold to a South American country. Amiad Brezner, private correspondence, April 5, 2011.

19. Brezner, *Fire Will Go before Him,* 166.

20. Eitan Haber and Ze'ev Schiff, *Lexicon of the Yom Kippur War* (Tel Aviv: Zmora Beitan Modan, 2003), 408.

21. Brezner, *Gallant Chargers,* 224, 281.

22. Ibid., 282.

23. Givati, *On the Path of Desert and Fire,* 97–98.

24. Zvi Alper, ed., *The Company that Changed the History of Armor in the 1956 Sinai Campaign* (privately published, 2005), 60.

25. Brezner, *Gallant Chargers,* 282.

26. Ibid., 160–61.

27. Uri Ben Ari, *"Get Moving, Over and Out!" Armor's Struggle* (Tel Aviv: Ma'arachot, 1998), 257.

28. Ibid., 324.

29. Brezner, private correspondence, April 5, 2011.

30. Carmit Guy, *Bar-Lev: A Biography* (Tel Aviv: Am Oved and Sifriyat Hapo'alim, 1998), 89.

31. Brezner, *Gallant Chargers,* 264–67.

32. Golani, *There Will Be War,* 2:499.

33. Brezner, *Gallant Chargers*, 264–67.
34. Golani, *There Will Be War*, 1:113.
35. Ibid., 213.
36. Brezner, *Gallant Chargers*, 180.
37. Ibid., 187.
38. Ibid., 267.
39. Yigal Shefi, *Warning Being Tested: The Rotem Incident and Israel's Security Concept, 1957–1960* (Tel Aviv: Ma'arachot, 2008), 202.
40. Yona Roznau, AMX-13 commander in the Sinai War, correspondence and conversation with the author, April 16, 2011.
41. Brezner, *Gallant Chargers*, 260–63.
42. Ibid., 263–64.
43. Golani, *There Will Be War*, 1:341–42.
44. Brezner, *Gallant Chargers*, 256. As stated, no armored brigades existed in 1954–1955.
45. Golani, *There Will Be War*, 1:341–42.
46. Brezner, *Gallant Chargers*, 287.
47. Ibid., 259.
48. Ibid., 291.
49. Ibid., 288.
50. Ibid., 290.
51. Golani, *There Will Be War*, 1:216.
52. Brezner, *Gallant Chargers*, 278.
53. Ibid., 378–80.
54. Ibid., 381.
55. This section is based on Elron, "Armor Threat."
56. Ibid., 121–23.
57. Ibid., 137–39.
58. Ibid., 142.
59. Ibid., 145.
60. Ibid., 150.
61. Ibid., 177–79.
62. Amos Carmel, *The General of Victory: Asaf Simchoni* (Tel Aviv: Yediot Achronot–Sifrei Hemed, 2009).
63. Elron, "Armor Threat," 124.
64. Golani, *There Will Be War*, 1:59.
65. Meir Amit, *Head to Head: A Personal Look at Major Events and Undisclosed Events* (Or Yehuda: Hed Artzi, 1999), 49.
66. Ibid., 52.
67. Elron, "Armor Threat," 125.
68. Carmel, *General of Victory*, 288.
69. Motti Habakuk, "The Development of the Air Force in Light of the Lessons of the Sinai Campaign," in Golan and Shai, *When the Engines Roared*, 309. See also Yitzhak

Shteigman, *The Sinai Campaign: The Air Force, 1950–1956 Growth and Operations* (IAF and Ministry of Defense, 1990), 71, 94.

70. The problems were loss of stability at high speeds, long takeoff distance, short flight time, and flawed carrying strength. Shteigman, *Sinai Campaign,* 63–64.

71. Ezer Weizman, *On Eagles' Wings: The Personal Story of the Leading Commander of the Israeli Air Force* (Tel Aviv: Ma'ariv, 1975) 138. According to Golani, the IAF delegation trained on these planes in the middle of 1955 and discovered serious defects in them. Golani, *There Will Be War,* 1:126.

72. Yitzhak Greenberg, "The IDF's Order of Battle between the Six-Day War and Yom Kippur War," *Iyunim Bitkumat Israel* 14 (2004): 393–427.

73. Golani, *There Will Be War,* 1:210.

74. Shteigman, *Sinai Campaign,* 94.

75. Weizman, *On Eagles' Wings,* 162.

76. Ehud Yunai, *Air Superiority: The Story of the Israeli Air Force* (Jerusalem: Keter, 1993), 128.

77. Golani, *There Will Be War,* 2:408.

78. Yitzhak Bar-On, *Umbrella on a Rainy Day: Security Relations between France and Israel, 1948–1956* (Tel Aviv: Effi Meltzer, 2010), 558–89.

79. Weizman, *On Eagles' Wings,* 154–55.

80. Ran Ronen (Pekker), *Eagle in the Sky* (Tel Aviv: Yediot Achronot–Sifrei Hemed, 2002), 45–46.

81. Ibid., 49–50.

82. Yunai, *Air Superiority,* 128.

83. Habakuk, "Development of the Air Force," 310.

84. Shteigman, *Sinai Campaign,* 89.

85. Eliezer (Cheetah) Cohen and Zvi Lavi, *Skies without Borders: The Story of the Israeli Air Force* (Tel Aviv: Ma'ariv, 1990) 143. See also Shteigman, *Sinai Campaign,* 76.

86. Habakuk, "Development of the Air Force," 310.

87. Golani, *There Will Be War,* 1:207–8.

88. This section is based on Brezner's *Fire Will Go before Him.*

89. Shimon Golan, *The Three Front War: Decision-Making in the High Command in the Six-Day War* (Tel Aviv: Ma'arachot, 2007), 21; Ami Gloska, *Eshkol, Give the Orders* (Tel Aviv: Ma'arachot, 2004), 249–50.

90. Brezner, *Fire Will Go before Him,* 212–13.

91. Ibid., 213.

92. Ibid., 255.

93. Ibid.

94. Ibid., 216.

95. Ibid., 255.

96. Ibid., 216–17.

97. Givati, *In Their Hands Steel Was Forged,* 136.

98. Yitzhak Greenberg, *Accounting and Strength: The Security Budget from War to War, 1957–1967* (Tel Aviv: Ministry of Defense, 1997), 100.

99. Brezner, *Fire Will Go before Him,* 257–58.

100. Ibid., 249.

101. Ibid., 246.

102. Avigdor Kahalani, *The Path of a Fighter* (Tel Aviv: Steimatzky, 1989), 83–84.

103. Yossi Peled, *Military Man* (Tel Aviv: Ma'ariv, 1993), 103.

104. Brezner, *Fire Will Go before Him,* 247.

105. Zalman Gandler (intelligence officer, Northern Command, during the Six-Day War), summary of an intelligence briefing carried out by the head of intelligence, Aharon Yariv, Ministry of Defense, Intelligence Heritage Center, June 2007, 12.

106. Haim Nadal, *Between Two Wars (1967–1973)* (Tel Aviv: Ma'arachot, 2006), 106.

107. Updating the Formation of the 210th Division—Organization Order 2-0731-MN, GHQ, May 14, 1973.

108. The 7th Brigade in "B" Standard—Organization Order 2-2780-MN GHQ, August 31, 1973.

109. The Blue-White alert's effects on the organization of the order of battle were unsubstantiated; for a general review of the Blue-White alert in Northern Command, see Dani Asher, ed., *Inside Israel's Northern Command: The Yom Kippur War on the Syrian Border* (Lexington: University Press of Kentucky, 2014), 55–60.

110. Nadal, *Between Two Wars,* 155.

111. Operational Activities Carried out in the Blue-White Alert, Ministry of Defense 22/2502, GHQ/Operations, June 1, 1973.

112. Agranat Commission Investigating Committee—Yom Kippur War, *Third and Final Report,* vol. 1 (Jerusalem, 1975), 122.

113. Blue-White, Progress Report (no. 5), GHQ Planning and Organization, August 2, 1973.

114. Givati, *In Their Hands Steel Was Forged,* 166–67.

115. Amira Shachar, *The Ordnance Branch as a Force Multiplier: The History of the Ordnance Corps, 1967–1985* (Ordnance Branch and Doctrine and Instruction Association, 2006), 265–67.

116. Avshalom Levi, ed., *All "Ayala" Stations in the Yom Kippur War* (n.p., n.d.).

117. Blue-White—Raising the Level of Alert for Mobilization of the Reserves, Ministry of Defense 21/2093, GHQ Planning and Organization, May 25, 1973.

118. Operational Activities Carried out in the Blue-White Alert, Ministry of Defense 22/2502, GHQ/Operations, June 1, 1973.

119. Sam Bronfeld, email correspondence, May 29, 2011.

120. Nadal, *Between Two Wars,* 109.

121. Israel Tal, *Israel's National Security: The Few against the Many* (Tel Aviv: Dvir, 1996), 168.

122. Yishay Cordova, *United States Policy in the Yom Kippur War,* Center of Gravity series (Tel Aviv: Ma'arachot, 1987), 188.

123. Uzi Eilam, *Eilam's Bow: Advanced Technology—The Secret of Israel's Strength* (Tel Aviv: Yediot Achronot–Sifrei Hemed, 2009), 193–94.

124. Ibid., 202–3.

125. Weapons Systems Evaluation Group (WSEG), *Evaluation of the Weapons and Tactics Used in the October 1973 Middle East War,* WSEG Report 249 (WSEG, October 1973), 53.

126. Givati, *In Their Hands Steel Was Forged,* 177.

127. Eilam, *Eilam's Bow,* 203.

128. WSEG, *Evaluation of the Weapons and Tactics Used,* 42.

129. Maozia Segal, *Testimony at the Sand Level: The Paratroopers Battle at the Chinese Farm* (Tel Aviv: Modan, 2007), 52.

130. Ze'ev Almog, *Bats in the Red Sea: Naval Commando Operations in the War of Attrition and Yom Kippur War* (Tel Aviv: Ministry of Defense, 2007), 196–98, 202–4.

131. Segal, *Testimony at the Sand Level,* 343.

132. Aharon Lapidot, ed., *The Antiaircraft Layout: The Sky Is the Limit.* (IAF and Ministry of Defense, 2002), 94–100.

133. Givati, *In Their Hands Steel Was Forged,* 147, 151.

2. The Effect of Prolonged Routine Security Operations on Wartime Capabilities

1. The IDF carried out reprisal operations in the 1950s and 1960s in response to frequent fedayeen attacks during which armed Arab militants infiltrated Israel from Syria, Egypt, and Jordan to strike at Israeli soldiers and civilians.

2. Retaliation operations until the Six-Day War, for example, were characterized by devotion to mission accomplishment, even at the cost of heavy losses to Israeli forces.

3. Another issue is the use of a "problematic" weapon in a small-scale war (such as cluster munitions in the Second Lebanon War) whose use may be limited in a full-scale war.

4. The IDF was already operating in Lebanon in the early 1970s.

5. Edward Luttwak and Dan Horowitz, *The Israeli Army* (London: Allen Lane, 1975), 333, 334. Although this source is outdated, the quotes presented here are supported by the thorough research recently published by Yoav Gelber, *Attrition: The Forgotten War* (Tel Aviv: Dvir, 2017).

6. Gelber, *Attrition,* 217–20.

7. Shmuel Gordon, *30 Hours in October—Crucial Decisions: The Air Force at the Start of the Yom Kippur War* (Tel Aviv: Ma'ariv, 2008), 406–7.

8. Ibid., 407. See also ibid., 421.

9. John I. Alger, *The Quest for Victory: The History of the Principles of War* (London: Greenwood, 1982), 51.

10. Hanan Shai (Schwartz), *IDF C2 at the Operational Level in Light of the Theoretical Foundations of the Modern System of Task-Oriented Decentralized Command* (IDF Command and Staff College, 1995), 381–92. Some of the operations between 1967 and 1973 were against regular armies (e.g., the Egyptian army in the canal sector), but they were similar to what Shai describes as "operations of limited scope and length," with significant restrictions dictated by the political level.

11. Guy, *Bar-Lev,* 165–66.

12. Shai, *IDF C2 at the Operational Level,* 384, 388. Shai's evaluation should be taken with a grain of salt. The senior IDF commanders were veterans of the Sinai Campaign and the Six-Day War.

13. Agranat Commission, *Third and Final Report,* vol. 4, 1269–70, 1276–77. If the commission was referring to the brigade level, the answer is clear. At the division level, it is difficult to judge whether commanding from the war room was the correct course of action.

14. Ibid., 1276.

15. Dani Shalom, *Apparition over Cairo: The Air Force in the War of Attrition (1967–1970)* (Rishon Lezion: B'avir Air and Space Publications, 2007), 1:340.

16. Ibid., 1:352.

17. Ibid., 2:668. See also ibid., 1:579.

18. Yiftach Spector, "The Fall of the Phantom," *Ma'arachot* 422 (2008): 34–39.

19. Yiftach Spector, *Loud and Clear* (Tel Aviv: Yediot Achronot, 2008), 162, 164.

20. Ibid., 159–60.

21. Shalom, *Apparition over Cairo,* 1:191.

22. Nadal, *Between Two Wars,* 234.

23. Ilan Amit, "An Effective Surprise Weapon Not Only When It's Brand New: Part 1," *Ma'arachot* 340 (April 1995): 11.

24. Ilan Amit, "Wisdom and Technology on the Future Battlefield," *Ma'arachot* 297 (January 1985): 37.

25. Amit, "Effective Surprise Weapon: Part 1," 16.

26. Ibid., 17.

27. Ilan Amit, "An Effective Surprise Weapon Not Only When It's Brand New: Part 2," *Ma'arachot* 341 (June 1995): 18–25.

28. Ze'ev Almog, "Israel's Maritime Theater—Evaluation and Lessons," *Ma'arachot* 299 (August 1985): 12.

29. Development of the Avshalom chaff rocket began in 1965 and was completed in 1968. The Amnon rocket was developed and became operational in 1972. See Ze'ev Bonen, *Rafael: From Systems Lab to a Campaign* (Israel: NND Media, 2003), 47. On the accelerated development of electronic weapons after the destroyer's loss, see Brigadier General Eli, "The Gabriel Ships, Force Design that Brought Naval Victory in the Yom Kippur War," *Ma'arachot* 296 (December 1984): 33.

30. Rami Lunz, "The Missile Boat—From Idea to Decisive Victory at Sea," *Ma'arachot* 362 (January 1999): 21.

31. Ibid., 19–20; Rami Lunz, "The Yom Kippur War at Sea," in *War Today: Studies in the Yom Kippur War,* ed. Hagai Golan and Shaul Shai (Tel Aviv: Ministry of Defense, 2003), 389–408.

32. Mahmoud Fawzi, *Harb October: Derasa wa Durous* (Cairo: al-Hayaa al-Misriyya al-Ama leil kitab, n.d.). Fawzi's book was never published in English or Hebrew. Hatzav, an agency within the Israeli intelligence branch, translated chapters from the book published by the Lebanese paper *Al Shara* during August–October 1988; see Hatzav 843 (April 23, 1989): 35.

33. Shalom, *Apparition over Cairo,* 2:665 (quoting the IAF journal).
34. Ibid., 1:419–20.
35. Ibid., 2:711.
36. Ibid., 763.
37. Ibid., 854.
38. Ibid., 863.
39. Ibid., 887, 904.
40. Ibid., 908.
41. Ibid., 912.
42. Ibid., 912–14.
43. Ibid., 918–19, 925.
44. Ibid., 957–59.
45. Ibid., 960.
46. Ibid., 967.
47. Ibid., 970.
48. Ibid., 1004.
49. Ibid., 1091–94.
50. Ibid., 1107.
51. Ibid., 1:545.
52. Ibid., 2:981.
53. Ibid., 1:544, n. 5.
54. Dima Adamsky, *Operation Kavkaz: Soviet Involvement and the Israeli Surprise in the War of Attrition* (Tel Aviv: Ma'arachot, 2006), 164.
55. Saad El Shazly, *The Crossing of the Suez,* rev. ed. (San Francisco: American Mideast Research, 2003), 81.
56. Author's correspondence with Meir Amitai, November 3, 2011.
57. Fawzi, *Harb October;* see Hatzav, 15–16.
58. Haitam al-Ayoubi, "The Revolutionary Nature of the Fourth Arab-Israeli War," *Ma'arachot* 234–35 (February 1974): 15–21.
59. Tal, *Israel's National Security,* 205.
60. Shai, *IDF C2 at the Operational Level,* 387.
61. Agranat Commission, *Third and Final Report,* 4:1347.
62. Shai, *IDF C2 at the Operational Level,* 388.
63. Ibid.
64. Winograd Commission, Investigating Commission on the Second Lebanon War, *Final Report* (2008), 390.
65. Ibid., 556.
66. Moshe Tamir, *War without a Badge* (Tel Aviv: Ma'arachot, 2005), 276.
67. Uzi Ben-Shalom and Eitan Shamir, "The Mission-Oriented Command between Theory and Practice," *Ma'arachot* 418 (April 2008): 33–39.
68. Winograd Commission, *Final Report,* 403.
69. Ibid., 404.
70. Ibid., 424.

71. Ibid., 556.

72. Gal Hirsch, *A War Story, a Love Story* (Tel Aviv: Yediot Sfarim, 2009), 330.

73. Tamir, *War without a Badge,* 193.

74. Asael Lubotzky, *From the Desert and Lebanon* (Tel Aviv: Yediot Sifrei Hemed, 2008), 60–61.

75. Based on Amira Shachar's unpublished manuscript "The History of the Merkava Tank," 134–36.

76. Ibid., 224.

77. Ibid.

78. Winograd Commission, *Final Report,* 253.

79. Ibid., 273.

80. Ibid., 277.

81. Ibid., 277–78.

82. Cited in Matt M. Matthews, "Hard Lessons Learned—A Comparison of the 2006 Hezbollah-Israeli War and Operation Cast Lead: A Historical Overview," in *Back to Basics: A Study of the Second Lebanon War and Operation Cast Lead,* ed. Lieutenant Colonel Scott C. Farquhar (Fort Leavenworth, KS: Combat Studies Institute, US Army Combined Arms Center, 2009), 5–44.

83. Yonatan Cohen, *I Never Made It to the Litani* (Tel Aviv: Sifriyat Ma'ariv, 2007), 17, 25–26.

84. Captains Nir and Yoav, "Flexibility and the Use of Force Design in Limited Conflicts: The Artillery Branch as a Test Case," *Ma'arachot* 401 (May 2005): 58–61.

85. Lubotzky, *From the Desert,* 105–6.

86. Winograd Commission, *Final Report,* 278.

87. Benjamin S. Lambeth, *Air Operations in Israel's War against Hizbollah: Learning from Lebanon and Getting It Right in Gaza* (Santa Monica, CA: Rand, 2011), 181–98, 259–76.

88. Boaz Zalmanovitch, "Establishing Special Forces in Low Intensity Conflicts," *Ma'arachot* 369 (February 2000): 32–35.

89. *The Story of a Brigade: The Kfir Brigade—The First Years* (Kfir Brigade Foundation, Afula Municipality, 2011).

90. Boaz Zalmanovitch, "The Tactical Combat Unit in Limited Conflicts, Testing and Experiment," *Ma'arachot* 405 (February 2006): 28–33.

91. Boaz Zalmanovitch, "Elucidation and Criticism of the Training of the Givati Brigade's Reconnaissance Battalion," *Mahatz* 15 (April 2004): 18.

92. Ibid., 20.

93. Erez Weiner, "From Bewilderment to Awareness—The Development of a Combat Doctrine and Counterinsurgency Fighting Model, 1996–2004," *Ma'arachot* 409–10 (December 2006): 4–19.

3. The Outbreak of War during Conceptual or Doctrinal Change

1. Moshe Ya'alon, *A Long Short Road* (Tel Aviv: Yediot Books, 2008), 259–60.

2. Starry, "FM 100–5 Operations," 305.

3. The IDF experienced this phenomenon a number of times. For example, a few weeks before the 1956 Sinai Campaign, a conceptual debate was resolved that went against the opinion of senior armor commanders, but in practice, the commanders applied their concept during the war.

4. IDF Operations Branch, Doctrine and Instruction Division, *Basic Security and Military Documents—Essence, Purpose and Organization* (GHQ, February 2011), 27.

5. David Fastebend, "That Elusive Operating Concept," *Army Magazine* 51, no. 6 (2001).

6. Nadal, *Between Two Wars,* 154.

7. Ibid., 156.

8. Guy, *Bar-Lev,* 174.

9. Avraham Adan, *On the Banks of the Suez* (Jerusalem: Idanim, 1979), 47.

10. Ibid.

11. Guy, *Bar-Lev,* 175.

12. Ibid., 176.

13. Ibid., 177.

14. Ibid., 179.

15. Emanuel Sakal, *Soldier in the Sinai* (Lexington: University Press of Kentucky, 2014), 28–29.

16. Adan, *On the Banks,* 48.

17. Ibid.

18. Moshe Dayan, *Milestones: An Autobiography* (Tel Aviv: Idanim-Dvir, Yediot Achronot, 1976), 515.

19. Ariel Sharon and David Chanoff, *Warrior* (New York: Simon and Schuster, 2001), 230.

20. Ibid., 237–38.

21. Adan, *On the Banks,* 50–51.

22. Ibid., 52.

23. Avraham Adan, testimony before the Agranat Commission, 33–34, IDF and Defense Establishment Archives website, http://www.archives.mod.gov.il/sites/English/docs/agranat2/Pages/default.aspx. All Agranat Commission testimony is from this source, unless otherwise noted.

24. Hanoch Bartov, *Dado: 48 Years and 20 Days,* vol. 2 (Tel Aviv: Ma'ariv, 1978), 199.

25. Ibid., 201.

26. Sharon and Chanoff, *Warrior,* 270.

27. Bartov, *Dado,* 259.

28. Dan Shomron, testimony before the Agranat Commission, 65–70.

29. Sakal, *Soldier in the Sinai,* 47.

30. Shmuel Gonen, testimony before the Agranat Commission (January 22, 1974), 1–4.

31. The strongholds Egrofit (southern sector), Lakekan (central sector), and Traklin (northern sector) were reopened before the war. See Sakal, *Soldier in the Sinai,* 49.

32. Bartov, *Dado,* 201.

33. Sharon and Chanoff, *Warrior,* 231.

34. Ze'ev Eitan, "'Dovecote,' the Test of Planning and Implementation under Fire," *Ma'arachot* 276–77 (October–November 1980): 39.

35. Sakal, *Soldier in the Sinai,* 31.

36. Nadal, *Between Two Wars,* 166.

37. Eitan, "'Dovecote,'" 42.

38. Adan, *On the Banks,* 71.

39. Bartov, *Dado,* 55; Adan, *On the Banks,* 36.

40. Dayan, *Milestones,* 597.

41. Adan, *On the Banks,* 75.

42. Dayan, *Milestones,* 592.

43. Adan, *On the Banks,* 80.

44. Ibid.

45. Sharon and Chanoff, *Warrior,* 294.

46. Bartov, *Dado,* 2:85–86.

47. See also Sharon's testimony before the Agranat Commission in ibid., 41–42.

48. Ibid., 86.

49. Shomron, testimony before the Agranat Commission, 16, 23–24, 24, 24–25.

50. Ibid., 25.

51. Ibid., 56.

52. Ibid., 61–62.

53. Ibid., 59–61.

54. Ibid., 62.

55. Amnon Reshef, testimony before the Agranat Commission, 35–36.

56. Ibid., 42–43, 50–51, 52–53.

57. Amnon Reshef, *14th Brigade Commander Yom Kippur War After Action Report,* 54, http://www.hativa14.com/.

58. Amiram Ezov, "'Ministerial Advice': Southern Command in the Yom Kippur War—October 7, 1973—from Blocking to Counterattack," in *War Today: Studies on the Yom Kippur War,* ed. Hagai Golan and Shaul Shai (Tel Aviv: Ministry of Defense, 2003), 205–58.

59. Reshef, *14th Brigade Report,* 58.

60. Author's interviews with Major General Emanuel Sakal, Latrun, May 29, 2011; Brigadier General Yom Tov Tamir, Glilot, June 19, 2011; Major General Amnon Reshef, Tel Aviv, August 15, 2011.

61. Haber and Schiff, *Lexicon,* 316.

62. Emanuel Sakal, testimony before the Agranat Commission, 37.

63. Sakal, *Soldier in the Sinai,* 149.

64. Haber and Schiff, *Lexicon,* 263.

65. Ofer Regev and Hadas Regev-Yarkoni, *Maoz Tzur: The 68th Battalion/Jerusalem Brigade and the Stronghold Battle in the Yom Kippur War* (Tzur Yigal: Porat Publishers, 2010), 126.

66. Ibid.

67. Ehud Michalson, *Stouthearted Men: The 184th Battalion* (Tel Aviv: Ministry of Defense, 2003).

68. Ibid., 189–90, 196.

69. Givati, *On the Path of Desert and Fire,* 421.

70. Ibid., 422, 424.

71. Eitan, "'Dovecote,'" 43.

72. Ezov, "'Ministerial Advice,'" 225.

73. Ibid., 226.

74. Eli Ze'ira, *Myth versus Reality: The Yom Kippur War; Failures and Lessons* (Tel Aviv: Yediot Achronot–Sifrei Hemed, 2004), 93, 85.

75. Sakal, *Soldier in the Sinai,* 60, 61.

76. Shmuel Gonen, interview with IDF history branch, February 14, 1977. I am grateful to Lieutenant Colonel Dr. Shimon Golan for his comments.

77. Winograd Commission, *Final Report,* 321.

78. Ibid., 323. My research supports Tamari's and Klifi's claims concerning the institutional effort to discuss and assimilate the concept. Some of the papers are located in the Dado Center, which replaced OTRI.

79. Dov Tamari and Meir Klifi, "The IDF Operational Concept," *Ma'arachot* 423 (February 2009): 26–41.

80. Dana Preisler, What Can Be Learned from the Development of the IDF's Operating Concept of 2006?" *Bein Haktavim* 10 (March 2017): 28.

81. Office of the IDF Chief of Staff, *IDF General Staff Operating Concept Investigation: Chief of Staff Summary* (December 11, 2006): "According to the chief of staff, although the operating concept was published in April 2006, it did not form the basis of these battles and its influence on the war was less than what was presented in the investigation."

82. Dan Halutz, *Eye to Eye* (Tel Aviv: Miskal–Yediot Achronoth and Hemed, 2010), 257.

83. Office of the IDF Deputy Chief of Staff, *Operating Concept Investigative Team—Summary* (December 2006), 3.

84. Ephraim Segoli, *Knowledge Development Processes in the Context of the Northern Theater in 2002–2006: Between Design and the "Final Leg"* (Dado Center, 2015), 18. The study is based on interviews with several officials who were serving at the time.

85. Winograd Commission, *Final Report,* 272.

86. Author's interview with Major General Meir Klifi, Glilot, April 1, 2012.

87. Gavriel Siboni, "The Military System in Lebanon," in *The Second Lebanon War,* ed. Meir Elran and Shlomo Brom (Tel Aviv: Yediot Sfarim and Institute for National Security Studies, 2007), 58–73.

88. Winograd Commission, *Final Report,* 322.

89. Ohad Laslau, *Development of the Operational Concept for the Lebanese Theater* (Dado Center, 2015), 77.

90. Winograd Commission, Investigating Commission on the Second Lebanon War, *Preliminary Report* (April 2007), 55–57; Halutz, *Eye to Eye,* 375.

91. Laslau, *Development of the Operational Concept,* 78.

92. Ibid., 82; author's interview with Major General Sami Turgeman (head of Operations Division/J3 before and during the war), Glilot, April 18, 2017.

93. Winograd Commission, *Final Report,* 348.

94. Ibid., 371.

95. Ibid., 372–73.

96. Hirsch, *War Story,* 217, 320.

97. Winograd Commission, *Final Report,* 407.

4. From Routine Security Operations to War

1. Oren Avman, "The Transition to Fighting from Routine and Daily Security Operations," *Ma'arachot* 441 (February 2012): 14–21.

2. The Capital A battle day took place on November 9. No information could be found on its action. My search in the IDF History Department and Archives for material on the Capital C battle day also proved fruitless.

3. Asher, *Inside Israel's Northern Command,* 74–75.

4. Aviram Barkai, *Blocking the Enemy: The Story of the 188th Brigade in the Yom Kippur War* (Tel Aviv: Sifriyat Ma'ariv, 2009), 28.

5. Asher, *Inside Israel's Northern Command,* 142.

6. Barkai, *Blocking the Enemy,* 168.

7. Ibid., 193.

8. Aryeh Arad and Haim Laskov, *Replay: Soldiers Talk about the Battles They Took Part in during the Yom Kippur War* (privately published by the Arad Family, 2003), 129–30.

9. Ibid., 163–71.

10. Avigdor Kahalani, *"I Swear to You": Conversations with Soldiers Who Fought in the Yom Kippur War* (Tel Aviv: Ministry of Defense, 2004), 270–80.

11. Ze'ev Oren, testimony before the Agranat Commission, 32, IDF and Defense Establishment Archives website, http://www.archives.mod.gov.il/sites/English/docs/agranat2/Pages/default.aspx.

12. Ibid., 41.

13. Uri Simchoni, *White Whale* (Binyamina: Glory, 2006), 63.

14. Asher, *Inside Israel's Northern Command,* 91.

15. Ibid., 63.

16. Barkai, *Blocking the Enemy,* 310.

17. Moshe Givati, *Alone on the Tel: The Tel e-Saki Battle in the Yom Kippur War* (Holon: Re'ut, 2009), 81–83.

18. Kahalani, *"I Swear to You,"* 327–28.

19. Barkai, *Blocking the Enemy,* 309.

20. Simchoni, *White Whale,* 65.

21. Asher, *Inside Israel's Northern Command,* 66–68.

22. Yehuda Wagman, "Chaos at Nafach—Analysis of an Event," in *War Today: Studies on the Yom Kippur War,* ed. Hagai Golan and Shaul Shai (Tel Aviv: Ministry of Defense,

2003), 311–58. Wagman served as a reservist battalion commander in the 679th Armored Brigade that rushed to save Nafach.

23. Barkai, *Blocking the Enemy,* 53.

24. Wagman, "Chaos at Nafach," 316.

25. Ibid., 317.

26. Rafael Eitan, *A Soldier's Story* (Tel Aviv: Ma'ariv, 1985), 128–29.

27. Quoted in Regev and Regev-Yarkoni, *Rock Stronghold,* 199.

28. Amnon Reshef, correspondence with the author, May 11, 2012.

29. Gideon Avidor, correspondence with the author, April 20, 2012.

30. Givati, *On the Path of Desert and Fire,* 406.

31. Arad and Laskov, *Replay,* 8–9.

32. Ibid., 28–29.

33. Ibid., 32.

34. Ibid., 32–33.

35. Sakal, *Soldier in the Sinai,* 306.

36. Agranat Commission, *Third and Final Report,* 1363.

37. Arad and Laskov, *Replay,* 12.

38. Michalson, *Stouthearted Men,* 130–43.

39. Ibid., 150.

40. Avidor, correspondence with the author.

41. Sakal, *Soldier in the Sinai,* 310.

42. Ibid., 151.

43. Michalson, *Stouthearted Men,* 126.

44. Ibid., 128.

45. Avidor, correspondence with the author.

46. Arad and Laskov, *Replay,* 40.

47. Gordon, *30 Hours in October,* 205.

48. Ibid.

49. Ibid., 208.

50. Ibid., 210–11.

51. Ibid., 211.

52. Benny Peled, *Days of Soul-Searching* (Ben Shemen: Modan, 2004), 362.

53. Gordon, *30 Hours in October,* 404.

54. Ibid., 266.

55. Ibid., 406–7.

56. Winograd Commission, *Final Report,* 297.

57. Halutz, *Eye to Eye,* 381.

58. Shimon Golan, *The Second Lebanon War: Decision Making at the Strategic Level* (IDF Doctrine and Instruction Division, History Department, 2014).

59. Ibid. Parts of the discussion appear in Winograd Commission, *Final Report,* 298 (citing the July 13, 2006, situation estimate).

60. Golan, *Second Lebanon War.*

61. Shlomo (Sami) Turgeman, interview with the author, Glilot, April 18, 2017.

62. Golan, *Second Lebanon War.*

63. Halutz, *Eye to Eye,* 386.

64. Ibid.

65. Ibid., 406.

66. Shaul Yardeni and Gal Oren, "The Air Force—The Mental Transition from Routine Security to a State of War," in *The Second Lebanon War: The Wisdom of Action,* vol. 2, ed. Zvi Ofer (IDF Institute for the Research of the Tactical Level, 2008), 135–42.

67. Winograd Commission, *Final Report,* 295–96.

68. Northern Command situation estimate, July 29, 2006 (internal IDF document).

69. Transcript of chief of staff's approval for the division's plan, August 3, 2006 (internal IDF document).

70. Winograd Commission, *Final Report,* 314–15.

71. Hirsch, *War Story,* 259, 260–61.

72. Ibid., 275.

73. Ibid., 284.

74. Ibid., 279.

75. Ibid., 290.

76. Ibid., 392–93.

77. Quoted in Yaron Sitbon, "The Influence of Daily Security Operations on the Second Lebanon War," in Ofer, *Second Lebanon War,* 124.

78. Nimrod Aloni, "The 35th Reconnaissance Battalion in the Second Lebanon War," in Ofer, *Second Lebanon War,* 168.

79. Sitbon, "Influence of Daily Security," 127.

80. Aloni, "35th Reconnaissance Battalion," 168.

81. Avman, "Transition to Fighting," 20.

5. The American Past, Present Challenges, and Future Lessons

1. Dima Adamsky, *The Culture of Military Innovation: The Impact of Cultural Factors on the Revolution in Military Affairs in Russia, the U.S and Israel* (Redwood City, CA: Stanford University Press, 2010), 76.

2. Eitan Shamir, *Transforming Command* (Redwood City, CA: Stanford University Press, 2011), 98.

3. Adamsky, *Culture of Military Innovation,* 117–18.

4. Shamir, *Transforming Command,* 98.

5. Patrick Bell, Rozlyn Engel, Darren Hudson, Julian Jamison, and William Skimmyhorn, "Risk Preferences in Future Military Leaders," March 1, 2017, https://ssrn.com/abstract=3055387 or http://dx.doi.org/10.2139/ssrn.3055387.

6. Leonard Wong and Stephen J. Gerras, *Lying to Ourselves: Dishonesty in the Army Profession* (Carlisle, PA: Strategic Studies Institute and US Army War College Press, 2015).

7. Marvin A. Kreidberg and Henry J. Merton, *History of Mobilization in the United States Army, 1775–1945,* Department of the Army Pamphlet 20-212 (June 1955), 317, cited in Betts, *Military Readiness,* 10.

8. Martin Blumenson, "Kasserine Pass," in *America's First Battles, 1776–1965,* ed. Charles E. Heller and William A. Stofft (Lawrence: University Press of Kansas, 1986), 236.

9. Ibid., 247–48.

10. George C. Herring, "Ia Drang Valley," in Heller and Stofft, *America's First Battles,* 300–326.

11. Thomas C. Graves, *Transforming the Force: The 11th Air Assault Division (Test) from 1963–1965* (Fort Leavenworth, KS: School of Advanced Military Studies, US Army Command and General Staff College, 1999), 34.

12. Betts, *Military Readiness,* 192.

13. Graves, *Transforming the Force,* 38.

14. Harold G. Moore and Jeff Galloway, *We Were Soldiers Once and Young* (New York: Random House, 1992), 25.

15. Theodore J. Crackel, "The Battle for Queenston Heights, 13 October 1812," in Heller and Stofft, *America's First Battles,* 33–56.

16. Ibid., 39.

17. Ibid., 51–52.

18. Ibid., 54.

19. Ibid., 55–56.

20. Walter E. Kretchik, *U.S. Army Doctrine: From the American Revolution to the War on Terror* (Lawrence: University Press of Kansas, 2011), 50.

21. Benjamin M. Jensen, *Forging the Sword: Doctrinal Change in the U.S. Army* (Redwood City, CA: Stanford University Press, 2016), chap. 2.

22. Robert A. Doughty, *The Evolution of U.S. Army Tactical Doctrine, 1946–1976,* Leavenworth Papers no. 1 (Fort Leavenworth, KS: Combat Studies Institute, 1979), 43.

23. John L. Romjue, *From Active Defense to AirLand Battle: The Development of Army Doctrine, 1973–1982,* TRADOC Historical Monographs (Fort Monroe, VA: Historical Office, US Army TRADOC, 1984).

24. Paul H. Herbert, *Deciding What Has to Be Done: General William E. Depuy and the 1976 Edition of FM 100-5, Operations,* Leavenworth Papers no. 16 (Fort Leavenworth, KS, 1988), 96.

25. Shamir, *Transforming Command,* 103–4.

26. Starry, "FM 100-5 Operations," 304.

27. Kretchik, *U.S. Army Doctrine,* 202.

28. Jennifer Tew, David Persselin, and Maren Leed, *Meeting Peace Operations' Requirements while Maintaining MTW Readiness* (Santa Monica, CA: Rand Arroyo Center, 1998), ix.

29. David E. Johnson, *Hard Fighting Israel in Lebanon and Gaza* (Santa Monica, CA: Rand, 2011), 170.

30. Ibid., 178.

31. Sean MacFarland, Michael Shields, and Jeffery Snow, "The King and I: The Impending Crisis in Field Artillery's Ability to Provide Fire Support to Maneuver Commanders" (artillery white paper, 2008), https://www.npr.org/documents/2008/may/artillerywhitepaper.pdf.

32. J. P. Clark, "Adapting to Strategic Change: Organizational Change and Adaptation in the US Army," *Parameters* 46, no. 3 (Autumn 2016): 23–39.

33. David Fitzgerald, *Learning to Forget: U.S. Army Counterinsurgency Doctrine and Practice from Vietnam to Iraq* (Redwood City, CA: Stanford University Press, 2013).

34. Macgregor, *Margin of Victory,* 7–40.

35. William Davis, *Task Force Smith, a Leadership Failure?* (Carlisle, PA: US Army War College, 1992).

36. Charles M. Azotea, *Operational Intelligence Failures of the Korean War* (Fort Leavenworth, KS: School of Advanced Military Studies, US Army Command and General Staff College, 2014).

37. John Garrett, *Task Force Smith: The Lesson Never Learned* (Fort Leavenworth, KS: School of Advanced Military Studies, US Army Command and General Staff College, 1999), 22.

38. Roy K. Flint, "Task Force Smith and the 24th Division," in Heller and Stofft, *America's First Battles,* 273.

39. Ibid., 274.

40. Davis, *Task Force Smith,* 17–18.

41. Flint, "Task Force Smith," 14.

42. Russel A. Gugeler, *Combat Actions in Korea* (Washington, DC: Combat Force Press, 1954), 17.

43. T. R. Fehrenbach, *This Kind of War: A Study of Unpreparedness* (1963; reprint, New York: Bantam Books, 1991), 106.

44. Macgregor, *Transformation under Fire,* 56.

45. Stephen R. Covington, *The Culture of Strategic Thought behind Russia's Modern Approaches to Warfare* (Cambridge, MA: Belfer Center for Science and International Affairs, Kennedy School, Harvard University, 2016), 36.

46. Ibid., 37.

47. Henrik Parks, *Hybrid or Not: Deterring and Defeating Russia's Ways of Warfare in the Baltics—The Case of Estonia* (Rome, Italy: NATO Defense College, 2015).

48. Covington, *Culture of Strategic Thought,* 38.

49. For example, see Ulrich Kühn, *Preventing Escalation in the Baltic: A NATO Playbook* (Washington, DC: Carnegie Endowment for International Peace, 2018); David A. Shalpak and Michael W. Johnson, *Reinforcing Deterrence on NATO's Eastern Flank* (Santa Monica, CA: Rand, 2016).

50. Shalpak and Johnson, *Reinforcing Deterrence.*

51. Kühn, *Preventing Escalation.*

52. David Johnson, "An Army Trying to Shake Itself from Intellectual Slumber, Part II: From 9/11 to Great Power Competition," *War on the Rocks,* February 6, 2018, https://warontherocks.com/2018/02/army-trying-shake-intellectual-slumber-part-ii-9-11-great-power-competition/.

53. Kühn, *Preventing Escalation.*

54. Jakub Grygiel and Wess Mitchell, "The Best Defense: A Preclusive Strategy to Defend the NATO Frontier," *American Interest,* December 2, 2014, https://www.the-american-interest.com/2014/12/02/a-preclusive-strategy-to-defend-the-nato-frontier/.

55. "Partner forces that are politically aligned and militarily integrated with the Joint Force provide essential capacity, unique capabilities, and key terrain required to defeat enemy systems in competition and armed conflict. Unique partner capabilities contribute immeasurably to friendly success in reconnaissance, countering UW, and information environment operations (IEO), while enhanced partner counter-A2/AD and conventional ground maneuver capabilities and capacities buy critical time for friendly forces to prevail against attacking adversary conventional forces." TRADOC, *Multi-Domain Battle,* 24.

56. Allan R. Millett, "Cantigny, 28–31 May 1918," in Heller and Stofft, *America's First Battles,* 149–85.

57. Jay Luvaas, "Buna, 19 November 1942–2 January 1943: A Leavenworth Nightmare," in Heller and Stofft, *America's First Battles,* 225.

58. Lazar Berman and Yaniv Friedman, "The Suppressed Sword: Legitimacy Challenges in Gray Zone Conflict," in *Conflicts in the Gray Zone: A Challenge to Adapt*(Conference Proceedings, Budapest, Hungary, May 9–10, 2017).

59. David Barno and Nora Benshael, "Fighting and Winning in the 'Gray Zone,'" *War on the Rocks,* May 19, 2015, https://warontherocks.com/2015/05/fighting-and-winning-in-the-gray-zone/.

60. White House Office, *National Security Strategy of the United States of America,* December 2017, 28, https://www.hsdl.org/?abstract&did=806478.

61. Sydney J. Freedberg Jr., "McMaster: Army Might Be Outnumbered and Outgunned in Next War," *Breaking Defense,* April 6, 2016, https://breakingdefense.com/2016/04/mcmaster-army-may-be-outnumbered-and-outgunned-in-next-war/.

62. TRADOC, *Multi-Domain Battle.*

63. See, for example, Shmuel Shmuel, "Multi-Domain Battle: AirLand Battle, Once More, with Feeling," *War on the Rocks,* June 20, 2017, https://warontherocks.com/2017/06/multi-domain-battle-airland-battle-once-more-with-feeling/.

64. David G. Perkins, "U.S. Army: Multi-Domain Battle Driving Change to Win in the Future," *Military Review,* July–August 2017, 6–12.

65. Ibid., 11.

66. David G. Perkins, "U.S. Army: Preparing for the Fight Tonight—Multi-Domain Battle and Field Manual 3-0," *Military Review,* September–October 2017, 7–13.

67. David G. Perkins, "U.S. Army: Multi-Domain Battle—The Advent of Twenty-First Century War," *Military Review,* November–December 2017, 8–13.

68. Daniel Wasserbly, "U.S. Army Chief Eyes 'Leap-Ahead' Technologies," *IHS Jane's Defense Weekly,* January 17, 2018.

69. Sydney J. Freedberg Jr., "Permanent Evolution: Sec Army Esper on Futures Command," *Breaking Defense,* May 7, 2018, https://breakingdefense.com/2018/05/permanent-evolution-secarmy-esper-on-futures-command-exclusive/.

70. Colin Gandy, "Time Is Always a Constraint: Transforming Headquarters Organization and Employment for the Multi-Domain Battle Environment," *Small Wars Journal,* July 20, 2017, http://smallwarsjournal.com/jrnl/art/time-is-always-a-constraint-transforming-headquarters-organization-and-employment-for-the-m.

71. Jensen, *Forging the Sword,* 151.

72. David Johnson, "An Army Trying to Shake Itself from Intellectual Slumber, Part I: Learning from the 1970s," *War on the Rocks,* February 2, 2018, https://warontherocks.com/2018/02/army-trying-shake-intellectual-slumber-part-learning-1970s/.

73. Kevin M. Woods and Thomas C. Greenwood, "Multi-Domain Battle: Time for a Campaign of Joint Experimentation," *Joint Force Quarterly* 88 (January 9, 2018): 14–21.

74. TRADOC, *Multi-Domain Battle,* 34.

75. Swedish Civil Contingencies Agency, *If a Crisis or War Comes,* 2018, www.msb.se.

76. Macgregor, *Transformation under Fire,* 161–68.

77. "Troops Put Rumsfeld in the Hot Seat," CNN, December 8, 2004. Rumsfeld was responding to the question: "Now why do we soldiers have to dig through local landfills for pieces of scrap metal and compromised ballistic glass to up-armor our vehicles, and why don't we have those resources readily available to us?"

Conclusions

1. Murray, *Military Adaptation in War,* 305.

2. Ron Ben-Yishay, "Hezbollah's Strategy: Rockets on Tel Aviv, Raids on the Galilee," *Ynet,* November 2, 2013, https://www.ynetnews.com/articles/0,7340,L-4343662,00.html.

3. Yaakov Lappin, "Hezbollah Planning 'Large Raids' into Galilee, Senior Army Source Says," *Jerusalem Post,* September 14, 2014, https://www.jpost.com/Arab-Israeli-Conflict/Hezbollah-planning-large-raids-into-Galilee-senior-army-source-says-375303.

4. Judah Ari Gross, "In a Surprise Drill, IDF Tests Reaction to Hezbollah Attack," *Times of Israel,* June 5, 2017, https://www.timesofisrael.com/in-surprise-drill-idf-tests-reaction-to-hezbollah-attack/.

5. Noa Landau, "Netanyahu Responds to Nasrallah: If Hezbollah Confronts Israel, They'll 'Get a Crushing Blow,'" *Haaretz,* September 29, 2018, https://www.haaretz.com/israel-news/.premium-netanyahu-responds-to-hezbollah-s-nasrallah-if-they-confront-israel-they-ll-get-a-crushing-blow-1.6492035.

6. Judah Ari Gross, "IDF Releases Photos of Alleged Hezbollah Missile Sites Near Beirut Airport," *Times of Israel,* September 27, 2018, https://www.timesofisrael.com/idf-releases-photos-of-alleged-hezbollah-missile-sites-near-beirut-airport/.

7. Macgregor, *Transformation under Fire,* 189–223.

8. Donald E. Vandergriff, "When Do We Teach the Basics?" *Joint Forces Quarterly* 58, no. 3 (2010): 69–74.

9. Clark, "Adapting to Strategic Change."

10. Ran Rimon, "Simulating Surprise," *Ms&T Magazine,* June 2016; Ran Rimon, "The Reflection Game," *Ms&T Magazine,* January 2018.

11. Clark, "Adapting to Strategic Change," 38.

Bibliography

Books and Articles

Adamsky, Dima. *The Culture of Military Innovation: The Impact of Cultural Factors on the Revolution in Military Affairs in Russia, the U.S. and Israel.* Redwood City, CA: Stanford University Press, 2010.

———. *Operation Kavkaz: Soviet Involvement and the Israeli Surprise in the War of Attrition.* Tel Aviv: Ma'arachot, 2006.

Adan, Avraham. *On the Banks of the Suez.* Jerusalem: Idanim, 1979.

Agranat Commission Investigating Committee—Yom Kippur War. *Third and Final Report.* Vols. 1 and 4. Jerusalem, 1975.

Alger, John I. *The Quest for Victory: The History of the Principles of War.* London: Greenwood, 1982.

Almog, Ze'ev. *Bats in the Red Sea: Naval Commando Operations in the War of Attrition and Yom Kippur War.* Tel Aviv: Ministry of Defense, 2007.

———. "Israel's Maritime Theater—Evaluation and Lessons." *Ma'arachot* 299 (August 1985): 10–18.

Aloni, Nimrod. "The 35th Reconnaissance Battalion in the Second Lebanon War." In *The Second Lebanon War: The Wisdom of Action.* Vol. 2, edited by Zvi Ofer, 163–86. IDF Institute for the Research of the Tactical Level, 2008.

Alper, Zvi, ed. *The Company that Changed the History of Armor in the 1956 Sinai Campaign.* Privately published, 2005.

Amit, Ilan. "An Effective Surprise Weapon Not Only When It's Brand New: Part 1." *Ma'arachot* 340 (April 1995): 11–19.

———. "An Effective Surprise Weapon Not Only When It's Brand New: Part 2." *Ma'arachot* 341 (June 1995): 18–25.

———. "Wisdom and Technology on the Future Battlefield." *Ma'arachot* 297 (January 1985): 35–38.

Amit, Meir. *Head to Head: A Personal Look at Major Events and Undisclosed Events.* Or Yehuda: Hed Artzi, 1999.

Arad, Aryeh, and Haim Laskov. *Replay: Soldiers Talk about the Battles They Took Part in during the Yom Kippur War.* Privately published by the Arad family, 2003.

Asher, Dani, ed. *Inside Israel's Northern Command: The Yom Kippur War on the Syrian Border.* Lexington: University Press of Kentucky, 2014.

Avman, Oren. "The Transition to Fighting from Routine and Daily Security Operations." *Ma'arachot* 441 (February 2012): 14–21.

Ayoubi, Haitam, al-. "The Revolutionary Nature of the Fourth Arab-Israeli War." *Ma'arachot* 234–35 (February 1974): 15–21.

Azotea, Charles M. *Operational Intelligence Failures of the Korean War.* Fort Leavenworth, KS: School of Advanced Military Studies, US Army Command and General Staff College, 2014.

Barkai, Aviram. *Blocking the Enemy: The Story of the 188th Brigade in the Yom Kippur War.* Tel Aviv: Sifriyat Ma'ariv, 2009.

Barno, David, and Nora Benshael. "Fighting and Winning in the 'Gray Zone.'" *War on the Rocks,* May 19, 2015. https://warontherocks.com/2015/05/fighting-and-winning-in-the-gray-zone/.

Bar-On, Yitzhak. *Umbrella on a Rainy Day: Security Relations between France and Israel, 1948–1956.* Tel Aviv: Effi Meltzer, 2010.

Bartov, Hanoch. *Dado: 48 Years and 20 Days.* Tel Aviv: Ma'ariv, 1978.

Bell, Patrick, Rozlyn Engel, Darren Hudson, Julian Jamison, and William Skimmyhorn. "Risk Preferences in Future Military Leaders," March 1, 2017. https://ssrn.com/abstract=3055387 or http://dx.doi.org/10.2139/ssrn.3055387.

Ben Ari, Uri. *"Get Moving, Over and Out!" Armor's Struggle.* Tel Aviv: Ma'arachot, 1998.

Ben-Shalom, Uzi, and Eitan Shamir. "The Mission-Oriented Command between Theory and Practice." *Ma'arachot* 418 (April 2008): 33–39.

Ben-Yishai, Ron. "Hezbollah's Strategy: Rockets on Tel Aviv, Raids on Galilee." November 2, 2013. https://www.ynetnews.com/articles/0,7340,L-4343662,00.html.

Berman, Lazar, and Yaniv Friedman. "The Suppressed Sword: Legitimacy Challenges in Gray Zone Conflict." In *Conflicts in the Gray Zone: A Challenge to Adapt.* Conference Proceedings, Budapest, Hungary, May 9–10, 2017.

Betts, Richard. *Military Readiness.* Washington, DC: Brookings Institution, 1995.

Blumenson, Martin. "Kasserine Pass." In *America's First Battles, 1776–1965,* edited by Charles E. Heller and William A. Stofft, 226–65. Lawrence: University Press of Kansas, 1986.

Bonen, Ze'ev. *Rafael: From Systems Lab to a Campaign.* Israel: NND Media, 2003.

Brezner, Amiad. *Fire Will Go before Him: Development and Change in Israeli Armor from the End of the Sinai Campaign to the Six-Day War.* Tel Aviv: Modan-Ma'arachot, 2017.

———. *Gallant Chargers: Development and Changes in Israeli Armor from the War of Independence to the Sinai Campaign.* Tel Aviv: Ma'arachot, 1999.

Carmel, Amos. *The General of Victory: Asaf Simchoni.* Tel Aviv: Yediot Achronot–Sifrei Hemed, 2009.

Clark, J. P. "Adapting to Strategic Change: Organizational Change and Adaptation in the US Army." *Parameters* 46, no. 3 (Autumn 2016): 23–39.

Cohen, Eliezer, and Zvi Lavi. *Skies without Borders: The Story of the Israeli Air Force.* Tel Aviv: Ma'ariv, 1990.

Cohen, Eliot A. *The Big Stick: The Limits of Soft Power and the Necessity of Military Force.* New York: Basic Books, 2016.

Cohen, Yonatan. *I Never Made It to the Litani.* Tel Aviv: Sifriyat Ma'ariv, 2007.

Cordova, Yishai. *United States Policy in the Yom Kippur War.* Center of Gravity series. Tel Aviv: Ma'arachot, 1987.

Covington, Stephen R. *The Culture of Strategic Thought behind Russia's Modern Approaches to Warfare.* Cambridge, MA: Belfer Center for Science and International Affairs, Kennedy School, Harvard University, 2016.

Crackel, Theodore J. "The Battle for Queenston Heights, 13 October 1812." In *America's First Battles, 1776–1965,* edited by Charles E. Heller and William A. Stofft, 33–56. Lawrence: University Press of Kansas, 1986.

Davis, William. *Task Force Smith, a Leadership Failure?* Carlisle, PA: US Army War College, 1992.

Dayan, Moshe. *Milestones: An Autobiography.* Tel Aviv: Idanim-Dvir, Yediot Achronot, 1976.

Doughty, Robert A. *The Evolution of U.S. Army Tactical Doctrine, 1946–1976.* Leavenworth Papers no. 1. Fort Leavenworth, KS: Combat Studies Institute, 1979.

Eilam, Uzi. *Eilam's Bow: Advanced Technology—The Secret of Israel's Strength.* Tel Aviv: Yediot Achronot–Sifrei Hemed, 2009.

Eitan, Rafael. *A Soldier's Story.* Tel Aviv: Ma'ariv, 1985.

Eitan, Ze'ev. "'Dovecote,' the Test of Planning and Implementation under Fire." *Ma'arachot* 276–77 (October–November 1980): 38–46.

Eli, Brigadier General. "The Gabriel Ships, Force Design that Brought Naval Victory in the Yom Kippur War." *Ma'arachot* 296 (December 1984): 31–48.

Elron, Ze'ev. "The Armor Threat (the Antitank Formation prior to the Sinai Campaign)." In *When the Engines Roared: 50th Anniversary to Sinai War,* edited by Hagai Golan and Shaul Shai, 117–62. Tel Aviv: Ma'arachot, 2006.

———. *Bracing for the Second Round: The Development of the IDF and the Change that Never Was in Israel's Strategic Doctrine, 1952 –1955.* Tel Aviv: Ma'arachot, Modan, 2016.

Ezov, Amiram. "'Ministerial Advice': Southern Command in the Yom Kippur War—October 7, 1973—From Blocking to Counterattack." In *War Today: Studies on the Yom Kippur War,* edited by Hagai Golan and Shaul Shai, 205–58. Tel Aviv: Ministry of Defense, 2003.

Fastebend, David. "That Elusive Operating Concept." *Army Magazine* 51, no. 6 (2001).

Fehrenbach, T. R. *This Kind of War: A Study of Unpreparedness.* 1963. Reprint, New York: Bantam Books, 1991.

Finkel, Meir. *On Flexibility: Recovery from Technological and Doctrinal Surprise on the Battlefield.* Redwood City, CA: Stanford University Press, 2011.

Fitzgerald David. *Learning to Forget: U.S. Army Counterinsurgency Doctrine and Practice from Vietnam to Iraq.* Redwood City, CA: Stanford University Press, 2013.

Flint, Roy K. "Task Force Smith and the 24th Division." In *America's First Battles, 1776–1965,* edited by Charles E. Heller and William A. Stofft, 266–99. Lawrence: University Press of Kansas, 1986.

Freedberg, Sydney J., Jr. "McMaster: Army Might Be Outnumbered and Outgunned in Next War." *Breaking Defense,* April 6, 2016. https://breakingdefense.com/2016/04/mcmaster-army-may-be-outnumbered-and-outgunned-in-next-war/.

———. "Permanent Evolution: Sec Army Esper on Futures Command." *Breaking Defense,* May 7, 2018. https://breakingdefense.com/2018/05/permanent-evolution-secarmy-esper-on-futures-command-exclusive/.

Gandy, Colin. "Time Is Always a Constraint: Transforming Headquarters Organization and Employment for the Multi-Domain Battle Environment." *Small Wars Journal,* July 20, 2017. http://smallwarsjournal.com/jrnl/art/time-is-always-a-constraint-transforming-headquarters-organization-and-employment-for-the-m.

Garrett, John. *Task Force Smith: The Lesson Never Learned.* Fort Leavenworth, KS: School of Advanced Military Studies, US Army Command and General Staff College, 1999.

Gelber, Yoav. *Attrition: The Forgotten War.* Tel Aviv: Dvir, 2017.

Givati, Moshe. *Alone on the Tel: The Tel e-Saki Battle in the Yom Kippur War.* Holon: Re'ut, 2009.

———. *In Their Hands Steel Was Forged: The Story of Repair and Maintenance Center 7100, 1948–1996.* Tel Aviv: Ministry of Defense, 1997.

———. *On the Path of Desert and Fire: The History of the 9th Armor Battalion, 1948–1984.* Tel Aviv: Ma'arachot, 1994.

Gloska, Ami. *Eshkol, Give the Orders.* Tel Aviv: Ma'arachot, 2004.

Golan, Shimon. *The Second Lebanon War: Decision-Making at the Strategic Level.* IDF Doctrine and Instruction Division, History Department, 2014.

———. *The Three Front War: Decision-Making in the High Command in the Six-Day War.* Tel Aviv: Ma'arachot, 2007.

Golani, Motti. *There Will Be War in the Summer: Israel on the Road to the Sinai Campaign, 1955–1956.* 2 vols. Tel Aviv: Ma'arachot, 1997.

Gordon, Shmuel. *30 Hours in October—Crucial Decisions: The Air Force at the Start of the Yom Kippur War.* Tel Aviv: Ma'ariv, 2008.

Graves, Thomas C. *Transforming the Force: The 11th Air Assault Division (Test) 1963–1965.* Fort Leavenworth, KS: School of Advanced Military Studies, US Army Command and General Staff College, 1999.

Greenberg, Yitzhak. *Accounting and Strength: The Security Budget from War to War, 1957–1967.* Tel Aviv: Ministry of Defense, 1997.

———. "The IDF's Order of Battle between the Six-Day War and Yom Kippur War." *Iyunim Bitkumat Israel* 14 (2004): 393–427.

Gross, Judah Ari. "IDF Releases Photos of Alleged Hezbollah Missile Sites Near Beirut Airport." *Times of Israel,* September 27, 2018. https://www.timesofisrael.com/idf-releases-photos-of-alleged-hezbollah-missile-sites-near-beirut-airport/.

———. "In Surprise Drill, IDF Tests Reaction to Hezbollah Attack." *Times of Israel,* June 5, 2017. https://www.timesofisrael.com/in-surprise-drill-idf-tests-reaction-to-hezbollah-attack/.

Grygiel, Jakub, and Wess Mitchell. "The Best Defense: A Preclusive Strategy to Defend the NATO Frontier." *American Interest,* December 2, 2014. https://www.the-american-interest.com/2014/12/02/a-preclusive-strategy-to-defend-the-nato-frontier/.

Gugeler, Russel A. *Combat Actions in Korea.* Washington, DC: Combat Force Press, 1954.

Guy, Carmit. *Bar-Lev: A Biography.* Tel Aviv: Am Oved and Sifriyat Hapo'alim, 1998.

Habakuk, Motti. "The Development of the Air Force in Light of the Lessons of the Sinai Campaign." In *When the Engines Roared: 50th Anniversary to Sinai War,* edited by Hagai Golan and Shaul Shai, 307–22. Tel Aviv: Ma'arachot, 2006.

Haber, Eitan, and Ze'ev Schiff. *Lexicon of the Yom Kippur War.* Tel Aviv: Zmora Beitan Modan, 2003.

Halutz, Dan. *Eye to Eye.* Tel Aviv: Miskal–Yediot Achronot and Hemed, 2010.

Heller, Charles E., and William A. Stofft, eds. *America's First Battles, 1776–1965.* Lawrence: University Press of Kansas, 1986.

Herbert, Paul H. *Deciding What Has to Be Done: General William E. DePuy and the 1976 Edition of FM 100-5, Operations.* Leavenworth Papers no. 16. Fort Leavenworth, KS, 1988.

Herring, George C. "Ia Drang Valley." In *America's First Battles, 1776–1965,* edited by Charles E. Heller and William A. Stofft, 300–326. Lawrence: University Press of Kansas, 1986.

Hirsch, Gal. *A War Story, a Love Story.* Tel Aviv: Yediot Sfarim, 2009.

Hoffman, Frank. "The Principle of Understanding." *Armed Forces Journal International* (February 2012). http://armedforcesjournal.com/in-this-issue-6/.

Jensen, Benjamin M. *Forging the Sword: Doctrinal Change in the U.S. Army.* Redwood City, CA: Stanford University Press, 2016.

Johnson, David. "An Army Trying to Shake Itself from Intellectual Slumber, Part I: Learning from the 1970s." *War on the Rocks,* February 2, 2018. https://warontherocks.com/2018/02/army-trying-shake-intellectual-slumber-part-learning-1970s/.

———. "An Army Trying to Shake Itself from Intellectual Slumber, Part II: From 9/11 to Great Power Competition." *War on the Rocks,* February 6, 2018. https://warontherocks.com/2018/02/army-trying-shake-intellectual-slumber-part-ii-9-11-great-power-competition/.

Johnson, David E. *Hard Fighting Israel in Lebanon and Gaza.* Santa Monica, CA: Rand, 2011.

Kahalani, Avigdor. *"I Swear to You": Conversations with Soldiers Who Fought in the Yom Kippur War.* Tel Aviv: Ministry of Defense, 2004.

———. *The Path of a Fighter.* Tel Aviv: Steimatzky, 1989.

Kreidberg, Marvin A., and Henry J. Merton. *History of Mobilization in the United States Army, 1775–1945.* Department of the Army Pamphlet 20-212, June 1955.

Kretchik, Walter E. *U.S. Army Doctrine: From the American Revolution to the War on Terror.* Lawrence: University Press of Kansas, 2011.

Kühn, Ulrich. *Preventing Escalation in the Baltic: A NATO Playbook.* Washington, DC: Carnegie Endowment for International Peace, 2018.

Lambeth, Benjamin S. *Air Operations in Israel's War against Hizbollah: Learning from Lebanon and Getting It Right in Gaza.* Santa Monica, CA: Rand, 2011.

Landau, Noa. "Netanyahu Responds to Nasrallah: If Hezbollah Confronts Israel, They'll 'Get a Crushing Blow.'" *Haaretz,* September 29, 2018. https://www.haaretz.com/israel-news/.premium-netanyahu-responds-to-hezbollah-s-nasrallah-if-they-confront-israel-they-ll-get-a-crushing-blow-1.6492035.

Lapidot, Aharon, ed. *The Antiaircraft Layout: The Sky Is the Limit.* IAF and Ministry of Defense, 2002.

Lappin, Yaakov. "Hezbollah Planning 'Large Raids' into Galilee, Senior Army Source Says." *Jerusalem Post,* September 14, 2014. https://www.jpost.com/Arab-Israeli-Conflict/Hezbollah-planning-large-raids-into-Galilee-senior-army-source-says-375303.

Laslau, Ohad. *Development of the Operational Concept for the Lebanese Theater.* Dado Center, 2015.

Levi, Avshalom, ed. *All "Ayala" Stations in the Yom Kippur War.* N.p., n.d.

Lubotzky, Asael. *From the Desert and Lebanon.* Tel Aviv: Yediot Sifrei Hemed, 2008.

Lunz, Rami. "The Missile Boat—From Idea to Decisive Victory at Sea." *Ma'arachot* 362 (January 1999): 16–25.

———. "The Yom Kippur War at Sea." In *War Today: Studies on the Yom Kippur War,* edited by Hagai Golan and Shaul Shai, 389–408. Tel Aviv: Ministry of Defense, 2003.

Luttwak, Edward, and Dan Horowitz. *The Israeli Army.* London: Allen Lane, 1975.

Luvaas, Jay. "Buna, 19 November 1942–2 January 1943: A Leavenworth Nightmare." In *America's First Battles, 1776–1965,* edited by Charles E. Heller and William A. Stofft, 186–225. Lawrence: University Press of Kansas, 1986.

MacFarland, Sean, Michael Shields, and Jeffery Snow. "The King and I: The Impending Crisis in Field Artillery's Ability to Provide Fire Support to Maneuver Commanders." Artillery white paper, 2008. https://www.npr.org/documents/2008/may/artillery-whitepaper.pdf.

Macgregor, Douglas. *Margin of Victory: Five Battles that Changed the Face of Modern War.* Annapolis, MD: Naval Institute Press, 2016.

———. *Transformation under Fire: Revolutionizing How America Fights.* Westport, CT: Praeger, 2003.

Matthews, Matt M. "Hard Lessons Learned—A Comparison of the 2006 Hezbollah-Israeli War and Operation Cast Lead: A Historical Overview." In *Back to Basics: A Study of the Second Lebanon War and Operation Cast Lead,* edited by Lieutenant Colonel Scott C. Farquhar, 5–44. Fort Leavenworth, KS: Combat Studies Institute, US Army Combined Arms Center, 2009.

Michalson, Ehud. *Stouthearted Men: The 184th Battalion.* Tel Aviv: Ministry of Defense, 2003.

Millett, Allan R. "Cantigny, 28–31 May 1918." In *America's First Battles, 1776–1965,* edited by Charles E. Heller and William A. Stofft, 149–85. Lawrence: University Press of Kansas, 1986.

Moore, Harold K., and Jeff Galloway. *We Were Soldiers Once and Young.* New York: Random House, 1992.

Murray, Williamson. *Military Adaptation in War, with Fear of Change.* New York: Cambridge University Press, 2011.

Nadal, Haim. *Between Two Wars (1967–1973).* Tel Aviv: Ma'arachot, 2006.

Nir and Yoav, Captains. "Flexibility and the Use of Force Design in Limited Conflicts: The Artillery Branch as a Test Case." *Ma'arachot* 401 (May 2005): 58–61.

Parks, Henrik. *Hybrid or Not: Deterring and Defeating Russia's Ways of Warfare in the Baltics—The Case of Estonia.* Rome, Italy: NATO Defense College, 2015.

Peled, Benny. *Days of Soul-Searching.* Ben Shemen: Modan, 2004.

Peled, Yossi. *Military Man.* Tel Aviv: Ma'ariv, 1993.

Perkins, David G. "U.S. Army: Multi-Domain Battle—The Advent of Twenty-First Century War." *Military Review,* November–December 2017, 8–13.

———. "U.S. Army: Multi-Domain Battle Driving Change to Win in the Future." *Military Review,* July–August 2017, 6–12.

———. "U.S. Army: Preparing for the Fight Tonight—Multi-Domain Battle and Field Manual 3–0." *Military Review,* September–October 2017, 7–13.

Preisler, Dana. "What Can Be Learned from the Development of the IDF's Operating Concept of 2006." *Bein Haktavim* 10 (March 2017): 9–50.

Regev, Ofer, and Hadas Regev-Yarkoni. *Maoz Tzur: The 68th Battalion/Jerusalem Brigade and the Stronghold Battle in the Yom Kippur War.* Tzur Yigal: Porat Publishers, 2010.

Reshef, Amnon. *14th Brigade Commander Yom Kippur War After Action Report.* http://www.hativa14.com/.

Rimon, Ran. "The Reflection Game." *Ms&T Magazine,* January 2018.

———. "Simulating Surprise." *Ms&T Magazine,* June 2016.

Romjue, John L. *From Active Defense to AirLand Battle: The Development of Army Doctrine, 1973–1982.* TRADOC Historical Monographs. Fort Monroe, VA: Historical Office, US Army TRADOC, 1984.

Ronen (Pekker), Ran. *Eagle in the Sky.* Tel Aviv: Yediot Achronot–Sifrei Hemed, 2002.

Sadat, Anwar. *In Search of Identity: An Autobiography.* New York: Harper and Row, 1978.

Sakal, Emanuel. *Soldier in the Sinai.* Lexington: University Press of Kentucky, 2014.

Segal, Maozia. *Testimony at the Sand Level: The Paratroopers Battle at the Chinese Farm.* Tel Aviv: Modan, 2007.

Segoli, Ephraim. *Knowledge Development Processes in the Northern Theater, 2002–2006: Between Design and the "Final Leg."* Dado Center, 2015.

Serena, Chad C. *A Revolution in Military Adaptation: The U.S. Army in the Iraq War.* Washington, DC: Georgetown University Press, 2011.

Shachar, Amira. *The Ordnance Branch as Force Multiplier: The History of the Ordnance Corps, 1967–1985.* Ordnance Branch and Doctrine and Instruction Association, 2006.

Shai (Schwartz), Hanan. *IDF C2 at the Operational Level in Light of the Theoretical Foundations of the Modern System of Task-Oriented Decentralized Command.* IDF Command and Staff College, 1995.

Shalom, Dani. *Apparition over Cairo: The Air Force in the War of Attrition (1967–1970).* Vols. 1 and 2. Rishon Lezion: B'avir Air and Space Publications, 2007.

Shalpak, David A., and Michael W. Johnson. *Reinforcing Deterrence on NATO's Eastern Flank.* Santa Monica, CA: Rand, 2016.

Shamir, Eitan. *Transforming Command.* Redwood City, CA: Stanford University Press, 2011.

Sharon, Ariel, and David Chanoff. *Warrior.* New York: Simon and Schuster, 2001.

Shazly, Saad El. *The Crossing of the Suez.* Rev. ed. San Francisco: American Mideast Research, 2003.

Shefi, Yigal. *Warning Being Tested: The Rotem Incident and Israel's Security Concept, 1957–1960.* Tel Aviv: Ma'arachot, 2008.

Shmuel, Shmuel. "Multi-Domain Battle: AirLand Battle, Once More, with Feeling." *War on the Rocks,* June 20, 2017. https://warontherocks.com/2017/06/multi-domain-battle-airland-battle-once-more-with-feeling/.

Shteigman, Yitzhak. *The Sinai Campaign: The Air Force, 1950–1956 Growth and Operations.* IAF and Ministry of Defense, 1990.

Shy, John. "First Battles in Retrospect." In *America's First Battles, 1776–1965,* edited by Charles E. Heller and William A. Stofft, 327–52. Lawrence: University Press of Kansas, 1986.

Siboni, Gavriel. "The Military System in Lebanon." In *The Second Lebanon War,* edited by Meir Elran and Shlomo Brom, 58–73. Tel Aviv: Yediot Sfarim and Institute for National Security Studies, 2007.

Simchoni, Uri. *White Whale.* Binyamina: Glory, 2006.

Simon, Jeffrey. *NATO–Warsaw Pact Force Mobilization.* Washington, DC: National Defense University Press, 1988.

Sitbon, Yaron. "The Influence of Daily Security Operations on the Second Lebanon War." In *The Second Lebanon War: The Wisdom of Action.* Vol. 2, edited by Zvi Ofer, 91–134. IDF Institute for the Research of the Tactical Level, 2008.

Spector, Yiftach. "The Fall of the Phantom." *Ma'arachot* 422 (2008): 34–39.

———. *Loud and Clear.* Tel Aviv: Yediot Achronot, 2008.

Starry, Donn. "FM 100–5 Operations." Inter-University seminar, Fort Leavenworth, KS, March 30, 1978. In *Press On: Selected Works of General Donn Starry.* Vol. 1, edited by Lewis Sorley. Fort Leavenworth, KS: Combat Studies Institute Press, US Army Combined Arms Center, 2009.

The Story of a Brigade: Kfir Brigade—First Years. Kfir Brigade Foundation, Afula Municipality, 2011.

Swedish Civil Contingencies Agency. *If a Crisis or War Comes.* 2018. www.msb.se.

Tal, Israel. *Israel's National Security: The Few against the Many.* Tel Aviv: Dvir, 1996.

Tamari, Dov, and Meir Klifi. "The IDF Operational Concept." *Ma'arachot* 423 (February 2009): 26–41.

Tamir, Moshe. *War without a Badge.* Tel Aviv: Ma'arachot, 2005.

Tew, Jennifer, David Persselin, and Maren Leed. *Meeting Peace Operations' Requirements while Maintaining MTW Readiness.* Santa Monica, CA: Rand Arroyo Center, 1998.

Vandergriff, Donald E. "When Do We Teach the Basics? *Joint Forces Quarterly* 58, no. 3 (2010): 69–74.

Wagman, Yehuda. "Chaos at Nafekh—Analysis of an Event." In *War Today: Studies on the Yom Kippur War,* edited by Hagai Golan and Shaul Shai, 311–58. Tel Aviv: Ministry of Defense, 2003.

Wasserbly, Daniel. "U.S. Army Chief Eyes 'Leap-Ahead' Technologies." *IHS Jane's Defense Weekly,* January 17, 2018.

Weapons Systems Evaluation Group (WSEG). *Evaluation of the Weapons and Tactics Used in the October 1973 Middle East War.* WSEG Report 249. WSEG, October 1973.

Weiner, Erez. "From Bewilderment to Awareness—The Development of a Combat Doctrine and Counterinsurgency Fighting Model, 1996–2004." *Ma'arachot* 409–10 (December 2006): 4–19.

Weizman, Ezer. *On Eagles' Wings: The Personal Story of the Leading Commander of the Israeli Air Force.* Tel Aviv: Ma'ariv, 1975.

Winograd Commission, Investigating Commission on the Second Lebanon War. *Preliminary Report.* April 2007.

———. *Final Report.* 2008.

Wong, Leonard, and Stephen J. Gerras. *Lying to Ourselves: Dishonesty in the Army Profession.* Carlisle, PA: Strategic Studies Institute and US Army War College Press, 2015.

Woods, Kevin M., and Thomas C. Greenwood. "Multi-Domain Battle: Time for a Campaign of Joint Experimentation." *Joint Force Quarterly* 88 (January 9, 2018): 14–21.

Ya'alon, Moshe. *A Long Short Road.* Tel Aviv: Yediot Books, 2008.

Yardeni, Shaul, and Gal Oren. "Air Force—The Mental Transition from Routine Security to a State of War." In *The Second Lebanon War: The Wisdom of Action.* Vol. 2, edited by Zvi Ofer, 135–42. IDF Institute for the Research of the Tactical Level, 2008.

Yunai, Ehud. *Air Superiority: The Story of the Israeli Air Force.* Jerusalem: Keter, 1993.

Zalmanovitch, Boaz. "Elucidation and Criticism of the Training of the Givati Brigade's Reconnaissance Battalion." *Mahatz* 15 (April 2004): 18–21.

———. "Establishing Special Forces in Low Intensity Conflicts." *Ma'arachot* 369 (February 2000): 32–35.

———. "The Tactical Combat Unit in Limited Conflicts, Testing and Experiment." *Ma'arachot* 405 (February 2006): 28–33.

Ze'ira, Eli. *Myth versus Reality: The Yom Kippur War; Failures and Lessons.* Tel Aviv: Yediot Achronot–Sifrei Hemed, 2004.

Military Doctrine

Headquarters, Department of the Army. *FM 100–5.* Washington, DC, 1976, 1993.

———. *FM 3–0.* Washington, DC, 2008.

IDF Operations Branch, Doctrine and Instruction Division. *Basic Security and Military Documents—Essence, Purpose and Organization.* GHQ, February 2011.

Ministry of Defense. *Joint Doctrine Publication 04 (JDP 04)—Understanding.* Shrivenham, UK: Development, Concepts and Doctrine Centre, December 2010.

Office of the IDF Chief of Staff. *IDF General Staff Operating Concept Investigation: Chief of Staff Summary.* December 11, 2006.

Office of the IDF Deputy Chief of Staff. *Operating Concept Investigative Team—Summary.* December 2006.

TRADOC. *Multi-Domain Battle: The Evolution of Combined Arms for the 21st Century —2025–2040.* December 2017.

US Joint Chiefs of Staff. *Joint Publication (JP) 5–0: Joint Operation Planning.* 2011.

White House Office. *National Security Strategy of the United States of America.* December 2017. https://www.hsdl.org/?abstract&did=806478.

Author's Interviews

Friedman, Brigadier General (res.) Alon. Glilot, March 26, 2017.
Klifi, Major General (res.) Meir. Glilot, April 1, 2012.
Reshef, Major General (res.) Amnon. Tel Aviv, August 15, 2011.
Sakal, Major General (res.) Emanuel. Latrun, May 29, 2011.
Tamir, Brigadier General (res.) Yom Tov. Glilot, June 19, 2011.
Turgeman, Major General (res.) Sami. Glilot, April 18, 2017.

Index